How India Earns, Spends and Saves

How India Earns, Spends and Saves

Unmasking the Real India

Rajesh Shukla

$SAGE www.sagepublications.com
Los Angeles ● London ● New Delhi ● Singapore ● Washington DC

Jointly published in 2010 by

SAGE Publications India Pvt Ltd   and
B1/I-1 Mohan Cooperative Industrial Area
Mathura Road, New Delhi 110 044, India
www.sagepub.in

N
NCAER

NCAER–CMCR
Parisila Bhawan
11 IP Estate
New Delhi 110 002

SAGE Publications Inc
2455 Teller Road
Thousand Oaks, California 91320, USA

SAGE Publications Ltd
1 Oliver's Yard, 55 City Road
London EC1Y 1SP, United Kingdom

SAGE Publications Asia-Pacific Pte Ltd
33 Pekin Street
#02-01 Far East Square
Singapore 048763

Published by Vivek Mehra for SAGE Publications India Pvt Ltd, Phototypeset in 10/14 pt Berthold Baskerville by Diligent Typesetter, Delhi and printed at Artxel, New Delhi.

Library of Congress Cataloging-in-Publication Data

Shukla, R.
  How India earns, spends and saves: unmasking the real India / Rajesh Shukla.
      p. cm.
Includes bibliographical references and index.
  1. Income–India–Statistics. 2. Consumption (Economics)–India–Statistics. 3. Saving and investment–India–Statistics. I. Title.

HC440.I5S564   339.2'20954–dc22   2010   2010011341

ISBN: 978-81-321-0476-6 (HB)

The SAGE Team: Rekha Natarajan, Vikas Jain, Vijay Sah and Trinankur Banerjee

Contents

List of Tables

List of Figures

List of Abbreviations

AIRHS	All India Rural Household Survey
CMCR	Centre for Macro Consumer Research
CSO	Central Statistical Organisation
GDP	Gross Domestic Product
IHDS	Indian Household Development Survey
HIS	Integrated Household Survey
MISH	Market Information Survey of Households
MPCE	Monthly Per Capita Income
NAS	National Accounts Statistics
NCAER	National Council of Applied Economic Research
NIC	National Industrial Classification
NCO	National Classification of Occupation
NSS	National Sample Survey
NSSO	National Sample Survey Organisation
NSC	National Statistical Commission
NSHIE	National Survey of Household Income and Expenditure
NDP	Net Domestic Product
PCA	Primary Census Abstracts
PPP	Purchasing Power Parity
UT	Union Territory

Foreword

Consumer India is a hydra-headed monster (or a many splendoured thing, depending on the beholder's point of view), and often begs the question: which India and whose India are we talking about? There is one India whose proud inhabitants enjoy higher per capita incomes than Brazil; a larger one that is slightly poorer than Indonesia and a third India that is double in size to the sum of the first two, but almost as poor as Bangladesh.

Most consumers in India do not work in the organised sector and their well being cannot be discerned from salary and wages data maintained by corporate houses. Many are not even salaried, but are self-employed or casual wage earners. Only 37 per cent of urban and 11 per cent of rural Indian households have a chief wage earner earning a regular salary/wage. Only in the top 20 cities is the salaried percentage close to half. In reality, most consumers are financially vulnerable. A quarter of them have loans outstanding; in case of a major drop in income, there is lack of sufficient savings to sustain them for even a year. What makes them spend is a financial (mis)optimism that something, somehow would work out. Yet, collectively, they account for the fourth largest economy in the world in purchasing power parity terms, and their consumption is a significant driver of India's economic growth.

It is not enough to simply have the potential to build global scale domestic businesses. The process of getting there begins with forming an understanding about our consumption economy. Indian households have come a long way in the post-reform period, absorbing dramatic changes to traditional thought processes governing consumption and savings. It is necessary to map households in terms of their earning, spending and saving patterns. What are the factors that determine the income of a household and thereby saving and expenditure patterns? What is the origin of income inequality? How do socio-economic characteristics like occupation, education and location impact a household's economic well being? There are, doubtless, constraints imposed by individual capabilities and behaviour–such as willingness and ability to take risks–but non-availability of capital, high cost of education and institutional factors, for example, inheritance laws and barriers to mobility too play a part.

To a large extent, the contributions of these elements are non-measurable. It is, however, important to distinguish between income levels associated with certain demographic and socio-economic characteristics of chief earners and households. It is indeed a given that age, education and occupation have a significant bearing on a chief earner's income. So, to gauge the extent of a household's well being, we must take into consideration employment, major sources of income and state of residence. It goes without saying that none of this would be possible without sophisticated and accurate data pouring in continuously from all corners of the country.

National Council of Applied Economic Research (NCAER) has done pioneering work in this area for over two decades and has been a dominant and highly respected voice in the arena of profiling and conceptualising India's changing consumer landscape. It was the first research body to link macroeconomic progress to obvious but unspotted changes caused at the household level in terms of income and consumption. Its pioneering contribution of culling data and generating informed insights into the consumption behaviour of India's vast and heterogeneous middle class is widely acknowledged. NCAER was also the first Indian think tank to announce income and consumption projections at the household level based on the long term outlook of India's economy. Its research findings on the stratification of the Indian consumer base into consumption behaviour-based segments (the widely used consuming classes model) was a trail blazer.

As far as the research challenge is concerned, measuring 'income' is a hard one in the Indian context. Valid data on incomes is hard to come by. NCAER has constantly sought to overcome this by applying newer and better ways of measuring income and expenditure.

This book is based on a survey which covered over 440,000 households in rural and urban India spread over 24 states. No previous research project has had such a formidable sample base. It is no overstatement that NCAER had at its disposal data from one of the most scientifically designed and meticulously conducted surveys of its kind in India. The effort, which marks the debut of the NCAER–Centre for Macro Consumer Research (NCAER–CMCR), explores the connection between national economic well being and phenomena like urbanisation, consumerism and rural market evolution. Included are insights based on longitudinal data collected through prolonged and painstaking door-to-door research done by NCAER teams. The highlights of the book include:

- **Primary data-based research:** This book presents the findings of an all-India household survey whose objective was to determine the current level of well being of Indian households through objective assessment of earnings, spending and saving patterns of households. A probability sample made up of 63,016 households out of a preliminary listed sample of 440,000 spread over 1,976 villages (250 districts) and 2,255 urban wards (342 towns) covering 64 NSS regions in 24 states/UTs was interviewed.

- **Objective analysis of household income, expenditure and saving:** There is deeper analysis of the economic well being of the Indian population based on socio-economic and demographic indicators at the level of the household (e.g. rural-urban, sector of employment, major source of income, state of residence, social group), and chief earners (their occupation, education and age, etc.). These have a significant bearing on earning, spending and saving.
- **Dynamics of income distribution:** Income distribution is presented through the Income Quintile Framework, which is universally accepted as it requires the least assumptions.
- **Rural well-being:** The dynamic changes happening in rural India, the transforming structure of the rural economy, their overall impact on consumerism and the larger ramifications carried for overall well being of households.
- **Urban well-being:** Finally, the book explores how our cities have been growing by studying rural-to-urban migration trends as well as population shifts from the smaller towns to the metro cities. How these set a trend for the future, apart from impacting the well being of households, was studied.

It is my privilege as the first non executive chairperson of NCAER–CMCR to write the foreword to this book authored by the Director of the newly formed centre, Dr Rajesh Shukla. I am sure it would be the first in a long line of impressive publications from the NCAER–CMCR team.

Rama Bijapurkar
Chairperson
NCAER–Centre for Macro Consumer Research (NCAER–CMCR)

Message

National Council of Applied Economic Research (NCAER) was founded to provide objective data and analysis to support India's economic development. Household demand is one of the key pillars of any economy, and business strategists and policy makers require continuous knowledge, insight and foresight on this crucial area. NCAER has been active in providing authoritative analyses on the Indian scenario for more than two decades now. To deepen its commitment, in March 2010 NCAER created a dedicated unit, NCAER–Centre for Macro Consumer Research (NCAER–CMCR), with the objective of building and disseminating seminal knowledge about India's consumer economy.

The first household survey on income and consumption, Market Information Survey of Households (MISH), was launched in 1985–86 and conducted almost every year since then until 2004–05 (1990–92, 2000–01 and 2002–04 were the exceptions). With each round, the scale, scope, methodology and rigour improved based on active and continuous user feedback and involvement at the design stages. In 2006, as part of a continuing effort to improve estimates of household income, the last round of MISH was redesigned (and re-christened National Survey of Household Income and Expenditure, or NSHIE). In particular, the questions on income were expanded and reformulated to reflect international conventions, and the sample design, the sample frame as it were, was similarly redesigned and expanded to reflect the greater interest in income.

Some of the important indicators and estimates in this study are fairly comparable with those of other reliable data sources such as NSS 61st Round, Census 2001 and National Accounts sources. Above all, a group of eminent economists and statisticians were associated as members of the Advisory Committee and as advisors throughout the study, and the findings of the study have been endorsed by them.

In 2007, NCAER brought out what is by far the most comprehensive report on India's consumer economy, *How India Earns, Spends and Saves*, which was released in Delhi by the Deputy-Chairperson of the Planning Commission, Mr Montek

Singh Ahluwalia, and forms the basis and inspiration for this book. This report was a worthy successor to the well-received earlier ones like *The Great Indian Middle Class*, *The India Market Demographics* and *The 10 Year White Book* (containing demand and user profile projections for various consumer durables).

This book is the first offering from NCAER–CMCR. The insights contained in it would help economic analysts, media, policy makers, the marketing community, development professionals, students and also the average Indian reader understand better how India's growth story has unfolded for its households.

Suman Bery
Director-General
NCAER

Acknowledgements

This book compiles research and data collated over several years. I wish to thank the NCAER Advisory Committee–chaired by Mr Suman Bery and consisting of members Mr S. L. Rao, Chairman, Institute for Social and Economic Change, Bangalore; Dr D. V. S. Sastry, Director-General, Insurance Regulatory and Development Authority, Hyderabad; and Dr Subhasis Gangopadhyay–for its guidance and support. I humbly and gratefully acknowledge the committee's generous contribution of time, effort and expertise under the most stringent schedules.

This initiative would not have been possible without the contribution of several researchers and policy makers. I extend my appreciation and gratitude to NCAER Advisors and Consultants, Dr N. S. Sastry, Former Director-General, National Sample Survey Organisation and Central Statistical Organisation, and Senior Advisor, NCAER; and Dr Anil Rai, Senior Scientist, Indian Agricultural Statistics Research Institute (IASRI).

The NCAER research team deserves a special mention, particularly Ms Preeti Kakar and Ms Adite Banerjie, for their constructive and analytical support and for their inputs that enriched this book. The NCAER field staff and state networking agencies and NCAER support staff worked overtime to collect data from all across the country.

This book also draws insights from the Max New York Life–NCAER India Financial Protection Survey (*How India Earns, Spends and Saves*), and I would like to extend my appreciation to the management team for allowing me to use the results from that survey.

Ms Rama Bijapurkar deserves a special thanks and appreciation for being instrumental in bringing the report into this shape.

Finally, I'm indebted to the Director-General, NCAER, Mr Suman Bery, for his unstinting support in making this book a reality.

Rajesh Shukla
Director
NCAER–Centre for Macro Consumer Research (NCAER–CMCR)

Introduction

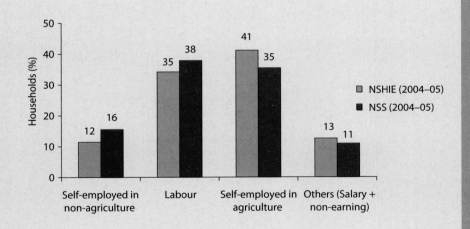

1.1 Background

Economic analysts and policy makers have identified three main purposes for compiling information on income distribution. The first is driven by a desire to understand how the pattern of income distribution can be related to patterns of economic activity and the returns to labour, capital and land, and to the way in which societies are organised. The second reflects the concern of policy makers to determine the need for both universal and socially targeted actions on different socio-economic groups and to assess their impact. The third is an interest in how different patterns of income distribution influence household well-being and people's ability to acquire goods and services that they need to satisfy their needs.

Unfortunately, there is a great dearth of reliable longitudinal data on household income in India. The National Sample Survey Organisation (NSSO) has made efforts in the past for collecting information on household income along with the consumer expenditure by using interview method of data collection in its ninth round (May 1955–September 1955) and fourteenth round (July 1958–June 1959). Later, it undertook collection of data on receipts and disbursements as part of the Integrated Household Survey (IHS) in its nineteenth round (July 1964–June 1965) and twenty-fourth round (July 1969–June 1970) with the aim of obtaining a complete picture of transactions of household income.

In 1983–84, the NSSO once again attempted a pilot enquiry on household income by following two approaches, viz. collection of data on household income directly from sources of earnings from one set of household, the collection of data on household consumption and saving from a second set of sample households, and data on income, consumption and saving from a third set of households. The objective was to explore the possibility of evolving an operationally feasible and sound technical methodology for collection of data on household income through the interview method by examining the effectiveness of direct income survey against the alternative approach of consumption and saving enquiry.

Experience showed that there were difficulties in collecting reliable income data in the field due to ambiguities in choice of unit of sampling, the sampling frame, the reference period of data collection, and even items of information.

Seasonality effect, lack of availability of accounts from employer households, significant amount of purchases through credit, hidden income generated through wages paid in kind, and so on, are other factors that come in the way of proper data collection. For these reasons, the NSSO has perhaps refrained from collection of data on household income. Greater emphasis was, therefore, placed on household expenditure surveys.

However, since the mid-1980s, another large scale survey—the Market Information Survey of Households (MISH) of National Council of Applied Economic Research (NCAER)—was initiated to estimate market size, penetration for a variety of consumer goods, and most importantly, to provide a profile of consuming households in terms of income, occupation and location. This survey is one of the few consistent sources that provides comparable household income data on a regular basis. Over time, more attention began to be paid to income data being generated as a by-product of the 'listing' exercise conducted to establish the sampling frame for each round. This income data started to generate public policy interest in its own right, as an additional perspective on poverty findings generated by the National Sample Survey (Bery and Shukla 2003).

NCAER's MISH data on income and demographics also provoked interest in the private sector as a benchmark for the 'growth of the middle class' (McKinsey Global Institute 2007). This interest was, for instance, reflected in McKinsey and Company's report 'The Bird of Gold,' to which NCAER contributed, and which used the NCAER classification of income categories in order to forecast income transitions in urban and rural India. The other major publications which were very well-received by the corporate world and policy makers include *The Great Indian Middle Class* (Shukla 2004), *The Great Indian Market* (Shukla 2005), *The India Market Demographics* and *The 10 Year Whitebook.*

The main concept of income that has been used in MISH is the concept of *perceived monetary income*, which includes all income received by the household as a whole and by each of its members during the reference year. A major concern about MISH surveys was the adequacy of a single income question 'What is your annual household income from all sources?' In *Data and Dogma: The Great Indian Poverty Debate* (Deaton and Kozel 2004), it has been emphasised that there is need for better income data, improvements in the data and broadening the indicators by which relevant policy issues may be objectively addressed. Also, the National Statistical Commission (NSC) recommended examining the feasibility of reintroducing the receipts and disbursement block with last 365 days as a reference period, as was the case when the NSSO adopted the integrated household schedule for its nineteenth to twenty-fifth rounds. However, it has still not happened.

In this backdrop, as part of its continuing effort to improve the estimates of household income, NCAER redesigned MISH in 2005 calling it the National Survey of Household Income and Expenditure (NSHIE), under the advice and guidance of outside statistical experts, to take better account of these emerging interests, while retaining comparability with the past. In particular, the questions on income were expanded and reformulated to reflect national and international conventions.[1] The sample design and the sample frame were also redesigned and expanded to reflect this greater interest in income.

1.2 About the Survey

The NSHIE was undertaken to generate a more robust and reliable estimate of household income. Survey procedures such as approach, concepts and definitions, sample design and sample size, content of the questionnaire and estimation procedure were executed after reviewing best international practices.[2] Details about concepts, definitions and survey methodology used in survey are given in Annexure. Some of the major features of NSHIE are as follows.

1.2.1 Accounting Period

The accounting period used for income distribution analysis is one year as per recommendation, and similarly, the household, defined as a group of two or more persons living together in the same house and sharing common food or other arrangements for essential living, has been adopted as the basic statistical unit.

---

[1] The major sources reviewed include: Situation Assessment Survey of Farmers (NSSO); Integrated Household Survey (NSSO); Employment and Unemployment Survey (NSSO); All India Rural Household Survey on Saving, Income and Investment (1962, NCAER); Survey on Urban Income and Saving (1962, NCAER); Market Information Survey of Households (1985–2001, NCAER); Micro-Impact of Macro and Adjustment Policies (NCAER); Rural Economic and Demographic Survey (NCAER); Expert Group on Household Income Statistics, Canberra Manual; Household Income and Expenditure Statistics (ILO); Chinese Household Income Project (1995) and Household Income and Expenditure Survey (Sri Lanka).

[2] For instance, Expert Group on Household Income Statistics (Canberra City Group of UN Statistical Commission): Over 70 experts from 26 national organisations and seven international organisations were involved in the work of the Canberra Group with the objective to enhance national household income statistics by developing standards on conceptual and practical issues related to the production of income distribution statistics. It carried out a metasurvey (survey about surveys) of 106 income components that are actually collected in 30 household income surveys in 25 countries from all continents.

1.2.2 Concept of Income

A hierarchy of components of income is built up which provides the definition of total disposable household income. The recommended practical definition of income has been adopted for use in making international comparisons of income. The major components of income covered in the survey are income from regular salary/wages, income from self-employment in non-agriculture, income from wages (agricultural labour and casual labour), income from self-employment in agriculture (crop production, forestry, livestock, fisheries, and so on), income from other sources such as rent (from leased out land and from providing accommodation and capital formation), interest dividends received, and employer-based pensions.

1.2.3 Sample Design

This survey was aimed at generating reliable estimates at the state level, covering both rural and urban India. Both quantitative (sample survey) and qualitative (PRA/RRA techniques) approaches were employed to generate the primary data. The target population of the survey was the total population in the country, with states and urban/rural categories as sub-populations or target groups. A three-stage stratified sample design has been adopted for the survey to generate representative samples. Sample districts, villages and households formed the first, second and third stage sample units, respectively, for selection of the rural sample, while cities/towns, urban wards and households were the three stages of selection for the urban sample. Sampling was done independently within each state/Union Territory (UT) and estimates were generated at state/UT level.

1.2.4 Sample Size and Its Allocation

The sample sizes at the first, second and third stages in rural and urban areas were determined on the basis of available resources and the derived level of precision for key estimates from the survey, taking into account the experience of NCAER in conducting the earlier surveys such as MISH, and so on. A total of 63,016 households were covered in NSHIE (about twice as that of MISH-2001), which is distributed over larger geographical area, particularly in rural areas to increase the reliability of estimates. For instance, in rural areas, the realised sample of 31,446 households out of the preliminary listed sample of 211,979 households was spread over 1,976 villages in 250 districts and 64 National Sample Survey (NSS) regions covering 24 states/UTs. Similarly, in urban areas, a sample of 31,570 households, out of the preliminary listed sample of 238,813 households, was spread over 2,255 urban wards in 342 towns and 64 NSS regions covering 24 States/UTs.

1.2.5 Selection of Households

In MISH, the listed households in each sample place (villages in the rural and urban blocks in urban) were stratified into five income bands on the basis of reported annual household income. These income bands were specific to NCAER and are adjusted in nominal terms each year to reflect constant levels of real household income as per the initial year. From each stratum (income band), households were selected independently with equal probability.

However, in NSHIE, there is major change in the selection and use of stratification variable. For instance, for the urban sample, all the listed households were grouped into seven strata, based on the principal source of income (regular salary/ wage earnings, self-employment and labour, and so on) and the level of monthly per capita income (MPCE) (Rs 800 or less, between Rs 801 and Rs 2,500, and above Rs 2,500). Similarly, in the case of rural sample, the land possessed and the principal source of income are used as stratification variables. All the listed households were grouped into eight strata based on the principal source of income (agriculture, salary/wage earnings and labour, and so on) and level of land possessed (less than two acres, two to 10 acres and more than 10 acres). From each of the strata, two households were selected at random with equal probability of selection.

For the purpose of increasing accuracy and ensuring adequate item response, the survey was conducted by adopting face-to-face interviews of heads of households as well as their members using a questionnaire-based approach. Non-response and non-sampling errors were reduced by conducting focus group discussions, proper training of interviewers and supervision.

Detailed information was collected on the demographic profiles of households and their composition, components of household income, consumption expenditure, and on relevant qualitative indicators related to economic activities of the households. An exclusive module containing aspects such as the motivation to save, reasons for saving, preferred mode of saving, investment, borrowing, household economic shocks, insurance, perception about well-being, and so on, were canvassed to all sample households to measure the level of financial vulnerability.

1.3 Validation of Choices and Reliability of Estimates

Income and expenditure surveys often tend to bring to fore certain stark trends and statistics. And invariably, doubts are raised over the reliability of such data. It should be admitted that there is no foolproof method by which one can establish the reliability or otherwise of all the survey results. There are, however, certain procedures by which it would be possible to make assessment of the degree of confidence that can be placed on the findings of the survey. The most widely used and fruitful procedure is to compare the survey estimates with the estimates generated by other reliable sources, despite the difficulty in obtaining estimates that are comparable from the point of view of concepts, coverage of population and period to which the data refer. However, such comparison provides some basis for judging the degree of reliability, and hence, an attempt is made to compare the survey results with the available external data. Using information collected through the NSHIE, two reports, namely, *How India Earns, Spends and Saves* (Shukla 2007) and *Next Urban Frontier: Twenty Cities to Watch* (Shukla and Purushothaman 2008) were published. These reports provide a fair degree of understanding of data quality and richness.

1.3.1 Demographic Characteristics

Information relating to key demographic characteristics of the Indian households is available from the sixty-first round of NSS (2004–05) and Census 2001, with which the NSHIE results can be checked. According to the NSHIE, there are 205.6 million households in the covered states[3] of the country, of which 30 per cent (61.4 million) are located in urban areas and the rest (144.2 million) in rural areas. The estimate of average household size from NSHIE (5.0 members) appears consistent with the estimates obtained from NSS sixty-first round (4.9 members) and Census 2001 (5.4 members) (Table 1.1). A similar pattern is also observed in the case of sex ratio. The NSHIE reported the sex ratio at 927 against 950 by the NSS sixty-first round and 933 by the Census 2001.

---

[3] Andhra Pradesh, Assam, Bihar, Chandigarh, Chhattisgarh, Delhi, Goa, Gujarat, Haryana, Himachal Pradesh, Jharkhand, Karnataka, Kerala, Madhya Pradesh, Maharashtra, Meghalaya, Orissa, Pondicherry, Punjab, Rajasthan, Tamil Nadu, Uttarakhand, Uttar Pradesh and West Bengal. Territories excluded were Jammu & Kashmir, Sikkim, Arunachal Pradesh, Nagaland, Manipur, Mizoram, Tripura, Andaman & Nicobar Islands, Daman & Diu, Dadra & Nagar Haveli and Lakshadweep. These states were left out due to operational difficulty. These states account for only 3 per cent to 4 per cent of the country's total population.

All the three data sources are also fairly comparable on some other parameters, such as the distribution of households by socio-religious groups. It is observed that the distribution of population for different religious groups in NSHIE appears to be slightly different compared to the NSS and Census estimates (Table 1.1). This is largely due to some states and UTs being left out in NSHIE.

Table 1.1: Demographic Profile of Indian Households

Characteristics	Rural			Urban		
	NSHIE (2004–05)	Census* (2001)	NSS** (2004–05)	NSHIE (2004–05)	Census* (2001)	NSS** (2004–05)
a. Estimated households (million)	144.2	137.7	147.8	61.4	55.8	56.2
b. Estimated population (million)	731.9	742.5	721.1	295.3	286.1	245.0
c. Household size	5.08	5.39	4.88	4.81	5.12	4.36
d. Distribution of households by social groups (per cent)						
Scheduled castes	18.3	17.9	21.5	12.8	11.8	15.3
Scheduled tribes	10.6	10.4	10.6	2.8	2.4	2.9
Others	71.2	71.7	67.8	84.4	85.8	81.8
Total	100.0	100.0	100.0	100.0	100.0	100.0
e. Distribution of households by religion (per cent)						
Hindu	88.3	82.3	85.1	83.7	75.6	80.6
Muslim	8.1	12.0	10.1	10.6	17.3	13.4
Christian	1.6	2.1	2.1	2.6	2.9	2.6
Sikh	1.6	1.9	1.8	2.2	1.8	1.6
Others	0.3	1.7	0.9	0.9	2.5	1.8
Total	100.0	100.0	100.0	100.0	100.0	100.0

Source: NSHIE 2004–05 data: NCAER–CMCR analysis.
Notes: * Author's calculation using Census 2001.
   ** Author's calculation using NSS 61st round of consumption expenditure survey unit record data.

1.3.2 Sources of Household Income

As per NSHIE, labourers constitute the largest segment of the population, heading a little over 31 per cent of the country's households. Self-employed agriculturists are the next largest segment (30.3 per cent). Salaried households account for a little over 18 per cent and the non-agricultural self-employed account for 17.5 per cent of the country's households. The figures differ for rural and urban areas.

While the salaried account for just 10.5 per cent of rural households, in urban areas they account for 36.9 per cent (Figures 1.1 and 1.2).

Figure 1.1: Distribution of Households by Source of Income: Urban

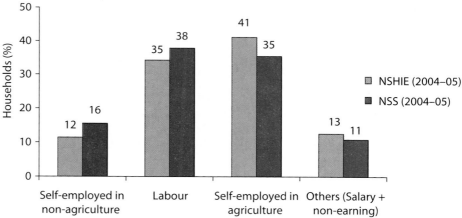

Source: NSHIE (2004–05): NCAER–CMCR analysis.
Note: Author's calculation using NSS 61st round of consumption expenditure survey data.

Figure 1.2: Distribution of Households by Source of Income: Rural

Source: NSHIE (2004–05): NCAER–CMCR analysis.
Note: Author's calculation using NSS 61st round of consumption expenditure survey data.

Similarly, the value of land owned by a rural household is perhaps an important indicator of the economic status of the household which is certainly more relevant in the context of rural Indian than urban India. Nearly 40 per cent of rural households in India do not possess any land while 30 per cent own between 0.1–2 acres of land (Figure 1.3).

Figure 1.3: Distribution of Households by Land Category: Rural

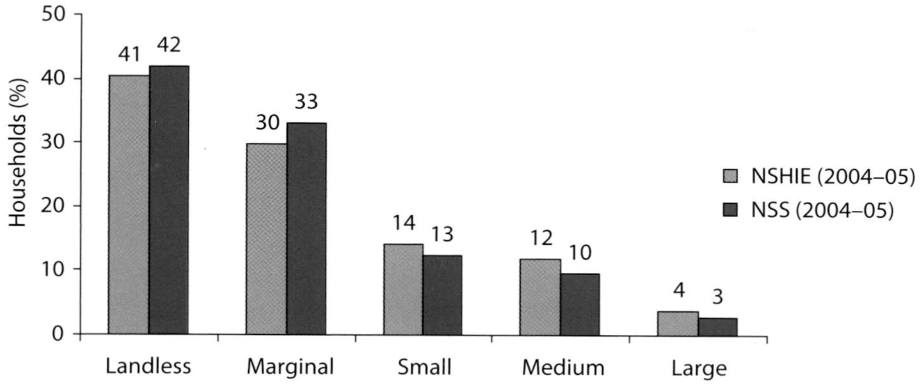

Source: NSHIE (2004–05): NCAER–CMCR analysis.
Note: Author's calculation using NSS 61st round of consumption expenditure survey data.

Distribution of households by major sources of household income and land category from NSHIE appears consistent and fairly comparable with the estimates obtained from NSS sixty-first round.

1.3.3 Estimates of Income, Expenditure and Saving

The average household in India had an annual income of Rs 65,041 in 2004–05, and an expenditure of Rs 48,558, leaving it with a surplus of Rs 16,483 to save and invest. Urban income levels are around 85 per cent more than rural ones (Rs 95,827 per annum versus Rs 51,922 per annum). Since expenses in urban areas are substantially higher (Rs 68,352 per annum in urban areas versus Rs 40,124 per annum in rural ones), the differences in the surplus income (of urban and rural areas) that can be saved or invested is not all that huge. As a result, the average urban household saves nearly double that of a rural household (Rs 27,475 per annum in urban areas versus Rs 11,798 for rural areas).

Household income estimated from NSHIE is compared with another income survey called Indian Household Development Survey (IHDS) carried out by NCAER with the same reference period. The mean per household income from the two surveys is quite close; the difference is about 0.5 per cent. However, the urban mean household income is significantly different in the two surveys. This could be due to the differences in survey design, the coverage of the two surveys as well as the smaller sample size in IHDS survey. However, the rural urban differences are far less pronounced when we compare the per capita incomes. The estimates of per capita income from the two NCAER surveys are given in Table 1.2.

Table 1.2: Estimates of Per Capita Income from Two NCAER's Surveys (Rs Per Annum)

	IHDS 2004–05	NSHIE 2004–05
Rural	8,413	10,227
Urban	15,915	19, 935
Total	10,366	13,018

Source: IHDS 2004–05 data and NSHIE 2004–05 data: NCAER–CMCR analysis.

A common problem faced by such surveys is the under-statement of economic data (income, expenditure and savings) by the respondents. The adopted concept of income in NSHIE includes wages, salaries, bonus, business, profession, farm income and other forms of labour income, pensions, rent, interest and dividend. The aggregate income of Indian households is estimated to be Rs 13,390 billion for the 12-month period—April 2004 to March 2005—which is around 53 per cent of the total personal disposable income provided by the National Accounts Statistics (NAS) for the entire country. An estimate of surplus income (as an indicator of savings) is arrived at by subtracting the total household expenditure from the total household income. Through this method, this survey found the estimates of savings as a proportion of disposable income to be 25.0 per cent, as against the official estimate of 27.1 per cent for the year 2004–05 (Table 1.3). It is important to note that for all practical purposes, the degree of under coverage of income, expenditure and saving in NSHIE in comparison to official estimates gives a fair degree of confidence for studying the distributional properties.

These differences in estimates can be attributed to the following factors. One, this survey did not cover some of the smaller states and UTs that account for about

Table 1.3: Estimates of Income, Expenditure and Saving

	NSHIE (2004–05) (24 states)	CSO (2004–05) (All India)	Ratio of NSHIE/CSO (per cent)
Estimated population (million)	1,027	1,090	94.2
Estimated households (million)	205.4	230.1	89.3
Personal disposable income (Rs billion)	13,390	25,330	52.9
Private final consumption expenditure (Rs billion)	10,044	18,900	53.1
Household saving (Rs billion)	3,346	6,870	48.7
Saving rate (per cent)	25.0	27.1	

Source: CSO, NSHIE 2004–05 data: NCAER–CMCR analysis.

4 per cent of the population. Two, according to the Central Statistical Organisation (CSO), the household sector by definition comprises individuals, non-government non-corporate enterprises of farm business and non-farm business like sole proprietorships and partnerships, and non-profit institutions. This survey, on the other hand, covers only households. Three, certain components of income are not perceived as income by the respondents, and hence, they get excluded from incomes reported in income surveys. Items like reimbursements for travel, medical and other such expenses are not reported correctly in this survey.

1.3.4 Estimates of Sampling Error

To check reliability of the data, a variety of methods are used. The most common amongst them are evaluation of sampling and non-sampling errors. Sampling errors are measurable within the framework of the sample design and are also controllable by varying the size of the sample. For instance, the average income per household is Rs 65,041 and its standard error is Rs 4; the average amount of life insurance payments made per household is Rs 1,227 and its sampling error is negligible at Re 1. Nearly 6.2 per cent of all urban households reported payments towards life insurance and their average insurance payment amounts to Rs 2,528. This estimate is subject to a standard error of Rs 2.

The standard error and coefficient of variation of the estimated average household income for various income quintiles is consistent and within permissible limits (Table 1.4). This generates a fair degree of confidence in the estimates presented in this book.

Table 1.4: Estimates of Standard Errors

Per capita income quintile	Percentage share in households	Percentage share in total income	Per capita income (Rs per annum)	Standard error of mean	Percentage standard error	Coefficient of variation (per cent)
Q1-Bottom quintile (0 per cent–20 per cent)	18.0	6.3	3,692	1.40	0.0072	45.9
Q2-Second quintile (21 per cent–40 per cent)	18.8	10.1	6,205	2.00	0.0063	40.7
Q3-Middle quintile (41 per cent–60 per cent)	20.4	14.4	8,905	2.90	0.0066	42.4
Q4-Fourth quintile (61 per cent–80 per cent)	20.7	21.3	13,311	4.50	0.0067	43.2
Q5-Top quintile (81 per cent–100 per cent)	22.1	48.0	33,020	9.60	0.0059	37.9
Total	100.0	100	13,018	3.60	0.0055	79.5

Source: NSHIE 2004–05 data: NCAER–CMCR analysis.

Another important source of error, which can vitiate the estimates, is the non-response rate. In the case of this survey, it was around 3 per cent and largely due to unanticipated reasons such as the psychology of the respondent. Non-sampling errors arise mainly from three sources. One, respondents refuse to cooperate and deny information, or they supply partial information that may not be usable, or they deliberately provide false information. Two, the interviewers are also prone to have some preconceived notions, whereby some biases creep into the schedules. Three, respondents may not remember all the relevant numbers sought by the interviewers, and this tends to considerably increase the margin of error in the data collected. There is no satisfactory procedure for a precise measurement of non-sampling errors. A team of trained interviewers (250), supervisors (50) and NCAER professionals (14) from different language groups were engaged for about four months to undertake the task of primary data collection. The field team was thoroughly trained through all the phases of the surveys. Every care was taken to implement maximum possible quality control in recording of the answers of the respondents.

1.4 Importance of the Study

As India is among the world's fastest growing economies, it is imperative to measure the economic well-being of its citizens on an ongoing basis. By tracking the various parameters that contribute towards the social and economic well-being of the people and their ability to protect themselves and their families against unforeseen crises, the findings of this study would help arrive at a true measure of economic well-being of India's populace.

Indian households have come a long way during the 20-year period that has seen dramatic changes in the way Indians live, earn, consume and save. And to truly understand the potential of Indian households, it is necessary to map them in terms of their earning and spending patterns. What are the factors that determine the income of a household and thereby its saving and expenditure trends? This book seeks to explore this question. As we will see in the following chapters, the level of well-being is dependent on a whole host of factors ranging from occupation to education, and location of households. Some of these factors include constraints imposed by individual capabilities and behaviour; for example, the willingness and ability to take risks. Other factors could be non-availability of capital, high cost of education and institutional factors such as inheritance laws and barriers to mobility. Since the impact of these factors is, to a large extent, non-measurable, we have focussed on discerning the differences in the income levels associated with certain demographic and socio-economic characteristics of chief earners and households. In respect of the chief earner, his occupation, education and age have significant bearing on his income, spending and saving levels. The sectors of employment, major sources of income, state of residence are also critical in ascertaining income, expenditure and saving levels in different parts of the country.

What light does this survey throw on the conduct of similar surveys in future? It has demonstrated that it is not impossible to collect reasonable data on income, expenditure and saving which cannot be obtained satisfactorily through other means and which are needed for an understanding of the economic process and also for policy purposes. It is true that all the data collected in any survey do not possess the same degree of accuracy and certain estimates are likely to be subject to large non-sampling errors. This, however, is likely to result in an underestimation of financial assets rather than overestimation. Finally, the only method of reducing non-sampling errors and increasing efficiency of survey estimates is to limit the scale of the survey operation and invest more time and energy in better training of the field staff in substantive matters and interviewing techniques, and improving survey instruments, the most important of which is the questionnaire.

All the estimates–income, expenditure, savings, and so on–presented in this book are based on two factors: the population covered by this survey and what was reported by the respondents. It is important to keep these limitations in mind while drawing any conclusion from the results presented in this book.

This book is a result of years of household level research that the author and his colleagues at NCAER have undertaken in an effort to track the dynamic changes that are taking place in our country. It is hoped that the insights in the following chapters will help economic analysts, policy makers, marketers, researchers, development professionals, international experts, Indologists and the average Indian reader get a better understanding of how the Indian growth story has unfolded for Indian households.

References

Bery, Suman and R. K. Shukla. 2003. 'NCAER's Market Information Survey of Households: Statistical Properties and Application for Policy Analysis', Special Issue of *Economic and Political Weekly*, 38(4 [25–31 January]): 350–54.

Deaton, Angus S. and Valerie Kozel. 2004. *Data and Dogma: The Great Indian Poverty Debate.* Oxford University Press and The World Bank.

McKinsey Global Institute. 2007. *The Bird of Gold: The Rise of India's Middle Class.* Available from http://www.mckinsey.com/mgi/publications/india_consumer_market/index.asp. Accessed on 22 February 2010.

Shukla, Rajesh. 2005. *The Great Indian Market: Results from the NCAER Market Information Survey of Households.* New Delhi: National Council of Applied Economic Research (NCAER) and *Business Standard.*

——. 2007. *How India Earns, Spends and Saves: Results from MNYL-NCAER Financial Protection Survey.* New Delhi: Max and NCAER.

Shukla, Rajesh and Roopa Purushothaman. 2008. *The Next Urban Frontier: Twenty Cities to Watch.* New Delhi: NCAER; Mumbai: Future Research Capital.

Earning Pattern of Indian Households

two

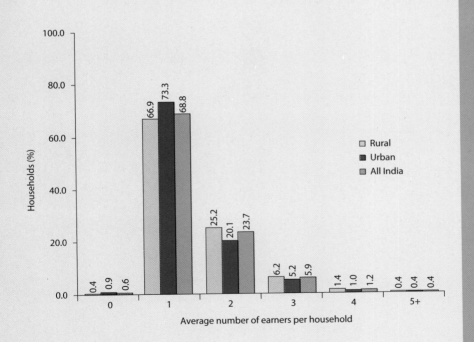

Household income is a valuable welfare indicator, useful to a wide range of users including planners, policy makers, employers and marketers. The large differences in earning patterns of households between rural and urban India are pointers to how things will unfold as urbanisation levels in the country increase. Urban households earn around 85 per cent more than rural ones, spend three-fourths more and, as a result, save nearly double that of rural households. Much of this can be explained by differences in the level of education of chief earners of households and their professions. Salary level for graduate households is 3.5 times more than that of illiterate households. In rural areas, households headed by labourers account for 34.6 per cent of the rural households, but only 20.2 per cent of rural incomes; in urban areas, the corresponding figures are 22.9 per cent and 9.7 per cent, respectively.

According to the National Survey of Household Income and Expenditure (NSHIE) 2004–05, there are 205.6 million households in India[1] of which nearly 70 per cent (144.2 million) are located in rural areas and the rest (61.4 million) in urban areas.[2] As urban families are marginally smaller than rural ones, the share of India's urban population is at 28.7 per cent (Table 2.1). While the average household size is

Table 2.1: Estimates of Household and Population

	Rural	Urban	All India
Households (million)	144.2	61.4	205.6
Population (million)	731.9	295.3	1027.3
Household size	5.08	4.81	5.00
Number of earners per household	1.43	1.34	1.40

Source: NSHIE 2004–05 data: NCAER–CMCR analysis.

---

[1] The survey covers all states and Union Territories (UTs) except Jammu & Kashmir, Sikkim, Arunachal Pradesh, Nagaland, Manipur, Mizoram, Tripura, Andaman & Nicobar Islands, Daman & Diu, Dadra & Nagar Haveli and Lakshadweep which account for 3–4 per cent of the country's total population.

[2] The definition of urban areas adopted here is the same as that used in the 2001 Census. Accordingly, urban areas include: *(a)* All places with a municipality/corporation, cantonment board or a notified town area committee; *(b)* All other places having minimum population of 5,000; at least 75 per cent of the male workforce is engaged in non-agricultural pursuits and a population density of over 400 per sq km (1,000 per sq mile).

five (5.08 in rural and 4.81 in urban), less than 1 per cent of Indian households are single-member units and around 10 per cent have more than seven members. The household size distribution is positively skewed, with both the urban and rural families showing similar distribution. The proportion of large families is higher in rural areas (Figure 2.1).

Figure 2.1: Distribution of Households by Household Size

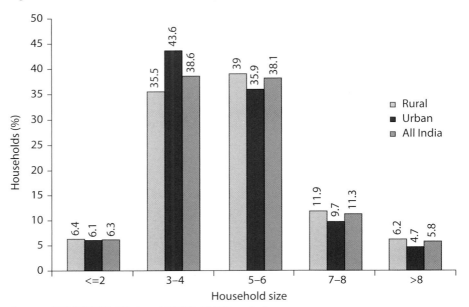

Source: NSHIE 2004–05 data: NCAER–CMCR analysis.

Earners comprise a little more than one fourth of the total population (28.1 per cent). Of this population, rural India's share is 71.5 per cent. The average number of earners per household is 1.41 (1.34 in urban areas and 1.43 in rural areas). A majority of the households are single-earner households (68.8 per cent), followed by two-earner households (23.7 per cent). The distribution of households by the number of earners is asymmetrical, where urban is more skewed than rural, that is, 2.03 and 1.76 respectively (Figure 2.2).

A household in India earns an average annual income of Rs 65,041 (in financial year 2004–05), spends Rs 48,558 and has a surplus of Rs 16,483 to save and invest (Figure 2.3). Urban income levels are around 85 per cent more than rural ones (Rs 95,827 versus Rs 51,922, per annum). Although expenses in urban areas are also substantially higher (Rs 68,352 versus Rs 40,124 per annum ones), an urban household manages to save nearly double that of a rural household (Rs 27,475 versus Rs 11,798 per annum).

Figure 2.2: Distribution of Households by Number of Earners

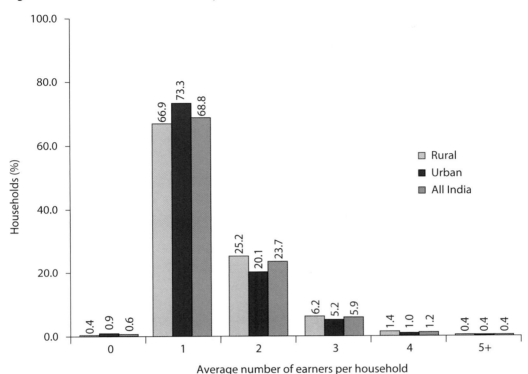

Source: NSHIE 2004–05 data: NCAER–CMCR analysis.

What are the factors that determine the income of a household or an individual? There is no easy answer to this question. As will be seen later, the income differential between different groups of population, particularly among different occupational groups, is so great that a number of factors come into play to produce the inequalities in income distribution. Some of these include constraints imposed by individual capabilities and behaviour, such as willingness and ability to take risks. Other factors could be non-availability of capital, high cost of education and institutional factors such as inheritance laws and barriers to mobility. Since the impact of these factors is, to a large extent, non-measurable, the focus of subsequent sections is on discerning the differences in the income levels associated with certain demographic and socio-economic characteristics of households and chief earners. The sector of employment, major source of income, state of residence, social group, and so on, are also critical in ascertaining a household's income level. In respect of the chief earner, his occupation, education and age have significant bearing on his income level.

Figure 2.3: Estimates of Income,* Expenditure** and Surplus Income***

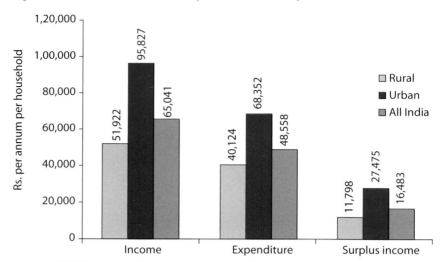

Source: NSHIE 2004–05 data: NCAER–CMCR analysis.

Notes: * Household income: It refers to total income received by the household as a whole by each of its members from all sources such as wages and salaries, income from self-employment; interest and dividends from invested funds, pensions or other benefits from social insurance and other current transfers receivable during the financial year 2004–05.

** Household expenditure: It includes both routine as well unusual consumption expenditure made by all members of the household during the financial year 2004–05. Routine expenditure includes consumption expenditure on food, housing, health, education, transport, clothing, durables and other such expenses that a household generally incurs. Unusual expenditure includes unplanned large expenditure on ceremonies (such as weddings, births, and so on), medical, higher education, leisure travel, and so on.

*** Surplus income: Total household income minus total household expenditure (routine plus unusual).

2.1 Socio-economic Profile of Household and Level of Earning

2.1.1 Sectors[3] as Major Source of Income for Households and Level of Earnings

The changing face of Indian households is also visible in terms of the sectors in which they are primarily engaged. Agriculture has been the dominant sector

---

[3] The National Industrial Classification (NIC 1998) is used for classifying the household which are akin in terms of process type, raw materials, used and finished goods produced. Sector of employment of a household is classified in any one of the sector which contributed maximum to household income among the following sectors. Agriculture: Agriculture, livestock, fishing, hunting and forestry; Industry: Mining, quarrying and manufacturing; Traditional services: Electricity, gas and water supply, hotel and restaurants, public administration and defence, financial intermediation, education, health and social work; and Modern services: Construction, transport, storage and communication, real estate, renting and business activities, wholesale/retail trade , repair household goods, private households, Others. Available from http://mospi.nic.in/nic_1998.htm. Accessed on 22 Feruary 2010.

Table 2.2: Estimates of Households, Population and Income by Sectors of Engagement: All India

Sectors of engagement	Households (million)	Population (million)	Household size	Average household income (Rs per annum)	Per capita income (Rs per annum)
Agriculture	86.7	437.9	5.05	48,097	9,518
Industry	19.7	97.8	4.95	71,372	14,411
Modern services	29.3	144.4	4.92	112,222	22,797
Traditional services	69.9	347.1	4.97	64,453	12,972
Total	205.6	1027.3	5.00	65,041	13,018

Source: NSHIE 2004–05 data: NCAER–CMCR analysis.

for decades and it still is a major source of income for 86.7 million households (Table 2.2). In other words, nearly 438 million people are dependent on agriculture for their income. Increasingly, however, services have started to play a significant role in terms of employment opportunities for households and as a generator of higher incomes. Nearly 100 million households covering a population of 491.5 million people are dependent on service sector for their income. Of these, traditional services sustain 69.9 million households, whereas modern services provide for the incomes of 29.3 million households.

Households in the agricultural sector have the lowest income. At the all-India level, the average household income is Rs 48,097. However, the household income of this sector, in urban areas, is a little more than 1.5 times the income in rural areas (Tables 2.3 and 2.4). The urban–rural divide is quite stark even among households

Table 2.3: Estimates of Households, Population and Income by Sectors of Engagement: Rural

Sectors of engagement	Households (million)	Population (million)	Household size	Average house-hold income (Rs per annum)	Per capita income (Rs per annum)
Agriculture	83.4	421.0	5.05	46,942	9,295
Industry	8.8	45.0	5.11	46,567	9,111
Modern services	13.0	67.4	5.17	102,345	19,793
Traditional services	39.0	198.6	5.09	46,921	9,210
Total	144.2	731.9	5.08	51,922	10,227

Source: NSHIE 2004–05 data: NCAER–CMCR analysis.

Table 2.4: Estimates of Households, Population and Income by Sectors of Engagement: Urban

Sectors of engagement	Households (million)	Population (million)	Household size	Average house-hold income (Rs per annum)	Per capita income (Rs per annum)
Agriculture	3.3	16.9	5.13	77,338	15,077
Industry	11.0	52.8	4.83	91,296	18,921
Modern services	16.3	77.0	4.72	120,117	25,426
Traditional services	30.9	148.5	4.81	86,578	18,001
Total	61.4	295.3	4.81	95,827	19,935

Source: NSHIE 2004–05 data: NCAER–CMCR analysis.

employed in the industrial and traditional services sectors which earn 96 per cent and 84 per cent, respectively, more than their rural counterparts. The inequality in earning capacity between rural and urban households is the least for those engaged in modern services (Rs 102,345 in rural versus Rs 120,117 in urban India).

Per capita income is much higher for households engaged in modern services (Rs 22,797) and industrial sectors (Rs 14,411) followed by traditional services and agricultural sectors. This trend has been observed for urban areas as well (Table 2.4). As for rural areas, per capita income across all household types is more or less similar, except in the case of modern services where it is significantly higher at Rs 19,793 (Table 2.3).

The declining stature of agriculture is even more apparent when the earning weights of the sectors are taken into account. The highest earning weight is that of modern services: 1.75. Households engaged in this sector contribute 14.1 per cent share to total population and 24.6 per cent to total household income (Table 2.5). For the rural areas, the earning weight is still higher (1.94) as 9.2 per cent households contribute 17.8 per cent to the total income. Traditional services with an earning weight of 1.0 also fare well, with 33.8 per cent population engaged in such services, contributing almost at the same rate to total household income. In contrast, the earning weight of the agricultural sector is just 0.73 pointing to the fact that this sector is making a lower contribution towards higher personal disposable income through household income (Table 2.5).

Significantly, though the industry sector has an earning weight of 1.11, its potential as a major contributor to personal disposable income continues to be underutilised. There are barely 9.5 per cent households engaged in this sector

Table 2.5: Distribution of Population, Income and Earning Weights by Sector of Engagement

Sectors of engagement	Distribution of population (per cent)			Distribution of income (per cent)			Earning weight*		
	Rural	Urban	All India	Rural	Urban	All India	Rural	Urban	All India
Agriculture	57.5	5.7	42.6	52.3	4.3	31.2	0.91	0.76	0.73
Industry	6.1	17.9	9.5	5.5	17.0	10.5	0.89	0.95	1.11
Modern services	9.2	26.1	14.1	17.8	33.3	24.6	1.94	1.28	1.75
Traditional services	27.1	50.3	33.8	24.4	45.4	33.7	0.90	0.90	1.00
Total	100.0	100.0	100.0	100.0	100.0	100.0	1.00	1.00	1.00

Source: NSHIE 2004–05 data: NCAER–CMCR analysis.
Note: * Earning weight is the ratio of share of income of a category of households to its population share, that is, the extent to which the category controls income beyond its 'natural share' in the population.

and their share of personal disposable income is about 10.5 per cent. Clearly, it is time for policy makers to focus on this sector in a bid to revive its potential as an income-generator, and in the process, enhance its contribution to economic growth.

For examining the sectoral impact on household income, we have taken the income for industry sector as the base income (Table 2.6). At the all-India level, if households that are currently engaged in industry sector are to switch to traditional services, their annual income would actually decline by 10 per cent, and if they adopt agriculture, it would reduce by as much as 33 per cent. On the other hand, their income would see a growth of 57 per cent if they opt for modern services. The impact is, however, much higher in rural areas (120 per cent increase in income) than in urban areas (32 per cent).

Table 2.6: Impact of Change of Sector of Engagement on Household Earnings (Percentage Increase in Income over Industry Sector Income)

Sectors of engagement	Increase in income (Rs)			Increase in income (per cent)		
	Rural	Urban	All India	Rural	Urban	All India
Modern services	55,778	28,821	40,850	120	32	57
Agriculture	375	–13,958	–23,276	01	–15	–33
Traditional services	354	–4,718	–6,919	01	–05	–10
Industry (Base income)	46,567	91,296	71,372			

Source: NSHIE 2004–05 data: NCAER–CMCR analysis.

2.1.2 Major Occupation[4] of Households and Level of Earnings

For an overwhelmingly large number of Indian households, self-employment is the major source of income. Nearly 82.3 million households (42 per cent) are engaged in farming, fishing, hunting and allied activities, and 45.6 million households (22.2 per cent) are involved in production related work or jobs pertaining to transportation (Table 2.7). These two groups have an average annual income

Table 2.7: Estimates of Households, Population and Income by Occupation: All India

Occupation	Households (million)	Population (million)	Household size	Average household income (Rs per annum)	Per capita income (Rs per annum)
Professional, technical and related workers	9.6	49.2	5.14	129,213	25,156
Administrative, executive and managerial workers	5.9	28.7	4.91	169,317	34,507
Clerical and related workers*	10.9	52.3	4.81	99,584	20,708
Sales workers**	25.9	132.4	5.12	86,409	16,876
Service workers***	11.6	56.6	4.88	81,741	16,753
Farmers, fishermen, hunters, loggers and related workers	82.3	416.5	5.06	48,295	9,544
Production and related workers	45.6	230.3	5.05	47,841	9,478
Workers not classified by occupation	13.9	61.2	4.40	51,769	11,754
Total	205.6	1027.3	5.00	65,041	13,018

Source: NSHIE 2004–05 data: NCAER–CMCR analysis.

Notes: * Clerical and related workers include book-keepers, typists, computer operators, shop assistance, and so on.

** Sales workers cover both wholesale and retail, including hawkers, pedlars, street vendors, real estate salesmen, insurance agents, manufacture's agents, and so on.

*** Service workers includes carpenters, masons, tailors, cobblers, mechanics, barbers, drycleaners, porters, watchman, and so on.

---

[4] The National Classification of Occupation (NCO 1968) is used for classifying in any specific occupation category which contributes maximum to household income. In an occupation classification, the groups of occupation have to be based on the fundamental criterion of 'type of work performed.' All the workers engaged in the same type of work are grouped together irrespective of the industrial classification of establishments where they are engaged. For example, all clerical workers have been classified in one occupational group whether they are engaged in a factory, mine, government office or a shop.

of nearly Rs 48,000. The next big group of households (25.9 million) earns its income from sales related jobs. But the top earning households (5.9 million) are those that are primarily dependent on administrative, executive or managerial jobs. The average annual household income of this group (Rs 169,317) is more than 3.5 times that of households engaged in production and related jobs, which in fact generates the lowest income (Rs 47,841). This high income group constitutes a population of about 28.7 million which forms just 2.8 per cent of the total population. Households of professional and technical workers too have a substantially high annual income of about Rs 129,213, which is 2.5 times that of the bottom most rung of occupation.

The top two highest income generating occupation groups comprise nearly 35 million people in rural areas and 43 million in urban India. In contrast, the farmers/fishermen group constitute a population of nearly 402 million people in rural India and only 14 million in urban India. Interestingly, the population of sales workers in rural and urban areas are nearly of the same size: 65 million in rural versus 67 million in urban India. However, the rural–urban divide in terms of household income is quite substantial. While urban sales workers have annual household incomes of Rs 106,842, their rural counterparts earn only Rs 64,568. This disparity in income is observed across all groups of workers (Tables 2.8 and 2.9).

Table 2.8: Estimates of Households, Population and Income by Occupation: Rural

Occupation	Households (million)	Population (million)	Household size	Average household income (Rs per annum)	Per capita income (Rs per annum)
Professional, technical and related workers	4.7	25.6	5.43	120,080	22,108
Administrative, executive and managerial workers	1.7	9.1	5.24	135,222	25,798
Clerical and related workers	4.1	20.8	5.05	98,878	19,595
Sales workers	12.5	65.3	5.22	64,568	12,362
Service workers	5.3	26.9	5.05	70,681	13,987
Farmers, fishermen, hunters, loggers and related workers	79.5	402.4	5.06	47,371	9,361
Production and related workers	28.7	147.7	5.15	34,746	6,746
Workers not classified by occupation	7.6	34.1	4.51	43,458	9,644
Total	144.2	731.9	5.08	51,922	10,227

Source: NSHIE 2004–05 data: NCAER–CMCR analysis.

Table 2.9: Estimates of Households, Population and Income by Occupation: Urban

Occupation	Households (million)	Population (million)	Household size	Average household income (Rs per annum)	Per capita income (Rs per annum)
Professional, technical and related workers	4.9	23.6	4.85	138,065	28,463
Administrative, executive and managerial workers	4.1	19.6	4.76	183,803	38,577
Clerical and related workers	6.8	31.5	4.66	100,016	21,445
Sales workers	13.4	67.1	5.02	106,842	21,266
Service workers	6.3	29.7	4.73	91,097	19,252
Farmers, fishermen, hunters, loggers and related workers	2.8	14.1	5.06	74,623	14,755
Production and related workers	16.9	82.6	4.87	70,011	14,368
Workers not classified by occupation	6.3	27.1	4.28	61,694	14,406
Total	61.4	295.3	4.81	95,827	19,935

Source: NSHIE 2004–05 data: NCAER–CMCR analysis.

Per capita incomes for all worker types are higher in urban areas as compared to rural areas. The administrative and managerial group has the highest per capita income followed by professional, technical and related workers. At the all-India level there is little difference among the clerical category, sales workers and service workers in terms of per capita income. There is also no difference between the farming group and the production related workers group. The urban and rural scenarios are quite different from the overall picture. In the rural areas, service workers earn more on per capita basis than sales workers but in urban area the situation is just the reverse. While in urban areas, the categories of 'farmers' and 'production related workers' do not show any difference in per capita earnings, in the rural areas, the farmers earn more on per capita basis than the 'production related workers.'

The share of the farming community (which includes fishermen, hunters and allied occupations) in total population is 40.5 per cent but their share in total household income is only 29.7 per cent. The earning weight of this group therefore, works out to a mere 0.73. The earning weight of the administrative/managerial group is the highest (2.6) as just 2.8 per cent of the population contributes 7.4 per cent to total household income. Households engaged in professional and technical jobs have the next highest earning weight (1.93) as their shares in population and household income are 4.8 per cent and 9.3 per cent, respectively (Table 2.10).

Table 2.10: Distribution of Population, Income and Earning Weights by Occupation

Occupation	Distribution of population (per cent)			Distribution of income (per cent)			Earning weight		
	Rural	Urban	All India	Rural	Urban	All India	Rural	Urban	All India
Professional, technical and related workers	3.5	8.0	4.8	7.6	11.4	9.3	2.16	1.43	1.93
Administrative, executive and managerial workers	1.2	6.6	2.8	3.2	12.8	7.4	2.52	1.94	2.65
Clerical and related workers	2.8	10.7	5.1	5.5	11.5	8.1	1.92	1.08	1.59
Sales workers	8.9	22.7	12.9	10.8	24.2	16.7	1.21	1.07	1.30
Service workers	3.7	10.1	5.5	5.0	9.7	7.1	1.37	0.97	1.29
Farmers, fishermen, hunters, loggers and related workers	55.0	4.8	40.5	50.3	3.5	29.7	0.92	0.74	0.73
Production and related workers	20.2	28.0	22.4	13.3	20.1	16.3	0.66	0.72	0.73
Workers not classified by occupation	4.7	9.2	6.0	4.4	6.6	5.4	0.94	0.72	0.90
Total	100.0	100.0	100.0	100.0	100.0	100.0	1.00	1.00	1.00

Source: NSHIE 2004–05 data: NCAER–CMCR analysis.

The impact of a change of occupation on household income can be quite dramatic. It is also a pointer to the need for vocational training. For instance, if the farmer/fishermen group's income of Rs 48,295 is taken as base income, switching to a sales job would instantly raise the household's annual income by 79 per cent (Table 2.11). Even a change to a service related job would help the household earn 69 per cent more. By switching to a professional/technical job, the household would get an additional 68 per cent. However, a switch from farming to a production/transport job may not be beneficial as it could lead to a 6 per cent fall in income in urban areas and 27 per cent fall in rural areas, though at the all-India level the decline is just 1 per cent. This clearly indicates that rural household incomes could be dramatically improved with some vocational and skill improvement, as agriculture is unable to provide sustainable incomes for large sections of the rural population.

Table 2.11: Impact of Change of Occupation Categories on Household Earnings (Increase in Income over Farming as Source of Income)

Occupation	Increase in income (Rs)			Increase in income (per cent)		
	Rural	Urban	All India	Rural	Urban	All India
Professional, technical and related workers	72,709	63,443	80,918	53	85	68
Administrative, executive and managerial workers	87,851	109,181	121,021	85	46	251
Clerical and related workers	51,507	25,393	51,289	109	34	106
Sales workers	17,197	32,219	38,113	36	43	79
Service workers	23,310	16,474	33,445	49	22	69
Production and related workers	−12,625	−4,612	−454	−27	−06	−01
Farmers, fishermen, hunters, loggers and related workers (Base income)	47,371	74,623	48,295			

Source: NSHIE 2004–05 data: NCAER–CMCR analysis.

2.1.3 State of Residence and Level of Earnings

The role of state governments in creating an enabling environment and creating economic opportunities for their people is an aspect that is rarely discussed or considered while analysing household income and expenditure levels. However, the fact remains that different states offer varying levels of economic opportunities, thus influencing household income levels. In the absence of vital infrastructure, many states continue to lag behind others in offering employment and growth opportunities. Some states are in a better position to attract corporate participation and thus offer the right opportunities for socio-economic prosperity to the people. Of late, the impact of good governance is being recognised by more and more economists in the nation's growth dynamics.

As per Central Statistical Organisation (CSO) estimates, the per capita net domestic product at current prices for 2004–05 varies significantly across the country, ranging from Rs 29,137 for Delhi to Rs 6,277 in Bihar, which means a difference of around five times between the richest and poorest states. If the various states are bunched into three categories[5] of low, middle and high income states

[5] **Low income states**: Assam, Bihar, Madhya Pradesh, Meghalaya, Orissa, Rajasthan, Uttar Pradesh, Chattisgarh, Uttaranchal and Jharkhand; **Middle income states**: Andhra Pradesh, Himachal Pradesh, Karnataka, Kerala, Tamil Nadu and West Bengal; and **High income states**: Goa, Gujarat, Haryana, Maharashtra, Punjab, Pondicherry, Chandigarh and Delhi.

Table 2.12: Estimates of Households, Population and Income by State of Residence: All India

State of residence	Households (million)	Population (million)	Household size	Average household income (Rs per annum)	Per capita income (Rs per annum)
Low income states	91.7	493.3	5.38	52,052	9,679
Middle income states	69.6	314.0	4.51	66,737	14,792
High income states	44.3	220.0	4.97	89,288	17,972
Total	205.6	1027.3	5.00	65,041	13,018

Source: NSHIE 2004–05 data: NCAER–CMCR analysis.

(based on the level of their per capita income), it is observed that 48 per cent of Indians live in low income states, 30.6 per cent in middle income sates and the balance in high income states (Table 2.12).

It follows that low income states are characterised by large populations, a majority of which occupy the lowest rungs of the socio-economic ladder. These states have nearly 91.7 million households, carrying a population of almost 493.3 million. In contrast, high income states have 44 million households and their population is about 220 million, which is less than half that of the low income states. Average annual household income of high income states is, however, 1.7 times the household income of low income states.

As expected, the per capita income increases as we move from low income to high income states. In high income states, the relative increase (over the lowest income) in the per capita rural income is of the same order as with urban per capita income (Tables 2.13 and 2.14). In middle income states, the proportionate increase in per capita income is much higher in the case of rural income (45 per cent) compared to urban income (34 per cent).

The high income states have a share of just 21.5 per cent of the total population in the country but their contribution to total disposable income is nearly 30 per cent

Table 2.13: Estimates of Households, Population and Income by State of Residence: Rural

State of residence	Households (million)	Population (million)	Household size	Average household income (Rs per annum)	Per capita income (Rs per annum)
Low income states	73.7	398.0	5.40	44,999	8,336
Middle income states	46.6	214.0	4.60	55,604	12,094
High income states	23.9	119.9	5.02	66,121	13,172
Total	144.2	731.9	5.08	51,922	10,227

Source: NSHIE 2004–05 data: NCAER–CMCR analysis.

Table 2.14: Estimates of Households, Population and Income by State of Residence: Urban

State of residence	Households (million)	Population (million)	Household size	Average household income (Rs per annum)	Per capita income (Rs per annum)
Low income states	18.0	95.2	5.29	80,948	15,295
Middle income states	23.0	100.0	4.34	89,223	20,566
High income states	20.4	100.1	4.91	116,421	23,720
Total	61.4	295.3	4.81	95,827	19,935

Source: NSHIE 2004–05 data: NCAER–CMCR analysis.

(Table 2.15). In contrast, low income states have a share of nearly 48 per cent of the total population in India and their share of the total disposable income is about 35.7 per cent. Almost half of the Indian population lives in low income states, 30.6 per cent in middle income and 21.4 per cent in high income states.

The earning weights worked out for the low, middle, and high income categories of states in India are also presented in Table 2.15. The earning weight of middle income states is 1.4 as against 0.7 for low income states, that is, double that of low income states. It may be noted that in high and middle income states the earning weight for rural areas is slightly higher than in urban areas. This may be due to better rural infrastructure and facilities provided by the state governments of these richer states, whereby the people are able to make useful and effective contributions to the total household income.

Table 2.15: Distribution of Population, Income and Earning Weights by State of Residence

State of residence	Distribution of population (per cent)			Distribution of income (per cent)			Earning weight		
	Rural	Urban	All India	Rural	Urban	All India	Rural	Urban	All India
Low income states	54.4	32.3	48.0	44.3	24.7	35.7	0.82	0.77	0.74
Middle income states	29.2	33.9	30.6	34.6	34.9	34.7	1.18	1.03	1.14
High income states	16.4	33.9	21.4	21.1	40.3	29.6	1.29	1.19	1.38
Total	100.0	100.0	100.0	100.0	100.0	100.0	1.00	1.00	1.00

Source: NSHIE 2004–05 data: NCAER–CMCR analysis.

The impact of the state of residence on household income quantified in terms of percentage increase in base income, that is, the low income state is given in Table 2.16. If a household residing in a low income state migrates to a middle income state, its annual income would rise by Rs 14,685 (28 per cent) and by Rs 37,236 (72 per cent) if the shift is to a high income state. The impact is relatively higher for rural households than for urban ones. This analysis once again corroborates the observed trend of rural people migrating from low income states to high income states in search of a livelihood.

Table 2.16: Impact of Change of State of Residence on Household Earning (Increase in Income over that of Low Income States)

State of residence	Increase in income (Rs)			Increase in income (per cent)		
	Rural	Urban	All India	Rural	Urban	All India
High income states	21,122	35,474	37,236	47	44	72
Middle income states	10,606	8,276	14,685	24	10	28
Low income states (Base income)	44,999	80,948	52,052			

Source: NSHIE 2004–05 data: NCAER–CMCR analysis.

2.2 Demographic Profile of Chief Earner[6] and Level of Earning

2.2.1 Occupation of Chief Earner and Level of Earning

Occupation is considered to be one of the important socio-economic characteristics in influencing an individual's status in society, standard of living and also to some extent his aspirations. It has been aptly described as a person's way of life. At the all-India level, 66.8 million households, with manual labourers as chief earners, are the biggest group comprising a population of nearly 321 million (Table 2.17). They constitute a little less than a third of total households in India. The average household size is 4.8 members, marginally smaller than households belonging to the other occupation categories. There are 59.4 million households with chief earners that are self-employed in farming related activities. Such households, forming the second largest group, comprise a population of 311.4 million with

---

[6] Chief earner is that member of a household who contributes maximum to the household income. In the majority of cases, the chief earner and head of the household is the same person.

Table 2.17: Estimates of Households, Population and Income by Occupation of Chief Earner: All India

Occupation of chief earner	Households (million)	Population (million)	Household size	Average household income (Rs per annum)	Per capita income (Rs per annum)
Regular salary/wages	37.9	186.0	4.90	110,344	22,501
Self-employment in non-agriculture	35.1	179.9	5.13	95,020	18,530
Labour	66.8	320.9	4.80	30,957	6,446
Self-employment in agriculture	59.4	311.4	5.24	55,653	10,622
Others	6.3	29.0	4.59	75,468	16,457
Total	205.6	1027.3	5.00	65,041	13,018

Source: NSHIE 2004–05 data: NCAER–CMCR analysis.

an average household size of 5.24 members. Households with salaried chief earners constitute about 18 per cent (37.9 million) of all households in India with a population of 186 million, whereas nearly 17 per cent of households (35.1 million) constituting a population of nearly 180 million depend on self-employment in non-agricultural activities for their income.

At the all-India level, there is a wide difference in income levels across occupation types. The lowest earners are labourers with an average annual household income of Rs 30,957 and a per capita income of Rs 6,446. The highest earners are salaried employees with an annual average household income (Rs 110,344) which is almost four times that of labourers, and a per capita income of Rs 22,501. Those who are self-employed in agriculture earn slightly more than labourers with household income of Rs 55,653 and per capita income of Rs 10,622. Those who are self-employed in non-farm occupations have annual household incomes of Rs 95,020 and per capita income of Rs 18,530.

Income levels vary significantly across rural and urban areas too, thus widening the gap between different socio-economic groups even further. Those that are self-employed in agriculture form the largest group in rural areas, accounting for 41.3 per cent of the population and 42.1 per cent of income (Table 2.20). In other words, they are the average rural household. In contrast, in urban India, this group accounts for just 3.1 per cent of the population and a mere 2.6 per cent of total urban income. This is despite the fact that urban agriculturist households earn nearly two-thirds more than their rural counterparts (Rs 91,218 versus Rs 54,622 per annum; Tables 2.18 and 2.19).

Table 2.18: Estimates of Households, Population and Income by Occupation of Chief Earner: Rural

Occupation of chief earner	Households (million)	Population (million)	Household size	Average household income (Rs per annum)	Per capita income (Rs per annum)
Regular salary/wages	14.7	76.9	5.24	103,687	19,793
Self-employment in non-agriculture	16.2	83.9	5.19	67,621	13,021
Labour	52.4	253.4	4.84	28,567	5,906
Self-employment in agriculture	57.8	302.3	5.23	54,622	10,438
Others	3.2	15.4	4.86	68,870	14,159
Total	144.2	731.9	5.08	51,922	10,227

Source: NSHIE 2004–05 data: NCAER–CMCR analysis.

In terms of per capita earning, salaried households in India earn 3.5 times more than the income of labour households. For the 'self-employed in non-agriculture' category, it is 2.9 times and for 'self-employed in agriculture' it is 1.6 times that of labour category. The per capita earnings are in general higher in the urban area for all classes of households but here, non-farm self-employment is more rewarding than manual labour (2.7 times per capita) than in rural areas (2.2 times per capita).

Table 2.19: Estimates of Households, Population and Income by Occupation of Chief Earner: Urban

Occupation of chief earner	Households (million)	Population (million)	Household size	Average household income (Rs per annum)	Per capita income (Rs per annum)
Regular salary/wages	23.2	109.1	4.69	114,551	24,411
Self-employment in non-agriculture	18.9	96.0	5.07	118,419	23,346
Labour	14.4	67.5	4.68	39,626	8,472
Self-employment in agriculture	1.7	9.1	5.46	91,218	16,721
Others	3.2	13.6	4.31	82,088	19,061
Total	61.4	295.3	4.81	95,827	19,935

Source: NSHIE 2004–05 data: NCAER–CMCR analysis.

At the all-India level, the labour class is the only category for which there is such a large difference between their share in the total population (31.2 per cent) and the corresponding share in total income (15.6 per cent; Table 2.20). The 'self-employed in agriculture' category is the only other group, where the population share (30.3 per cent) is higher than the income share (24.7 per cent). But the share-difference here is lower than labourer households.

Table 2.20: Distribution of Population, Income and Earning Weights by Occupation of Chief Earner

Occupation of chief earner	Distribution of population (per cent)			Distribution of income (per cent)			Earning weight		
	Rural	Urban	All India	Rural	Urban	All India	Rural	Urban	All India
Regular salary/wages	10.5	36.9	18.1	20.3	45.2	31.3	1.93	1.22	1.73
Self-employment in non-agriculture	11.5	32.5	17.5	14.6	38.1	24.9	1.27	1.17	1.42
Labour	34.6	22.9	31.2	20.0	9.7	15.6	0.58	0.42	0.50
Self-employment in agriculture	41.3	3.1	30.3	42.1	2.6	24.7	1.02	0.84	0.82
Others	2.1	4.6	2.8	2.9	4.4	3.6	1.38	0.96	1.28
Total	100.0	100.0	100.0	100.0	100.0	100.0	1.00	1.00	1.00

Source: NSHIE 2004–05 data: NCAER–CMCR analysis.

There is not much difference in income levels of the 'self-employed in non-agriculture' category and the salaried class in urban areas, but the difference is as high as 53 per cent in rural areas. Salaried households constitute around 37 per cent of urban households and account for a little over 45 per cent of the total income. In the case of the 'self-employed in non-agriculture' category, the second largest group with 32.5 per cent of urban households, the share of total urban income is 38.1 per cent. The proportion of households with labourers as chief earners, not surprisingly, is much higher but they contribute a much lower share to the total income, especially in urban areas.

Households headed by labourers form 34.6 per cent of rural households but they earn only 20.0 per cent of rural incomes. In urban areas, the figures are 22.9 per cent and 9.7 per cent, respectively. While a labour household in the urban area earns 39 per cent more than what its rural counterpart earns, its relatively lower share in urban income is a function of much higher incomes for other occupational categories.

The value of contribution of each occupational group to personal disposable income is best assessed in terms of its earning weight, which is the ratio of its share in total household income to its share in the total population. The earning weights so computed for different occupations are also presented in Table 2.20 for rural, urban and all India levels.

At the aggregate level, salaried households have the greatest earning weight (1.73). With just 18.1 per cent share in total population, they contribute 31.3 per cent to the country's total income. In other words, salaried population possessed 73 per cent higher share in income than its natural share in population. Interestingly, the earning weight of the salaried household in rural India (1.93) is higher than that of its urban counterpart (1.22). Given their low income levels, labour households contribute the least to the personal disposable income. Nearly a third of all Indian households list labour as their primary source of income, and incomes from this segment account for around one-seventh of the country's total income. Labourer families, not surprisingly, have the least earning weight (0.50) among the five occupational categories. For the agriculture dependent households with 30.3 per cent of share in the population and 24.7 per cent share in the personal disposable income, the earning weight works out to 0.82.

To understand the impact of the occupation of chief earner on household income, labour households' earnings of Rs 30,957 per annum is taken as base income and the percentage changes in income by switching to other occupations are worked out. For example, if the labour household switches to agriculture, their income may rise annually by Rs 24,696, that is, by 80 per cent. If labour households opt for self-employment in non-agricultural activities, its income may grow by about Rs 64,064, an increase of 207 per cent over the base income (Table 2.21). The sharpest hike (256 per cent) is observed when the change is made from labour household to a regular wage-earning one.

Table 2.21: Impact of Change of Occupation of Chief Earner on Household Earning (Increase in Income over Labour Household Income)

Occupation of chief earner	Increase in income (Rs)			Increase in income (per cent)		
	Rural	Urban	All India	Rural	Urban	All India
Regular salary/wages	75,120	74,924	79,387	263	189	256
Self-employment in non-agriculture	39,053	78,793	64,064	137	199	207
Self-employment in agriculture	26,055	51,592	24,696	91	130	80
Labour household income (Base income)	28,567	39,626	30,957			

Source: NSHIE 2004–05 data: NCAER–CMCR analysis.

2.2.2 Level of Education of Chief Earner and Level of Earning

The importance of education cannot be over-emphasised. Rising literacy and progress in education are key indicators of human development, and to a large extent, it is the level of education which determines the nature of occupation and, thereby, the earning and standard of living of an individual and household.

The break-up of estimates of households, population and income depending on the education level of the chief earner, in terms of all India, rural and urban areas is presented in Tables 2.22, 2.23 and 2.24, respectively. There are 42.3 million (or nearly 21 per cent) households in the country, where the chief earner has had no formal education or is illiterate. There are more such households in rural areas (26 per cent) compared to urban areas (8 per cent). The largest chunk of Indian households (74.8 million, 36.4 per cent) belongs to the category where the chief earner is a matriculate (Class 10), comprising a population of 371.92 million. Households headed by primary school passed individuals constitute 19.3 per cent (39.6 million) of all households, with the rural and urban break-up being 32.5 million (22.5 per cent) and 7.1 million (11.6 per cent), respectively. There are also 28.1 million households comprising 13.7 per cent of the total households, where the chief earner is a graduate.

Education makes a big difference to earning levels in all cases, though the impact of education is truly visible only when combined with opportunity. This is why the levels of earning vary significantly with the level of education as well as location, that is, rural versus urban. For instance, at the aggregate level, annual earnings range from Rs 37,062 for illiterate chief earner households to Rs 134,539 (more than 3.5 times) for graduate[+] households.

Table 2.22: Estimates of Households, Population and Income by Education Level of Chief Earner: All India

Education level of chief earner	Households (million)	Population (million)	Household size	Average household income (Rs per annum)	Per capita income (Rs per annum)
Illiterate	42.3	215.1	5.08	37,062	7,292
Up to primary (5th)	39.6	201.1	5.08	44,677	8,790
Up to matric (10th)	74.8	371.9	4.97	59,897	12,044
Up to higher secondary (12th)	20.9	102.8	4.93	85,334	17,303
Graduate and above (Graduate+)	28.1	136.3	4.85	134,539	27,718
Total	205.6	1027.3	5.00	65,041	13,018

Source: NSHIE 2004–05 data: NCAER–CMCR analysis.

Table 2.23: Estimates of Households, Population and Income by Education Level of Chief Earner: Rural

Education level of chief earner	Households (million)	Population (million)	Household size	Average household income (Rs per annum)	Per capita income (Rs per annum)
Illiterate	37.5	190.4	5.08	35,455	6,974
Up to primary (5th)	32.5	165.0	5.08	41,783	8,229
Up to matric (10th)	52.5	264.4	5.04	52,640	10,444
Up to higher secondary (12th)	11.6	59.7	5.14	75,526	14,690
Graduate and above (Graduate+)	10.1	52.4	5.17	114,514	22,161
Total	144.2	731.9	5.08	51,922	10,227

Source: NSHIE 2004–05 data: NCAER–CMCR analysis.

For each level of education, the income in urban areas is higher. The average income of an illiterate earner household is Rs 35,455 per annum in rural areas (Table 2.23) while it is Rs 49,416 in urban areas (Table 2.24); for 'graduate[+]' category, the average income of a rural household is Rs 114,514 as compared to Rs 145,859 for urban household (Tables 2.23 and 2.24). On an average, urban earnings at each level of education are nearly one-third higher compared to rural earnings.

The rise in per capita income across different educational levels, relative to the illiterate class, is strikingly similar for both rural and urban areas. But the national picture is quite different with Graduate+ households showing a 3.8 fold rise, despite both rural and urban households showing a uniform increase of 3.2

Table 2.24: Estimates of Households, Population and Income by Education Level of Chief Earner: Urban

Education level of chief earner	Households (million)	Population (million)	Household size	Average household income (Rs per annum)	Per capita income (Rs per annum)
Illiterate	4.9	24.7	5.07	49,416	9,738
Up to primary (5th)	7.1	36.0	5.11	58,015	11,357
Up to matric (10th)	22.3	107.5	4.82	76,948	15,980
Up to higher secondary (12th)	9.2	43.2	4.67	97,648	20,916
Graduate and above (Graduate+)	17.9	83.9	4.68	145,859	31,189
Total	61.4	295.3	4.81	95,827	19,935

Source: NSHIE 2004–05 data: NCAER–CMCR analysis.

per cent. This discrepancy is the result of the much larger population of Graduate+ households and much smaller population of illiterates in urban areas than in rural areas.

Earning weights calculated for various educational levels of chief earner are presented in Table 2.25. Not surprisingly, the earning weight (2.13) of graduate+ households is the highest, as 13.3 per cent population from graduate households contribute 28.2 per cent of the total household income. Similarly, 10.0 per cent population from households, whose chief earners have studied up to higher secondary, contribute 13.3 per cent of the income, taking their earning weight to 1.33. Matriculate headed households, with 36.2 per cent population share, contribute 33.5 to the total household income and have thus recorded an earning weight of 0.93.

The chief earner's education level has enormous impact on the household's income level—even more than the impact shown by occupations. While it may seem frivolous to state the obvious, that is, the higher the education the better the opportunity, it is definitely interesting to actually quantify the changes in household incomes brought about by different levels of education, by proceeding in the same manner as in the case of occupational impact.

For this the illiterate household's income, at Rs 37,062 per annum, is taken as the base income (Table 2.26). The percentage rise in income level as a result of a switch over from illiterate status upwards on the education hierarchy are given in Table 2.26. If the illiterate household attains primary level education, its annual income increases by about Rs 7,615 or 21 per cent and it further rises to Rs 22,834 (62 per cent), Rs 48,272 (130 per cent) and Rs 97,477 (263 per cent) at the educational levels of matriculation, higher secondary and graduation, respectively.

Table 2.25: Distribution of Population, Income and Earning Weights by Education Level of Chief Earner

Education level of chief earner	Distribution of population (per cent)			Distribution of income (per cent)			Earning weight		
	Rural	Urban	All India	Rural	Urban	All India	Rural	Urban	All India
Illiterate	26.0	8.4	20.9	17.7	4.1	11.7	0.68	0.49	0.56
Up to primary (5th)	22.5	12.2	19.6	18.1	7.0	13.2	0.80	0.57	0.68
Up to matric (10th)	36.1	36.4	36.2	36.9	29.2	33.5	1.02	0.80	0.93
Up to higher secondary (12th)	8.2	14.6	10.0	11.7	15.3	13.3	1.44	1.05	1.33
Graduate and above (Graduate+)	7.2	28.4	13.3	15.5	44.4	28.2	2.17	1.56	2.13
Total	100.0	100.0	100.0	100.0	100.0	100.0	1.00	1.00	1.00

Source: NSHIE 2004–05 data: NCAER–CMCR analysis.

Table 2.26: Impact of Change of Level of Education of Chief Earner on Household Earnings (Percentage Increase in Income over that of Illiterate Chief Earners)

Education level of chief earner	Increase in income (Rs)			Increase in income (per cent)		
	Rural	Urban	All India	Rural	Urban	All India
Graduate and above (Graduate+)	79,059	96,442	97,477	223	195	263
Up to higher secondary (12th)	40,071	48,232	48,272	113	98	130
Up to matric (10th)	17,184	27,531	22,834	48	56	62
Up to primary (5th)	6,327	8,598	7,615	18	17	21
Illiterate (Base income)	35,455	49,416	37,062			

Source: NSHIE 2004–05 data: NCAER–CMCR analysis.

2.2.3 Age of Chief Earner and Level of Earning

Age of the chief earner is an important demographic factor associated with household earning patterns and per capita income levels. Though India's demographic profile is getting younger, it is the higher age groups that earn more. Households whose chief earners are in the 56–65 years age bracket, for instance, comprise 8.9 per cent of the population at the all-India level and contribute 10.4 per cent to total income whereas the 66+ group with 2.6 population share contribute 3.0 per cent to total income. Those in the 46–55 years age group comprise 21.9 per cent of total population and contribute 25.3 per cent to total household income (Table 2.30).

Average household incomes, at the all-India level, rise from Rs 47,745 per annum in the case of households where the chief earner is below 25 years old, to Rs 55,830 in the 26–35 years age group, and maintaining an upward trend reaches the level of Rs 80,964 per annum in households where the chief earner is above 66 years old (Table 2.27).

In urban areas, nearly 45 per cent of household income flows from regular salaries, and as the chief earner approaches the age of superannuation, incomes are likely to decline. As a result, urban household income falls to Rs 107,524 (for the 56–65 years age group) from Rs 115,676. A rise in household income in the 66+ category may be the result of additional earning members contributing to the household income.

The per capita income figures display certain interesting features across different household categories (Tables 2.27, 2.28 and 2.29). Maximum increase in per capita income is observed in the case of households with chief earners in the age group of 46–55 years both in rural (18 per cent) and urban (23 per cent), and all-India (21 per cent) levels. In urban areas, where 45 per cent of household income

Table 2.27: Estimates of Households, Population and Income by Age of Chief Earner: All India

Age of chief earner (years)	Households (million)	Population (million)	Household size	Average household income (Rs per annum)	Per capita income (Rs per annum)
Less than 25	11.5	51.9	4.51	47,745	10,591
26–35	53.7	257.3	4.79	55,830	11,652
36–45	75.0	375.3	5.01	62,231	12,433
46–55	43.5	225.3	5.17	77,553	14,990
56–65	17.0	91.3	5.37	81,616	15,203
66+	4.9	26.2	5.38	80,964	15,042
Total	205.6	1027.3	5.00	65,041	13,018

Source: NSHIE 2004–05 data: NCAER–CMCR analysis.

is contributed by wage earners, the per capita income of the 26–35 years category shows 12 per cent increase, pointing to the contribution of young professionals in this age group in boosting the household income, and hence, per capita income.

In rural India, the increase was only to the order of 6 per cent. In the urban 56–65 years category, the per capita income is 7 per cent less than the 46–55 category, resulting from a decline of household income possibly due to retirement of salaried individuals between 55 and 60 years. Urban per capita income receives a further boost in the 66+ category (12 per cent increase) as a result of younger family members stepping in to raise the income level.

In both rural and urban areas, households with chief earners in the 36–45 years age bracket account for the highest share of the total population as well as total income. At the all-India level, 36.5 per cent households are headed by a person in the 36–45 years age group. These households account for 34.9 per cent of the

Table 2.28: Estimates of Households, Population and Income by Age of Chief Earner: Rural

Age of chief earner (years)	Households (million)	Population (million)	Household size	Average household income (Rs per annum)	Per capita income (Rs per annum)
Less than 25	8.5	38.4	4.51	39,685	8,809
26–35	37.8	183.6	4.86	44,510	9,164
36–45	52.5	266.4	5.07	49,247	9,705
46–55	30.0	158.3	5.28	60,295	11,417
56–65	11.7	65.2	5.55	70,017	12,613
66+	3.6	20.0	5.54	68,943	12,454
Total	144.2	731.9	5.08	51,922	10,227

Source: NSHIE 2004–05 data: NCAER–CMCR analysis.

Table 2.29: Estimates of Households, Population and Income by Age of Chief Earner: Urban

Age of chief earner (years)	Households (million)	Population (million)	Household size	Average household income (Rs per annum)	Per capita income (Rs per annum)
Less than 25	3.0	13.5	4.52	70,794	15,675
26–35	15.9	73.7	4.64	82,759	17,852
36–45	22.5	108.9	4.84	92,563	19,106
46–55	13.6	67.0	4.94	115,676	23,434
56–65	5.3	26.1	4.96	107,524	21,675
66+	1.3	6.2	4.94	115,531	23,379
Total	61.4	295.3	4.81	95,827	19,935

Source: NSHIE 2004–05 data: NCAER–CMCR analysis.

total household income (Table 2.30). The average household income for this age group is Rs 62,231 (Table 2.27). In rural areas, such households account for 36.4 per cent share in total population and 34.5 per cent share in household income (Table 2.30). For urban areas, the figures are 36.9 per cent and 35.3 per cent, respectively (Table 2.30).

The earning weights for different age group categories of chief earners are also presented in (Table 2.30). It is observed that the earning weight of households whose chief earner is above 65 years of age is the highest at 1.16, followed by 56–65 year olds and 46–55 year olds, which show earning weights of 1.17 and 1.15, respectively. This shows that the intensity of contribution of the three highest age groups to the total household income is significant and more effective as compared to the lower age groups.

Table 2.30: Distribution of Population, Income and Earning Weights by Age of Chief Earner

Age of chief earner (years)	Distribution of population (per cent)			Distribution of income (per cent)			Earning weight		
	Rural	Urban	All India	Rural	Urban	All India	Rural	Urban	All India
Less than 25	5.3	4.6	5.1	4.5	3.6	4.1	0.86	0.79	0.81
26–35	25.1	24.9	25.0	22.5	22.3	22.4	0.90	0.90	0.90
36–45	36.4	36.9	36.5	34.5	35.3	34.9	0.95	0.96	0.96
46–55	21.6	22.7	21.9	24.1	26.7	25.3	1.12	1.18	1.15
56–65	8.9	8.8	8.9	11.0	9.6	10.4	1.23	1.09	1.17
66+	2.7	2.1	2.6	3.3	2.5	3.0	1.22	1.17	1.16
Total	100.0	100.0	1000	100.0	100.0	100.0	1.00	1.00	1.00

Source: NSHIE 2004–05 data: NCAER–CMCR analysis.

At the all-India level, the income increases from 17 per cent to 70 per cent between the 26–35 years and 66+ categories (Table 2.31). Per capita earnings are expected to be much higher in households whose chief earner is above 65 years of age; this is particularly so in urban India. In rural India, the increase in household income ranges from 12 per cent to 74 per cent as we move from 26–35 years to 66+ categories. In the urban case the corresponding income increases from 17 per cent to 63 per cent up to the 46–55 age group, then takes a dip to 52 per cent for the 56–65 years age group, and finally, it peaks again showing a 63 per cent increase for the 66+ age category over the 'less than 25 years age' category.

Table 2.31: Impact of Increase in the Age of Chief Earner on Household Earnings (Increase in Income over that of below 25 Years Category)

Age of chief earner (years)	Increase in income (Rs)			Increase in income (per cent)		
	Rural	**Urban**	**All India**	**Rural**	**Urban**	**All India**
26–35	4,825	11,965	8,085	12	17	17
36–45	9,562	21,769	14,486	24	31	30
46–55	20,610	44,882	29,808	52	63	62
56–65	30,332	36,730	33,871	76	52	71
66+	29,258	44,737	33,219	74	63	70
Less than 25 years (Base income)	39,685	70,794	47,745			

Source: NSHIE 2004–05 data: NCAER–CMCR analysis.

Spending Pattern of Indian Households

three

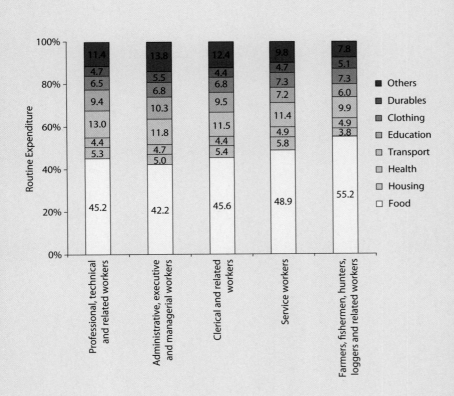

Expenditure patterns change as household incomes grow. For lower income households, the emphasis is on basic needs and food items but as their disposable income grows, purchase of durables, expenditure on health and education, and investment related spending come into play. Given the wide disparity in income between rural and urban India as well as across low, middle and high income states, differences in expenditure and saving patterns are also to be expected. This diversity is visible across all sections of the Indian society. Occupation profiles, educational qualifications and age of chief earners have a strong bearing on the manner in which households spend their income. Perhaps, one common feature among Indian households is the preponderance of 'unusual expenditure.' The urban–rural disparity is also reflected in the ownership profile of most consumer durables.

An average Indian household spends about three-fourths of its income on routine[1] and unusual[2] expenditure (for financial year 2004–05) (Table 3.1). The rural–urban divide is evident in spending patterns of households. While rural households spend, on an average, Rs 18,266 on food items in a year, urban households spend about Rs 26,524. In other words, rural households spend a little more than a third of their income on food, whereas for urban households it is slightly more than a quarter of their income. These expenses constitute 55 per cent of total routine expenditure for rural households (Figure 3.1) and 45 per cent of routine expenditure for urban households.

Rural households spend less on non-food items (Rs 14,788 per annum) compared to urban households' annual spend of Rs 31,893. While unusual expenditure accounts for 13.6 per cent of total household income in rural areas, it is slightly lower, at 10.4 per cent, in urban India, and 12.2 per cent for the country as a whole.

In the routine expenditure segment (Figure 3.1), urban households spend much more than rural households on housing (5.9 per cent versus 3.8 per cent) and education (8.7 per cent versus 6.4 per cent), while the difference is marginal in the case of transport (11.1 per cent versus 10 per cent). But expenditure on health (4.7 per cent versus 4.6 per cent), clothing (7.1 per cent versus 6.8 per cent) and

---

[1] Routine expenditure includes consumption expenditure on food, housing, health, education, transport, clothing, durables and other such expenses household generally incurs.

[2] Unusual (or non-routine) expenditure includes unplanned large expenditure on ceremonies (such as weddings, births, and so on), medical, higher education, leisure travel, and so on.

Table 3.1: Estimates of Income and Expenditure by Location

	Rural	Urban	All India
a. Annual household income (Rs)	51,922	95,827	65,041
b. Annual household expenditure (Rs)			
Food	18,266	26,524	20,733
Non-food	14,788	31,893	19,899
Total (routine)	33,054	58,417	40,632
Non-routine	7,070	9,935	7,926
Total (routine and non-routine)	40,124	68,352	48,558
c. Share of expenditure to income (per cent)			
Food	35.2	27.7	31.9
Non-food	28.5	33.3	30.6
Total (routine)	63.7	61.0	62.5
Non-routine	13.6	10.4	12.2
Total (routine and non-routine)	77.3	71.3	74.7

Source: NSHIE 2004–05 data: NCAER–CMCR analysis.

consumer durables (4.9 per cent versus 5.0 per cent) is more or less at par, pointing to the growing influence of urban ways on rural lifestyles.

Ceremonies and rituals are a big part of Indian households. As there are more joint families in rural areas, their significance is greater for rural citizens. Almost

Figure 3.1: Distribution of Routine Expenditure

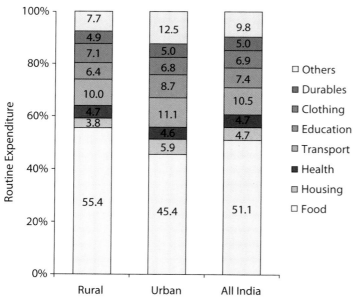

Source: NSHIE 2004–05 data: NCAER–CMCR analysis.

Figure 3.2: Distribution of Unusual Expenditure

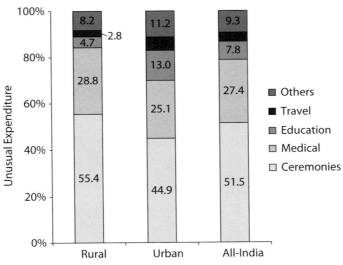

Source: NSHIE 2004–05 data: NCAER–CMCR analysis.

half the unusual expenditure (51.5 per cent) in India is incurred on account of rituals and ceremonies (Figure 3.2). Medical emergencies account for nearly 27 per cent of all unusual expenses. Education (8 per cent) and travel (4 per cent) are two other important items of unusual expenses for Indian households. Rural households spend more on ceremonies (55 per cent) than urban ones (45 per cent), while urban families have a much higher spend on education (13 per cent) than their rural counterparts (4.7 per cent). Medical emergencies too account for a slightly higher share of unusual expenses (29 per cent) for rural households compared to urban ones (25 per cent). Lack of access to health care is a key reason for rural families spending more on medical emergencies as compared to their urban cousins.

3.1 Socio-economic Profile of Household and Level of Spending

3.1.1 Sectors of Engagement of Household and Level of Spending

Agriculture as a sector of economy generates the lowest income compared to industry, modern services and traditional services. These differential income levels also influence the spend levels of households that earn their livelihood through these sectors. Households that are engaged in agriculture are the ones that spend the highest proportion of their income (36.6 per cent) on food items (Table 3.2), while households that earn their living from modern services spend the lowest proportion (24.8 per cent) and those that are employed in industry spend 31.0 per cent.

Table 3.2: Estimates of Income and Expenditure by Sectors of Engagement: All India

	Agriculture	Industry	Modern services	Traditional services
a. Annual household income (Rs)	48,097	71,372	112,222	64,453
b. Annual household expenditure (Rs)				
Food	17,600	22,113	27,804	21,260
Non-food	14,299	23,530	33,598	20,065
Total (routine)	31,899	45,643	61,403	41,325
Non-routine	6,960	6,994	12,300	7,550
Total (routine and non-routine)	38,859	52,637	73,703	48,876
c. Share of expenditure to income (per cent)				
Food	36.6	31.0	24.8	33.0
Non-food	29.7	33.0	29.9	31.1
Total (routine)	66.3	64.0	54.7	64.1
Non-routine	14.5	9.8	11.0	11.7
Total (routine and non-routine)	80.8	73.7	65.7	75.8

Source: NSHIE 2004–05 data: NCAER–CMCR analysis.

It appears that households in the highest earning sector (modern services) are also saving much more than those engaged in other sectors. Despite being the highest earners, their routine and non-routine expenses are just 66 per cent of their income, compared to nearly 81 per cent for agriculturist households, 76 per cent for households engaged in traditional services and 74 per cent for those in the industrial sector.

Households earning their livelihood from industry, modern services and traditional services have almost the same level of expenditure on housing (5 per cent of routine expenses) while agriculture dependent households spend only 3.8 per cent on this item (Figure 3.3). Health, durables and clothing expenditure are more or less similar across all household types classified according to sectors of engagement. Education expenditure is the only component which exhibits variation across the household segments; for agricultural sector households, educational expenditure constitutes just 6 per cent of routine expenditure, whereas for those in traditional services, industry and modern services, sectors the expenditure levels are 6.9 per cent, 7.7 per cent and 9.3 per cent, respectively.

Expenses on social ceremonies are very high for all household segments. Nevertheless, households in modern services sector spend the least proportion (46 per cent of unusual expenditure) on ceremonies, whereas households

Figure 3.3: Distribution of Routine Expenditure by Sectors of Engagement

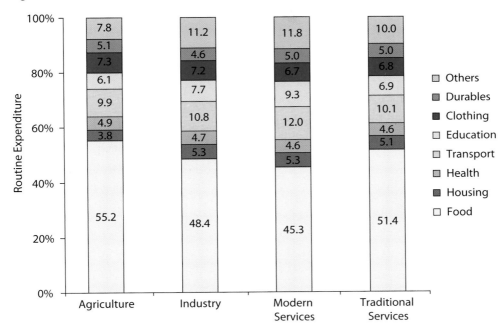

Source: NSHIE 2004–05 data: NCAER–CMCR analysis.

engaged in industry, traditional services, and agriculture sectors spend 50 per cent, 52 per cent and 55 per cent, respectively, on this account (Figure 3.4). Medical emergencies constitute 27 per cent of unusual expenses for households employed in modern services sector as against 30 per cent for those engaged in agricultural sector, and 25 per cent to 26 per cent for the other two sectors. The unusual expenditure on education is pretty high (11 per cent) for households that earn their income from modern services and industry sectors, but it as low as 5 per cent in agricultural sector households.

Consumption patterns seem to be more influenced by the location of the household than the sector of engagement, the only exception being households engaged in modern services (Table 3.3). The four household sectors show more or less the same spending pattern in both rural and urban areas, with urban households spending larger share of their income on non-food items and a smaller share on food items than their rural counterparts. For households engaged in modern services, urban households definitely spend more on non-food items than rural ones but the difference in spending rates on food is not so drastic as to draw any clear conclusion.

Figure 3.4: Distribution of Unusual Expenditure by Sectors of Engagement

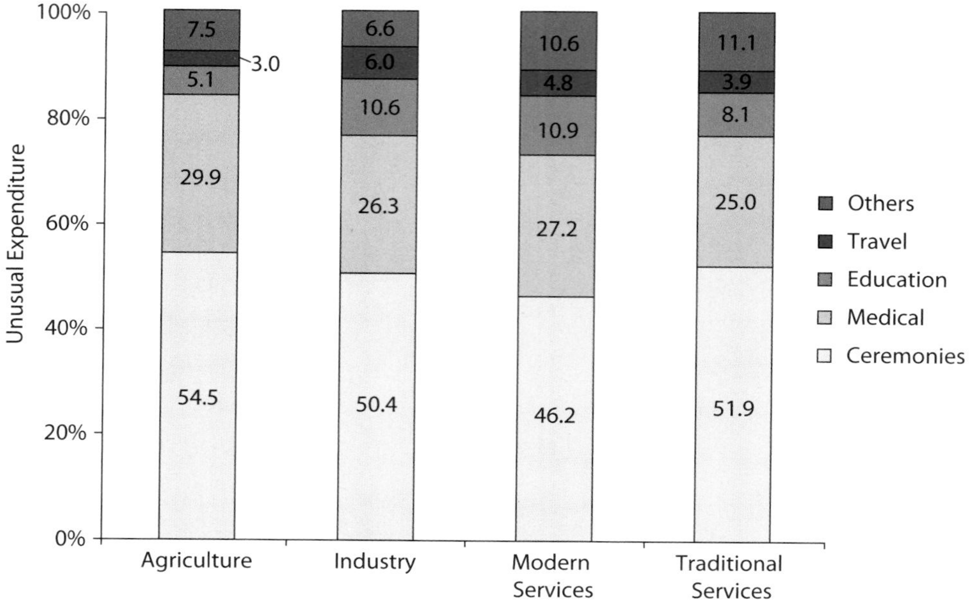

Source: NSHIE 2004–05 data: NCAER–CMCR analysis.

Table 3.3: Estimates of Income and Expenditure by Sectors of Engagement and Location

	Agriculture		Industry		Modern services	
	Rural	**Urban**	**Rural**	**Urban**	**Rural**	**Urban**
a. Annual household income (Rs)	46,942	77,338	46,567	91,296	102,345	120,117
b. Annual household expenditure (Rs)						
Food	17,371	23,405	17,570	25,762	24,740	30,254
Non-food	13,802	26,880	14,305	30,939	25,959	39,705
Total (routine)	31,173	50,285	31,875	56,701	50,699	69,958
Non-routine	6,627	15,406	4,903	8,674	12,980	11,756
Total (routine and non-routine)	37,799	65,690	36,778	65,375	63,679	81,715
c. Share of expenditure to income (per cent)						
Food	37.0	30.3	37.7	28.2	24.2	25.2
Non-food	29.4	34.8	30.7	33.9	25.4	33.1
Total (routine)	66.4	65.0	68.5	62.1	49.5	58.2
Non-routine	14.1	19.9	10.5	9.5	12.7	9.8
Total (routine and non-routine)	80.5	84.9	79.0	71.6	62.2	68.0

Source: NSHIE 2004–05 data: NCAER–CMCR analysis.

3.1.2 Major Occupation of Households and Level of Spending

The occupational profile of the household determines its social standing. In fact, spending patterns are almost always a reflection of not just income but also the social status of the household. In terms of household income, the farmers and fishermen group with an annual income of Rs 48,295 is at the lowest rung, whereas the group of administrative and managerial workers, earning Rs 169,317 per annum is at the top of the ladder (Table 3.4). Their income is more than three times that of the farmers/fishermen group. Food items constitute a major proportion of routine expenditure for the farmers/fishermen group. This group spends nearly 37 per cent of its income on food items, as against 22 per cent by the top earning group, 24 per cent by the professional and technical workers' group, and 27 per cent to 29 per cent by other groups. No substantial difference in spend levels (percentages) of non-food items is observed, although in absolute terms, the difference is huge: Rs 50,322 for the administrative and managerial workers group, as against Rs 14,364 for the farmers/fishermen group. This observed trend may indicate that the emphasis from food items is slowly shifting to non-food items even among the lower income categories of households.

Table 3.4: Estimates of Income and Expenditure by Occupation: All India

	Professional, technical and related workers	Administrative, executive and managerial workers	Clerical and related workers	Service workers	Farmers, fishermen, hunters, loggers and related workers
a. Annual household income (Rs)	129,213	169,317	99,584	81,741	48,295
b. Annual household expenditure (Rs)					
Food	31,105	36,704	26,776	23,409	17,708
Non-food	37,729	50,322	31,945	24,427	14,364
Total (routine)	68,834	87,026	58,721	47,836	32,072
Non-routine	16,042	14,150	8,909	9,337	7,092
Total (routine and non-routine)	84,876	101,176	67,630	57,173	39,165
c. Share of expenditure to income (per cent)					
Food	24.1	21.7	26.9	28.6	36.7
Non-food	29.2	29.7	32.1	29.9	29.7
Total (routine)	53.3	51.4	59.0	58.5	66.4
Non-routine	12.4	8.4	8.9	11.4	14.7
Total (routine and non-routine)	65.7	59.8	67.9	69.9	81.1

Source: NSHIE 2004–05 data: NCAER–CMCR analysis.

Let us now consider how routine expenses are distributed among its constituents in the major occupational groups. In all the groups, except the farmer/fishermen group, housing consumes 5.0 per cent to 5.8 per cent of their routine expenditure (Figure 3.5) and transport account for 11.5 per cent to 13 per cent of their routine expenditure. Health expenses constitute about 4 per cent to 5 per cent of routine expenditure across all the five occupational groups. Spending on durables is almost at the same level (5 per cent) for all the groups. This implies that the lowest earning group of farmers and fishermen is also spending at the same level on consumer durables as are the higher income groups, which is an indicator of the welfare and social justice available to the lowest strata of the society. Administrative and managerial workers, professionals and technical workers, and clerical workers spend about 9 per cent to 10 per cent of their income on education, while the two lowest earning groups of service workers and farmers/fishermen households spend about 6 per cent to 7 per cent.

Social status is also reflected in the spending pattern of households. For instance, richer households tend to spend more on leisure and travel, and education

Figure 3.5: Distribution of Routine Expenditure by Occupation

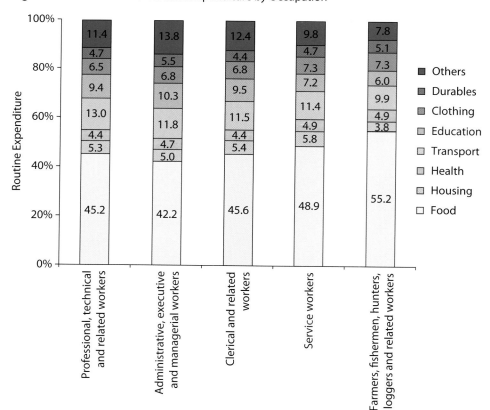

Source: NSHIE 2004–05 data: NCAER–CMCR analysis.

Figure 3.6: Distribution of Unusual Expenditure by Occupation

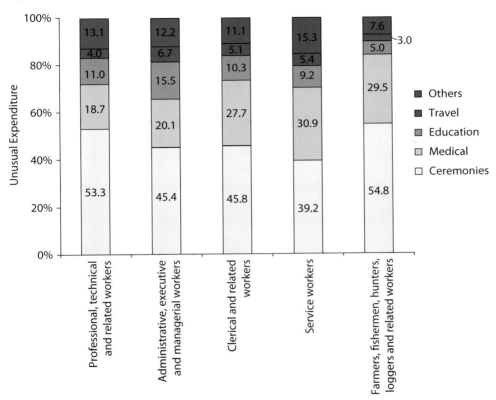

Source: NSHIE 2004–05 data: NCAER–CMCR analysis.

related items. Social standing and expenditure on ceremonies is directly linked and it is not surprising that even in lower income households, ceremonies entail a high percentage of total unusual expenses. In fact, 55 per cent of farmer and fishermen group's unusual expenses is incurred on social ceremonies as against 53 per cent spent by the second highest income group, that is, professionals and technical workers (Figure 3.6). For the other three groups, the spending on account of ceremonies ranges from 39 per cent to 46 per cent.

For the service workers and farmers/fishermen categories, medical emergencies account for nearly 31 per cent and 30 per cent, respectively, of their total unusual expenditure, and for clerical workers, it is about 28 per cent. In contrast, only 19 per cent to 20 per cent of non-routine expenses of administrative and managerial workers and professionals/technical workers is attributed to medical emergencies. Education is an important component of unusual expenditure for administrative workers (15.5 per cent), while for farmers and fishermen, it seems to be a low priority item entailing just 5 per cent of their unusual expenses. Travel related expenditure levels (out of total unusual expenditure) is highest for administrative workers at 7 per cent, 5 per cent each for clerical workers and service workers, and just 3 per cent for farmers and fishermen.

Location matters. This is clearly evident if you consider the fact that across three major occupational types–professional workers, administrative workers and farmers–the percentage of total routine expenditure allocated to non-food items by urban households is invariably more than that allocated by their rural counterparts (Table 3.5). Rural professional households and rural administrative workers also spend a higher share of their income on non-routine expenses, once again confirming the rural–urban divide in household expenditure levels.

Table 3.5: Estimates of Income and Expenditure by Occupation and Location

	Professional, technical and related workers		Administrative, executive and managerial workers		Farmers, fishermen, hunters, loggers and related workers	
	Rural	Urban	°Rural	Urban	Rural	Urban
a. Annual household income (Rs)	120,080	138,065	135,222	183,803	47,371	74,623
b. Annual household expenditure (Rs)						
Food	28,025	34,089	29,350	39,828	17,534	22,663
Non-food	28,821	46,364	33,751	57,363	13,960	25,887
Total (routine)	56,846	80,453	63,101	97,191	31,494	48,550
Non-routine	18,782	13,387	19,038	12,073	6,798	15,489
Total (routine and non-routine)	75,628	93,840	82,140	109,264	38,291	64,039
c. Share of expenditure to income (per cent)						
Food	23.3	24.7	21.7	21.7	37.0	30.4
Non-food	24.0	33.6	25.0	31.2	29.5	34.7
Total (routine)	47.3	58.3	46.7	52.9	66.5	65.1
Non-routine	15.6	9.7	14.1	6.6	14.3	20.8
Total (routine and non-routine)	63.0	68.0	60.7	59.4	80.8	85.8

Source: NSHIE 2004–05 data: NCAER–CMCR analysis.

3.1.3 State of Residence and Level of Spending

To bring in another layer of variability in the analysis of household spending, we now consider the impact of state of residence on a household's expenditure pattern. Just as households in the high income states have a higher income earning capacity–the average annual household income is Rs 89,288 compared to Rs 66,737 in the middle income states and Rs 52,052 in the low income states–their spending patterns show a similar trend. However, the degree of variation is much lower. For instance, households in high income states spend Rs 55,887 compared to Rs 49,872 by households in middle income states and Rs 44,025 by households in low income states (Table 3.6). The expenditure in high income states is 1.27 times that of the low income states, as against a 1.71 fold increase in income. Household expenditure on food items in the three state groups does not show much variation. It ranges from Rs 19,819 in the low income states to Rs 22,083 in high income states. The real difference in spend levels is with regard to non-food items. High income state households spend Rs 26,886 on non-food items compared to Rs 21,377 spent in middle income states and Rs 15,405 by low income state households.

Table 3.6: Estimates of Income and Expenditure by State of Residence: All India

	Low income states	Middle income states	High income states
a. Annual household income (Rs)	52,052	66,737	89,288
b. Annual household expenditure (Rs)			
Food	19,819	21,080	22,083
Non-food	15,405	21,377	26,886
Total (routine)	35,224	42,457	48,969
Non-routine	8,801	7,415	6,917
Total (routine and non-routine)	44,025	49,872	55,887
c. Share of expenditure to income (per cent)			
Food	38.1	31.6	24.7
Non-food	29.6	32.0	30.1
Total (routine)	67.7	63.6	54.8
Non-routine	16.9	11.1	7.7
Total (routine and non-routine)	84.6	74.7	62.6

Source: NSHIE 2004–05 data: NCAER–CMCR analysis.

Share of food expenses in total routine expenditure is about 45 per cent in high income states, which rises to 50 per cent in middle income states and peaks to 56 per cent in the low income states (Figure 3.7). Looking at the amounts spent by these three state groups on different items such as housing, health, transport, education, clothing, durables, and so on, it is evident that transport accounts for a much higher share of routine expenditure for households in high income states (13 per cent) compared to the middle income (10 per cent) and low income (9.5 per cent) states. In high income states, housing is another key component of household expenditure. Spending on housing, which is 4.7 per cent at the all-India level, is much lower at 4.1 per cent (Rs 1,446) in low income states and this rises to 6.1 per cent (Rs 3,032) in high income states.

Expenditure on health ranges between 4 per cent to 5 per cent as we move from low income states to high income states, whereas education expenses are

Figure 3.7: Distribution of Routine Expenditure by State of Residence

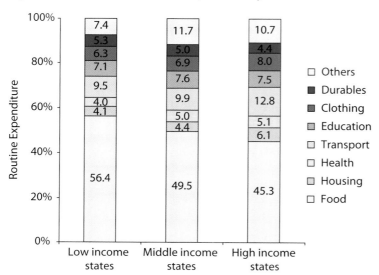

Source: NSHIE 2004–05 data: NCAER–CMCR analysis.

more or less stable at about 7.1 per cent to 7.5 per cent across the state types. Interestingly, expenditure on consumer durables also does not vary much across the state types, though it is marginally higher in low income and middle income states (5 per cent each) compared to 4.4 per cent in high income states.

Weddings, births and other ceremonies account for the bulk of unusual expenditure in low income states. More specifically, expenses on weddings and other social ceremonies account for around 56.8 per cent of total unusual expenses of households in low income states and this falls to 49.1 per cent in high income states and further decreases to 44.7 per cent in middle income states. Medical expenses account for nearly 26 per cent of unusual expenditure in low income and high income states as against 29 per cent in middle income states. Travel expenses which form 1.2 per cent of unusual expenses in low income states rise to 8.5 per cent in high income states (Figure 3.8).

Total routine expenditure, in rural areas, of low, middle and high income states range between Rs 30,816 and Rs 35,501. Non-routine expenditure of rural households does not show much variation; it is Rs 8,257 in low income states and Rs 5,327 in high income states. This is not the case with food consumption. Rural households in low income states spend nearly 41 per cent of their income on food items compared to 34 per cent in middle income states, and 25 per cent in the high income states (Table 3.7).

Figure 3.8: Distribution of Unusual Expenditure by State of Residence

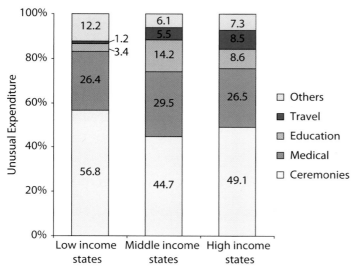

Source: NSHIE 2004–05 data: NCAER–CMCR analysis.

Table 3.7: Estimates of Income and Expenditure by State of Residence and Location

	Low income states		Middle income states		High income states	
	Rural	**Urban**	**Rural**	**Urban**	**Rural**	**Urban**
a. Annual household income (Rs)	44,999	80,948	55,604	89,223	66,121	116,421
b. Annual household expenditure (Rs)						
Food	18,374	25,741	18,970	25,342	16,561	28,551
Non-food	12,442	27,545	16,373	31,485	18,940	36,192
Total (routine)	30,816	53,286	35,342	56,827	35,501	64,743
Non-routine	8,257	11,025	6,083	10,105	5,327	8,780
Total (routine and non-routine)	39,073	64,311	41,425	66,932	40,828	73,523
c. Share of expenditure to income (per cent)						
Food	40.8	31.8	34.1	28.4	25.0	24.5
Non-food	27.7	34.0	29.4	35.3	28.6	31.1
Total (routine)	68.5	65.8	63.6	63.7	53.7	55.6
Non-routine	18.4	13.6	10.9	11.3	8.1	7.5
Total (routine and non-routine)	86.8	79.4	74.5	75.0	61.7	63.2

Source: NSHIE 2004–05 data: NCAER–CMCR analysis.

There is not much difference between expenditure patterns of urban house-holds in low and middle income states in the sense that urban households in both types spend a higher share of income on non-food items and a lower share on food items. The share of non-food items for urban households in low income and middle income states is actually slightly higher than that of their counterparts in high income states. In low income and middle income states, the percentage of routine expenditure spent on non-food items by an urban household is consider-ably large compared to a rural household. In the case of expenditure on food items, the trend is just the reverse.

3.2 Demographic Profile of Chief Earner and Level of Spending

3.2.1 Occupation of Chief Earner and Level of Spending

There is a marked difference in consumption patterns across different types of households that are classified by occupation. The highest earning group is that of households headed by salary/wage earners. In this group, nearly 66 per cent of the household income is spent on routine as well as non-routine expenses

Table 3.8: Estimates of Income and Expenditure by a Occupation of Chief Earner: All India

	Regular salary/ wages	Self-employment in non-agriculture	Labour	Self-employment in agriculture
a. Annual household income (Rs)	110,344	95,020	30,957	55,653
b. Annual household expenditure (Rs)				
Food	27,745	26,180	14,766	19,376
Non-food	33,363	28,700	10,217	16,342
Total (routine)	61,108	54,880	24,983	35,719
Non-routine	11,160	10,122	3,306	8,747
Total (routine and non-routine)	72,268	65,002	28,289	44,466
c. Share of expenditure to income (per cent)				
Food	25.1	27.6	47.7	34.8
Non-food	30.2	30.2	33.0	29.4
Total (routine)	55.4	57.8	80.7	64.2
Non-routine	10.1	10.7	10.7	15.7
Total (routine and non-routine)	65.5	68.4	91.4	79.9

Source: NSHIE 2004–05 data: NCAER–CMCR analysis.

(Table 3.8). For the second highest earner group made up of households headed by chief earners engaged in non-agricultural activities, the share of expenditure (68 per cent) is quite close to that of the highest earner. The other two occupation groups, viz. labour households and self-employed agriculturists, spend 91 per cent and 80 per cent of their income, respectively, on routine and non-routine expenses. In absolute terms, the expenditure levels of the salary earner and the businessman/trader (Rs 72,268 and Rs 65,002, respectively) are much higher than for self-employed in agriculture and labour dependent households (Rs 44,466 and Rs 28,289, respectively).

Expenditure on housing which is 4.7 per cent at the all-India level (Figure 3.9) is at a much lower level (3.8 per cent) among households headed by agriculturists. It rises to 5.6 per cent among salary earner households. There is little difference on health related (4.4 per cent to 4.8 per cent), clothing (6.7 per cent to 7.2 per cent) or durables (4.8 per cent to 5.1 per cent) expenditure among households. The share of expenses on transport and education, however, varies significantly.

Figure 3.9: Distribution of Routine Expenditure by Occupation of Chief Earner

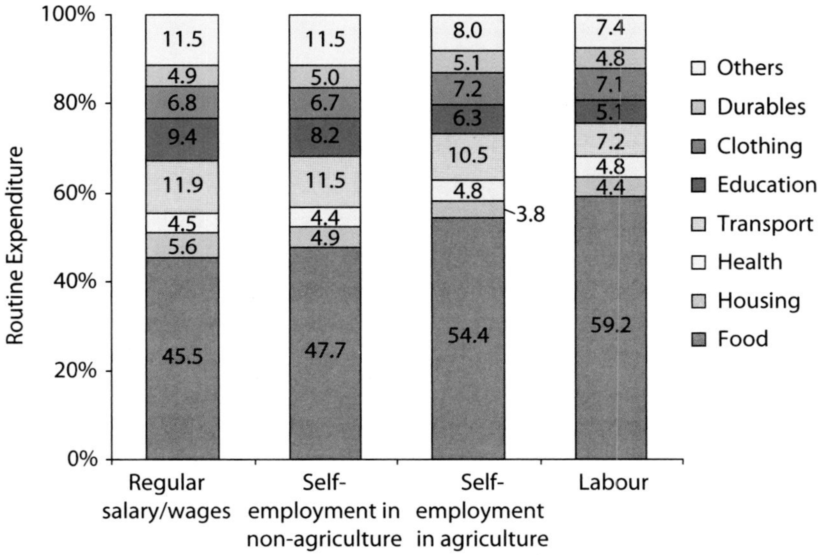

Source: NSHIE 2004–05 data: NCAER–CMCR analysis.

While households headed by labourers spend just 7.2 per cent of their routine expenses on transport, it rises to 11.9 per cent for the salaried households. Expenditure on education forms 5.1 per cent of routine expenses for a labourer household, whereas it is 9.4 per cent for the salaried category.

Figure 3.10: Distribution of Unusual Expenditure by Occupation of Chief Earner

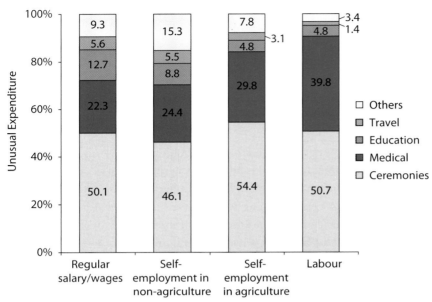

Source: NSHIE 2004–05 data: NCAER–CMCR analysis.

Unusual expenditure in connection with weddings and other social events is a common feature among all occupational groups. While salary earner and labour households each spend nearly 50 per cent of their non-routine expenditure on social ceremonies, the self-employed in agriculture and non-agriculture spend 54 per cent and 46 per cent, respectively, on this account. On medical emergencies, labour households spend nearly 40 per cent as against 22 per cent expenditure incurred by the salary earners group, and 30 per cent and 24 per cent by households engaged in agriculture and non-agriculture activities, respectively. While the salary earner households spend nearly 13 per cent on education, labour as well as agriculture dependent households spend a meagre 5 per cent on this priority item; the percentage spending by non-agriculture category is 9 per cent (Figure 3.10).

Just as urban incomes are higher than rural incomes across all occupation types, expenditure is also higher among urban households, irrespective of the occupation they are engaged in (Table 3.9). For instance, the total expenditure of a rural salary earning household is about Rs 63,000 compared to almost Rs 78,000 for an urban household. This works out to a spending rate of 61 per cent of the salary earner's income in rural areas as compared to 68 per cent in urban India. This also implies that the rural salary earner household has more surplus income for saving/investment than that available to its urban counterpart.

Table 3.9: Estimates of Income and Expenditure by Occupation of Chief Earner and Location

	Regular salary/wages		Labour		Self-employed in non-agriculture	
	Rural	**Urban**	**Rural**	**Urban**	**Rural**	**Urban**
a. Annual household income (Rs)	103,687	114,551	28,567	39,626	54,622	118,419
b. Annual household expenditure (Rs)						
Food	24,940	29,518	14,074	17,278	19,165	29,922
Non-food	25,898	38,080	8,810	15,321	15,890	36,959
Total (routine)	50,838	67,598	22,883	32,599	35,056	66,881
Non-routine	12,368	10,397	3,045	4,255	8,351	11,608
Total (routine and non-routine)	63,206	77,995	25,928	36,854	43,407	78,489
c. Share of expenditure to income (per cent)						
Food	24.1	25.8	49.3	43.6	35.1	25.3
Non-food	25.0	33.2	30.8	38.7	29.1	31.2
Total (routine)	49.0	59.0	80.1	82.3	64.2	56.5
Non-routine	11.9	9.1	10.7	10.7	15.3	9.8
Total (routine and non-routine)	61.0	68.1	90.8	93.0	79.5	66.3

Source: NSHIE 2004–05 data: NCAER–CMCR analysis.

Among the non-agricultural category of households, rural households have much lower surplus income compared to urban households in this category. While rural households spend 79 per cent of their income, urban households spend just 66 per cent of their income on routine and non-routine items. There is not much difference in rural–urban spend levels for labour-dependent housesholds, demonstrating that such families have very little surplus income.

It is interesting to note that the major share of the labour household's routine expenditure is incurred on food items both in rural and urban areas, the rural share (61 per cent) being slightly higher than the urban share (53 per cent). In contrast, the regular salaried class spend more on non-food items both in rural (51 per cent) and urban (56 per cent) areas. With the 'self-employed in non-agriculture' category, the proportion spent on food is higher in rural areas (55 per cent) but lower in urban areas (45 per cent).

3.2.2 Chief Earner's Education Profile and Expenditure

The strong linkage between household income, and occupation and education profiles of the chief earner is clearly evident. Households with graduate+ chief earners are likely to have salary/wages as the main source of income, and consequently,

consumption pattern too varies from those of households headed by chief earners with lower educational qualifications. The two highest earning groups are the
graduate+ households and those with higher secondary passed chief earners. They
spend 65 per cent and 71 per cent, respectively, of their incomes towards routine
and non-routine expenses (Table 3.10). These groups, therefore, have 35 per cent
and 29 per cent, respectively, of surplus income as against just 14 per cent surplus
income in the case of the lowest earning group of illiterate households.

Food expenses constitute 51 per cent of all routine expenditure at the all-India level.
But, for households headed by illiterates, it rises to 59 per cent, and for graduate+
households, it falls to 43 per cent (Figure 3.11). The distinction between the two
groups becomes clearer, when one considers the fact that illiterate households' food
expenditure is as much as 43 per cent of their total income compared to graduate+
households' 23 per cent. In absolute terms, graduate+ households spend Rs 31,058
on food items, which is twice that of illiterate households (Rs 15,796) and incur
non-food expenditure of Rs 41,282 which is nearly four times the expenditure of
illiterate households on non-food items (Rs 11,029).

Expenditure on housing, which is 4.7 per cent at the all-India level, is much
lower (3.5 per cent) among households headed by illiterates, whereas it is 5.5
per cent for graduates+ households. Health related expenses and spending on
clothing and durables do not vary significantly between illiterate and graduate+

Table 3.10: Estimates of Income and Expenditure by Education Level of Chief Earner: All India

	Illiterate	Up to primary (5th)	Up to matric (10th)	Up to higher secondary (12th)	Graduate and above
a. Annual household income (Rs)	37,062	44,677	59,897	85,334	134,539
b. Annual household expenditure (Rs)					
Food	15,796	17,705	20,285	24,204	31,058
Non-food	11,029	13,147	18,431	27,185	41,282
Total (routine)	26,825	30,852	38,716	51,389	72,340
Non-routine	5,111	6,598	7,358	9,198	14,609
Total (routine and non-routine)	31,936	37,450	46,074	60,587	86,949
c. Share of expenditure to income (per cent)					
Food	42.6	39.6	33.9	28.4	23.1
Non-food	29.8	29.4	30.8	31.9	30.7
Total (routine)	72.4	69.1	64.6	60.2	53.8
Non-routine	13.8	14.8	12.3	10.8	10.9
Total (routine and non-routine)	86.2	83.8	76.9	71.0	64.6

Source: NSHIE 2004–05 data: NCAER–CMCR analysis.

Figure 3.11: Distribution of Routine Expenditure by Education Level of Chief Earner

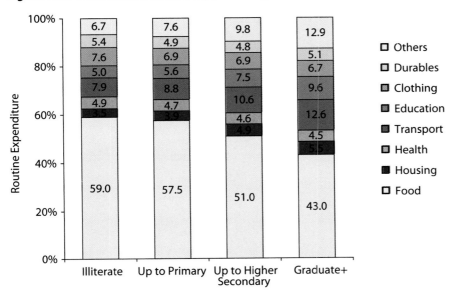

Source: NSHIE 2004–05 data: NCAER–CMCR analysis.

households. Education and transport expenses, however, show marked differences between the two categories. While households headed by illiterates spend just 7.9 per cent of their routine expenses on transport, graduate+ households spend 12.6 per cent on this item, with expenditures on education being 5 per cent and 9.6 per cent, respectively.

Interestingly, the proportion of total unusual expenditure that is incurred on ceremonies is nearly the same for graduate+ and illiterate households: 51 per cent and 53 per cent, respectively (Figure 3.12). On medical emergencies, the illiterate households spend 32 per cent of their income as against 20 per cent spent by graduate+ households. Educational expenses form another important component of graduate+ household's unusual expenditure (12.1 per cent) while it is not the case with the illiterate households, which spend only a meagre 2.8 per cent on this component.

As noted earlier, the location of a household—whether rural or urban—has a strong bearing on its earning level. This difference in earnings reflects on the household's spending levels as well. Just how much of a difference location makes is apparent from the fact that while a rural graduate+ household spends Rs 74,279 per annum, its urban counterpart spends a sum of Rs 94,112 per annum (Table 3.11). A similar trend is observed among poorer households as well. For instance, a rural illiterate household spends an amount of Rs 30,362 per annum compared to Rs 44,038 spent by a similar household in urban areas.

Figure 3.12: Distribution of Unusual Expenditure by Education Level of Chief Earner

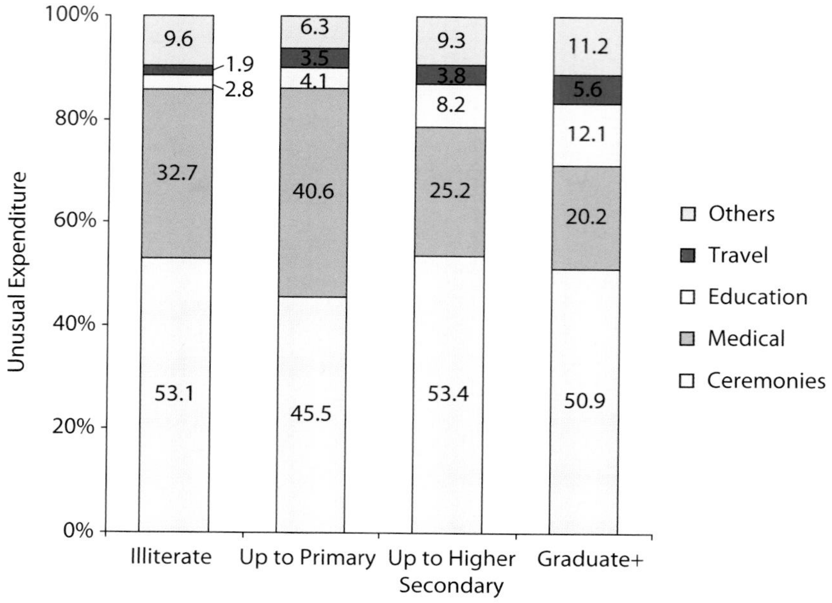

Source: NSHIE 2004–05 data: NCAER–CMCR analysis.

Table 3.11: Estimates of Income and Expenditure by Level of Education of Chief Earner and Location

	Illiterate		Up to matric (10th)		Graduate and above	
	Rural	Urban	Rural	Urban	Rural	Urban
a. Annual household income (Rs)	35,455	49,416	52,640	76,948	114,514	145,859
b. Annual household expenditure (Rs)						
Food	15,281	19,752	18,754	23,885	26,643	33,554
Non-food	10,261	16,932	15,292	25,804	30,820	47,196
Total (routine)	25,543	36,684	34,046	49,689	57,464	80,750
Non-routine	4,819	7,354	6,717	8,863	16,815	13,362
Total (routine and non-routine)	30,362	44,038	40,763	58,552	74,279	94,112
c. Share of expenditure to income (per cent)						
Food	43.1	40.0	35.6	31.0	23.3	23.0
Non-food	28.9	34.3	29.1	33.5	26.9	32.4
Total (routine)	72.0	74.2	64.7	64.6	50.2	55.4
Non-routine	13.6	14.9	12.8	11.5	14.7	9.2
Total (routine and non-routine)	85.6	89.1	77.4	76.1	64.9	64.5

Source: NSHIE 2004–05 data: NCAER–CMCR analysis.

Interestingly, while graduate+ households have the same level of food expenses in rural and urban areas (23 per cent of income), an illiterate household in urban area spends a slightly higher proportion of its income on non-food items and a little less on food items as compared to its rural counterpart.

The graduate+ households spend the major share of their routine expenditure on non-food items both in rural (54 per cent) and urban (58 per cent) areas whereas the illiterate households spend more on food items the rural share being higher (60 per cent) than the urban share (54 per cent). Among the matriculate chief earner category the proportionate expenditure on non-food items is more in urban areas (52 per cent) and less in rural areas (45 per cent).

3.3 Pattern of Product Ownership

Marketers are increasingly looking towards rural consumers in a bid to grow sales of their products. Given that rural India today contributes 56 per cent to total national income, 57 per cent to total expenditure and 33 per cent to surplus income, marketers are more than justified in reaching out to rural households (Table 3.12). What's more, a not insignificant proportion of the salaried (38.7 per cent) and

Table 3.12: Understanding Dynamics of Consumer Market

	Demographics	Share of rural to total (per cent)	Consumer goods	Share of rural to total stock (per cent)
Economic profile	Household	70.1	Computer	21.6
	Population	71.3	Fridge	28.7
	Income	56.0	Credit card	29.4
	Expenditure	57.0	Car	31.7
	Surplus income	33.0	Mobile	32.6
Occupation profile	Salaried	38.7	Telephone (L)	43.5
	Self-employed in non-agriculture	46.1	Television (Colour)	46.0
	Labour	78.4	Pressure cooker	52.6
	Agriculturists	97.2	Two wheeler	53.9
Education profile	Illiterate	88.5	Ceiling fan	55.9
	Up to primary (5th)	82.2	Wrist watch	67.0
	Up to matric (10th)	70.1	Television (B&W)	73.6
	Up to higher secondary (12th)	55.7	Radio	74.1
	Graduate and above	36.1	Bicycle	75.4

Source: NSHIE 2004–05 data: NCAER–CMCR analysis.

non-agricultural self-employed households (46.1 per cent) are located in rural areas. While an overwhelming share of illiterate households are based in rural areas (88.5 per cent), there are also 36.1 per cent households whose chief earners are graduate+.

Product ownership among rural households too is undergoing significant change. For instance, nearly 73.6 per cent of all black-and-white televisions sold in India are owned by rural households. Higher priced products such as refrigerators are also finding more buyers in rural areas with nearly 28.7 per cent of refrigerators sold being owned by rural households. Similarly, nearly 46 per cent of colour televisions, 53.9 per cent of two wheelers and 43.5 per cent of telephone instruments have been purchased by rural households.

Not surprisingly, the difference that is seen between rural and urban households in terms of earning and spending is also reflected in the ownership profile of most consumer durables. So, for instance, in the lower category of durables like pressure cookers and ceiling fans, urban ownership levels are much higher than those for rural areas (Figure 3.13). Just 38 per cent of rural households, for instance, own a pressure cooker/pan as compared with 80 per cent for urban areas. The penetration rate for fans is 48 per cent in rural areas and 89 per cent in urban, which perhaps also reflects the poor availability of electricity in villages. For items like wrist watches and bicycles, where electricity is not needed, the difference in rural and urban consumption is not that stark: 76 per cent versus 88 per cent in the case of wrist watches and 69 per cent versus 53 per cent in the case of bicycles.

Ownership of high-end consumer products such as colour televisions (regular and small), cars, mobile phones, refrigerators, credit cards, and so on, is growing in rural areas. Regular colour televisions, for instance, have penetrated a third of Indian homes, with ownership being much higher (67 per cent) in urban households. In rural areas, just 24 per cent of the households own colour television. Two wheeler ownership is 27 per cent in rural India as against 55 per cent in urban areas. The lower penetration of refrigerators in rural India is an indication of infrastructure constraints (such as lack of electricity) rather than a reflection of purchasing power. The rural–urban divide is visible also in the cases of mobile and landline phones.

Product ownership patterns also vary drastically between rural areas of low, middle and high income states (Figure 3.14). For instance, colour televisions are found in just 12 per cent rural households in low income states compared to 36 per cent and 41 per cent, respectively, in middle and high income states. Ceiling fans have penetrated into 70 per cent of rural homes in high income

Figure 3.13: Ownership of Selected Consumer Durable Goods: Rural and Urban (Per Cent of Households that Own Products)

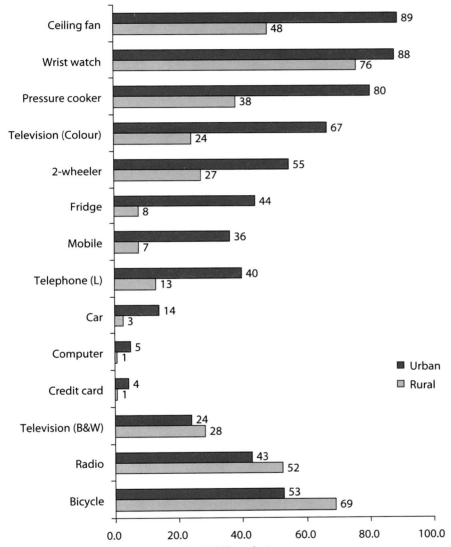

Source: NSHIE 2004–05 data: NCAER–CMCR analysis.

states as against just 30 per cent in low income states. In case of pressure cooker, the ownership is 65 per cent and 35 per cent for high and low income states, respectively, while for two wheelers, the corresponding shares are 44 per cent and 19 per cent.

Figure 3.14: Ownership of Selected Consumer Durable Goods by State of Residence: Rural (Per Cent of Households that Own Products)

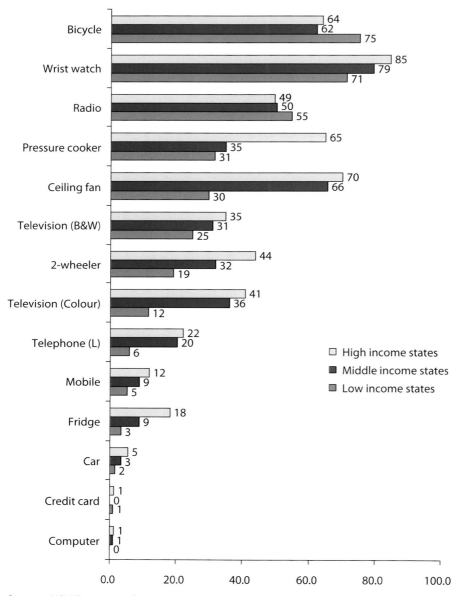

Source: NSHIE 2004–05 data: NCAER–CMCR analysis.

There is, however, not much difference between middle and high income states in the ownership levels of colour television, black and white television, ceiling fan, telephone, mobile phone, wrist watch and bicycle (Figure 3.14).

Figure 3.15: Ownership of Selected Consumer Durable Goods by State of Residence: Urban (Per Cent of House-holds that Own Products)

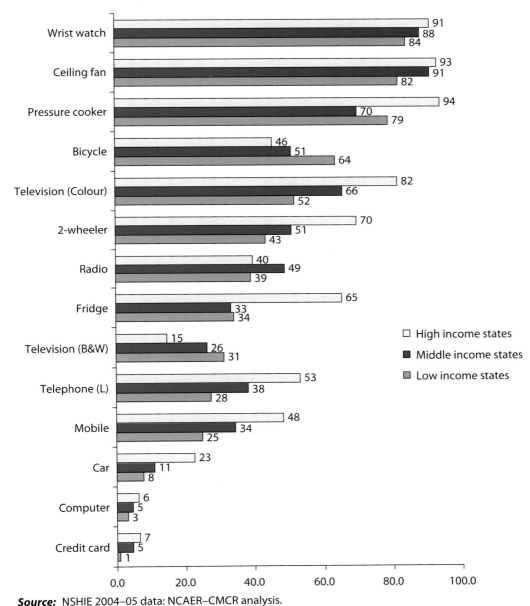

Source: NSHIE 2004–05 data: NCAER–CMCR analysis.

Ownership trends in urban households also show major differences when they are categorised according to low, middle and high income states. Consider, for in-stance, the case of black and white television. Only 15 per cent urban households in high income states own these, whereas 31 per cent households in low income states still own black and white television (Figure 3.15). This indicates that while the former (that is, high income states) have switched over to colour television, the latter have not yet done so. While low end products such as wrist watches, ceiling fans and pressure cookers have penetrated into urban households across all state types, high-end products such as two wheelers, refrigerators and cars are owned by a much larger segment of urban households in high income states than in low income states. Two wheeler ownership is growing rapidly among urban households in middle and low income states (at 51 per cent and 43 per cent, respectively). A quarter of the urban households in low income states, and nearly half the urban households in high income states own cellular phones. Ownership levels in middle and high income states are almost similar in the case of ceiling fan, wrist watch and bicycle.

Dissecting product ownership by households of various occupation types provides still more insights into consumption patterns. For instance, 48 per cent of urban salaried households own cellular phones (Figure 3.16) as against 22 per cent in the case of rural salaried households. Similarly, refrigerators are owned by nearly 58 per cent of urban salaried households compared to just 24 per cent of rural salaried households. Colour televisions are to be found in 83 per cent urban salaried households, while rural salaried households are fast catching up with nearly 57 per cent ownership. Three times more salaried households in urban areas own cars than their rural counterparts. The proportion of urban salaried households (18 per cent) owning a car is three times than that of the salaried households in rural areas (6 per cent). However, for wrist watch and two wheeler ownership, the rural–urban divide is not quite apparent.

Labour households in rural as well as urban areas tend to own similar kinds of products. But the penetration level of these products is higher among urban households. For instance, mobile phones, landline phones and refrigerators are owned by a minuscule segment of rural labour households (Figure 3.17). Ceiling fan ownership is much higher for urban labour households (73 per cent) compared to rural households (31 per cent). Similarly, 44 per cent urban labour households own black and white televisions compared to just 20 per cent among their rural counterparts. In the case of bicycle and radio, ownership levels in rural and urban areas are almost at par.

Figure 3.16: Ownership of Selected Consumer Durable Goods by Salaried Households and Location (Per Cent of Households that Own Products)

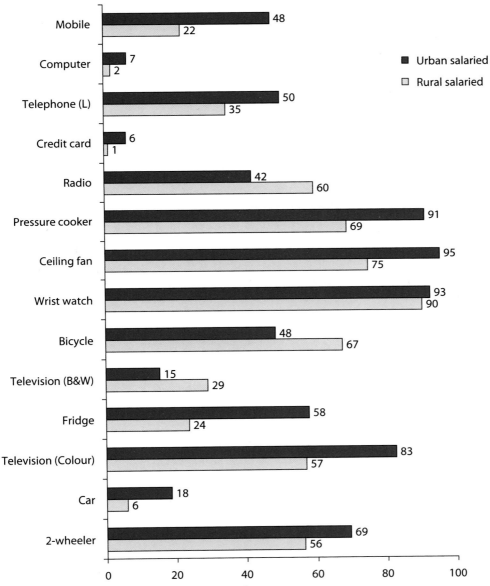

Source: NSHIE 2004–05 data: NCAER–CMCR analysis.

Figure 3.17: Ownership of Selected Consumer Durable Goods by Labour Households and Location (Per Cent of Households that Own Products)

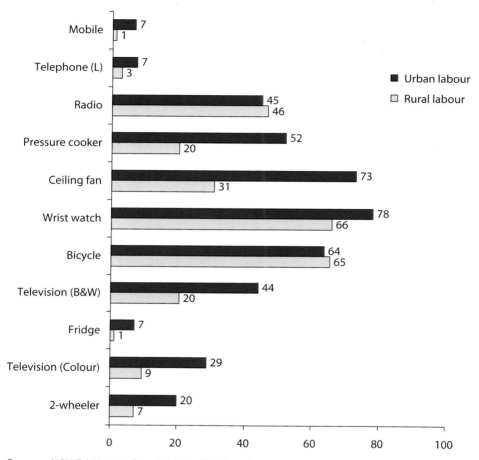

Source: NSHIE 2004–05 data: NCAER–CMCR analysis.
Note: Ownership of computer, credit card and car are negligible.

Saving Pattern of Indian Households

four

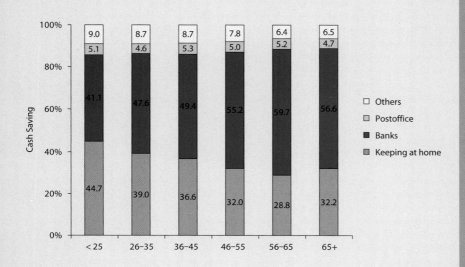

Traditionally India has been a nation of savers. Profligacy has been looked down upon and the saving habit has been lauded as a virtue through most of our fables and stories. Not surprisingly, India boasts one of the highest rates of national savings at 28 per cent. In recent years though, as the Indian economy has grown rapidly, and new employment opportunities have risen, particularly in the communications and technology sectors leading to higher disposable incomes, consumption rates have also grown. Purchase of consumer durables and the higher adoption of credit cards, as also the impact of increased advertising and access to a wider range of products and services, have led to increased expenditure levels in the households. Significantly, household savings are also used to meet business related expenses.

4.1 Saving Behaviour

Indian households save for a variety of reasons. Most households prefer to have an easily accessible corpus for emergencies, marriages and social occasions, children's education and gifting. Though India does not have a social security scheme, saving for old age is still not a priority for its households. Nearly 83 per cent of Indian households save for emergencies (in financial year 2004–05). Children's education emerges as a key priority with 81 per cent households saving to meet this requirement. About 69 per cent households save for reasons of old age financial security whereas 63 per cent households save to meet future expenses towards marriages, births and other social ceremonies. Significantly, 47 per cent households save to buy or build a house and an equal percentage of households save to expand their business operations. Almost 22 per cent households save to buy consumer durables and 18 per cent to meet expenses towards gifting, donations and pilgrimage.

Rural and urban households display some differences in their saving behaviour but there are more similarities than differences. While 87 per cent urban households put away some money for emergencies, only 81 per cent of rural households do so (Figure 4.1). More urban households (74 per cent) than rural ones (68 per cent) save for old age. Saving for purchasing large consumer durable items is observed among 29 per cent urban households as against 20 per cent rural households. Weddings, births, social events and ceremonies have special significance among

Indian families, particularly rural ones. Not surprisingly, 64 per cent rural and 60 per cent urban households save specifically for this cause.

Bank deposits and keeping money at home have emerged as the two most preferred modes of saving for Indian households. Half of all households keep more than half of their savings (51 per cent) in bank deposits, 36 per cent prefer to keep cash at hand and 5 per cent opt for post-office deposits. Cooperative society deposits, chit funds and purchasing bonds are some other modes of saving. Only 2 per cent households opt for purchasing insurance policies.

Owning an account in a financial institution[1] depends as much on the source of income as on age and education of the chief earner. Predictably, fewer rural Indians hold accounts in any financial institution as opposed to urban Indians. At the all-India level, 66 per cent households own accounts in a financial institution. The figures for rural and urban India are 59 per cent and 82 per cent, respectively.

Nearly a fourth of all Indians have outstanding loans: one-fifth in the case of urban households and one-fourth among rural ones. There are, however, variations

Figure 4.1: Motivation to Save for Future

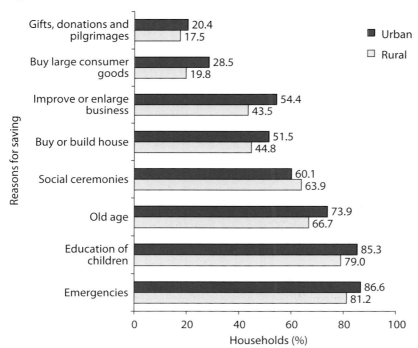

Source: NSHIE 2004–05 data: NCAER–CMCR analysis.

[1] Financial institution includes commercial banks, post-office, regional rural banks, registered societies, and so on.

depending on education and occupation levels of the chief owner. Other factors such as land ownership also determine whether or not a household is likely to have an outstanding loan. Households where the chief earner is self-employed in agriculture tend to be the most indebted. Over 27 per cent of such households have outstanding loans compared to just 17.6 per cent for households where the chief earner gets a regular salary. Over a fourth of households headed by labourers have outstanding loans and over 26 per cent of households with illiterate chief earners too have debts as compared to 18.8 per cent graduates+ households.

4.2 Demographic Profile of Household and Level of Surplus Income

Nearly 81.4 per cent of households at the all-India level save a part of their earnings. The figure is 88 per cent for urban India and 78.5 per cent for rural India. At the all-India level, the average household income is Rs 65,041, annual expenditure is Rs 48,558 and surplus income is Rs 16,483. Surplus income is almost a quarter of the total income and a significant proportion of this (16.4 per cent) is saved as liquid cash. Only 5.8 per cent of the surplus income is saved in physical assets and only 3.1 per cent in financial instruments (Table 4.1).

Table 4.1: Estimates of Earning, Spending and Savings by Location

	Rural	Urban	All India
a. Household income (Rs/annum)	51,922	95,827	65,041
b. Household expenditure (Rs/annum)	40,124	68,352	48,558
c. Surplus income (Rs/annum)			
Financial investment*	1,217	3,857	2,003
Physical investments**	2,886	5,912	3,792
Saving in cash	7,694	17,706	10,688
Total	11,798	27,475	16,483
d. Share of surplus income to income (per cent)			
Financial investment	2.3	4.0	3.1
Physical investments	5.6	6.2	5.8
Saving in cash	14.8	18.5	16.4
Total	22.7	28.7	25.3

Source: NSHIE 2004–05 data: NCAER–CMCR analysis.
Notes: * Financial instruments include investment made in stock market, small savings and life insurance only for the year 2004–05.
** Physical instruments include investment made in jewellery, consumer durable and others only for the year 2004–05.

The average income of rural households is Rs 51,922 compared to Rs 95,827 for urban households. Of this, Rs 40,124 is spent as routine and unusual expenses by rural households and Rs 68,352 by urban households. This shows a surplus income[2] of nearly 23 per cent in rural households and 29 per cent in urban ones. A major portion of the surplus income (15 per cent to 19 per cent) is saved as cash, while about 6 per cent is saved in physical assets, such as consumer goods, jewellery, and so on, and only 2 per cent to 3 per cent goes as financial investments. The share of physical investments in surplus income is relatively more in rural households (25 per cent) than in urban ones (22 per cent), while the share of financial investments is lesser in rural households (10 per cent) compared to urban ones (14 per cent). Investment priorities for rural and urban households are different. Looking at specific investment types, life insurance policies and stock holdings are more popular among urban households while jewellery and consumer durables are preferred options in rural households (Figure 4.2).

In terms of mode of saving, urban households put nearly 63 per cent of their cash in bank accounts, while rural households save 45 per cent of their income as bank deposits (Figure 4.3). A much higher share of the savings is kept as liquid cash by rural households (41.7 per cent) than by urban ones (23.4 per cent).

Figure 4.2: Distribution of Investment by Location (Per Cent of Total Investment)

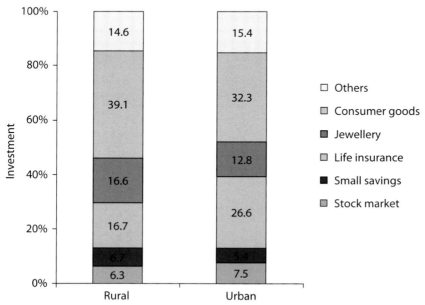

Source: NSHIE 2004–05 data: NCAER–CMCR analysis.

---

[2] Surplus income = Total household income – expenditure (routine+unusual). In this book, 'saving' is used frequently as a synonym to 'surplus income' to provide a better readability.

Figure 4.3: Preferred Form of Cash Saving by Location (Per Cent of Cash Saving)

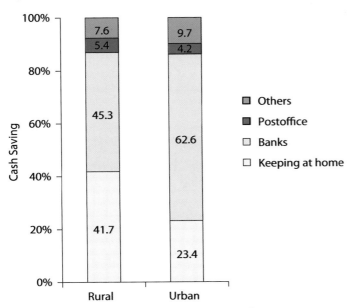

Source: NSHIE 2004–05 data: NCAER–CMCR analysis.

4.2.1 Occupation of Chief Earner and Level of Surplus Income

Salaried households constitute only 18 per cent of the households in the country, but account for the highest amount of savings. Out of an average annual income of Rs 110,344, a salary earning household saves nearly 35 per cent of this income (Table 4.2). The next high income earning group, that is, those who are self-employed in non-agricultural activities, saves 32 per cent (Rs 95,020). For the next two groups–agriculture and labour dependent households–the saving rate drops to 20 per cent and 8 per cent, respectively.

Saving in the form of physical investments is more common among the agriculture dependent (32 per cent of surplus) and labour dependent (22 per cent) households than those deriving their income from salary or non-agricultural activities (19 per cent to 20 per cent). The two highest income generating occupations save 68 per cent to 69 per cent of their surplus income in cash, whereas in the non-agriculture and labour categories cash savings forms 59 per cent and 55 per cent, respectively.

Life insurance and investing in consumer goods are the two most preferred options of financial investment for salary earning households (Figure 4.4). Such households allocate a fourth of their total savings to paying insurance premium but only 6.7 per cent towards shares and debentures. Financial investments form

Table 4.2: Estimates of Earning, Spending and Savings by Occupation of Chief Earner: All India

	Regular salary/ wages	Self-employment in non-agriculture	Self-employment in agriculture	Labour
a. Household income (Rs/annum)	110,344	95,020	55,653	30,957
b. Household expenditure (Rs/annum)	72,268	65,002	44,466	28,289
c. Surplus income (Rs/annum)				
Financial investment	4,563	3,476	1,028	610
Physical investments	7,147	6,005	3,560	600
Saving in cash	26,366	20,537	6,599	1,458
Total	38,076	30,018	11,187	2,668
d. Share of surplus income to income (per cent)				
Financial investment	4.1	3.7	1.8	2.0
Physical investments	6.5	6.3	6.4	1.9
Saving in cash	23.9	21.6	11.9	4.7
Total	34.5	31.6	20.1	8.6

Source: NSHIE 2004–05 data: NCAER–CMCR analysis.

Figure 4.4: Distribution of Investment by Occupation of Chief Earner: All India

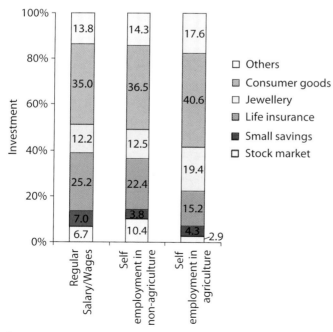

Source: NSHIE 2004–05 data: NCAER–CMCR analysis.

only a minuscule percentage of savings for these households as they prefer to keep the major chunk of their surplus incomes in cash, mostly in banks (68 per cent), and 20 per cent as cash on hand (Figure 4.5). Households engaged in non-agricultural activities also have more or less similar savings pattern as regular salary earning households. Investment in life insurance and debentures together constitutes 33 per cent of their surplus income, and this is on par with the corresponding share for the salaried category.

But in the 'self-employed in agriculture' category, the situation is quite different. These households have nearly 55 per cent of their cash savings kept at home and only 32 per cent is deposited in banks.

Figure 4.5: Preferred Form of Cash Saving by Occupation of Chief Earner: All India

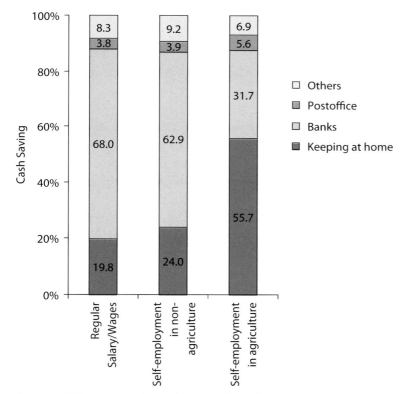

Source: NSHIE 2004–05 data: NCAER–CMCR analysis.

4.2.2. Education Level of Chief Earner and Surplus Income

Graduate+ households have the highest level of total surplus income in absolute terms (Rs 47,590 per annum), and in percentage terms too, this translates into a

Table 4.3: Estimates of Earning, Spending and Savings by Education Level of Chief Earner: All India

	Illiterate	Up to primary	Up to higher secondary	Graduate+
a. Household income (Rs/annum)	37,062	44,677	85,334	134,539
b. Household expenditure (Rs/annum)	31,936	37,450	60,587	86,949
c. Surplus income (Rs/annum)				
Financial investment	861	662	2,854	6,085
Physical investments	1,451	1,490	5,690	10,746
Saving in cash	2,814	5,075	16,204	30,759
Total	5,126	7,227	24,747	47,590
d. Share of surplus income to income (per cent)				
Financial investment	2.3	1.5	3.3	4.5
Physical investments	3.9	3.3	6.7	8.0
Saving in cash	7.6	11.4	19.0	22.9
Total	13.8	16.2	29.0	35.4

Source: NSHIE 2004–05 data: NCAER–CMCR analysis.

35 per cent share of their household income (Table 4.3). This is all the more significant when we recall that graduate+ households constituting just 13.7 per cent of total households in the country contribute 28.3 per cent to the total household income. Households of 'up to higher secondary' category are the next best performers, saving as much as 29 per cent of their income.

It is interesting to note that the proportions allocated to the three forms, viz. cash, financial investments and physical investments, are almost identical in the two top categories: 65 per cent cash saving and 23 per cent physical investments. While the 'illiterate' category' saves 55.0 per cent of their surplus income as cash on hand and 28.3 per cent as physical investments, the 'up to primary' category saves 70.3 per cent and 20.4 per cent, respectively. It is interesting to note that the illiterate chief earner households have the highest share of their surplus income (16.7 per cent) in financial investments while the graduate+ households have only a 13.0 per cent share.

The educated households invest a higher percentage in insurance policies (21 per cent to 25 per cent) as well as consumer durables (36 per cent to 37 per cent) as compared to the illiterate households (14 per cent and 29 per cent, respectively). Interestingly, it is the illiterate households that invest a higher share on debentures (10.2 per cent), the shares of graduate+ and 'up to higher secondary' categories being 5.3 per cent and 8.3 per cent, respectively. On an average,

Figure 4.6: Distribution of Investment by Education Level of Chief Earner: All India

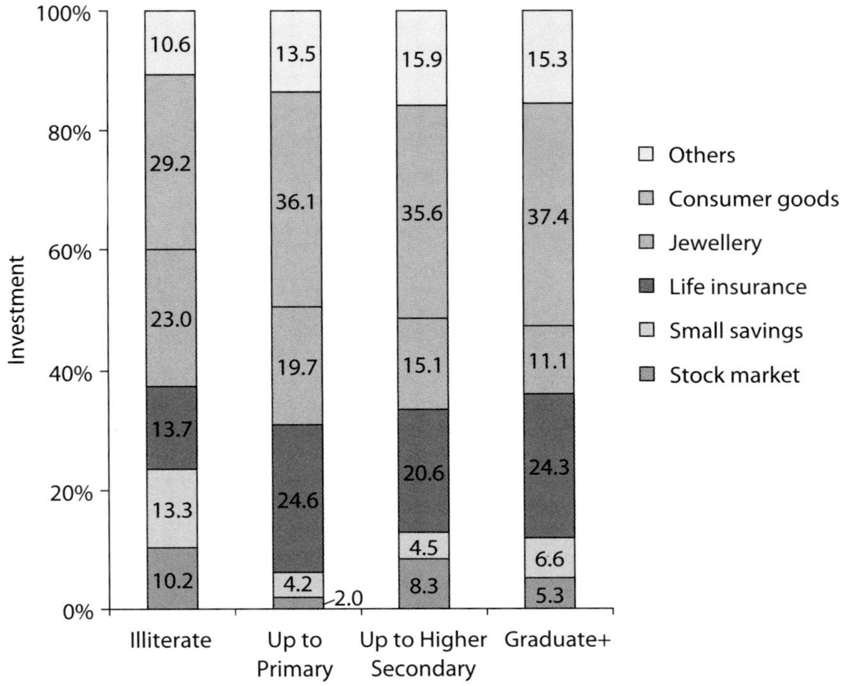

Source: NSHIE 2004–05 data: NCAER–CMCR analysis.

5.3 per cent of all graduate+ households tend to invest in shares/debentures and around 24.3 per cent in insurance policies. The levels of investment in jewellery among different household categories bear an inverse relationship with the levels of education of the chief earner. While 23 per cent illiterate chief earner households invest in jewellery, only 11 per cent of the graduate+ households do so (Figure 4.6).

Cash savings for the graduate+ group is also the highest at Rs 30,759 compared to Rs 16,204 for the 'up to higher secondary' group. In terms of percentage share, it works out to 23 per cent and 19 per cent of their incomes, respectively (Table 4.3). The share of the illiterate chief earner household group is 8 per cent. An overwhelming 73 per cent of the cash savings of the graduate+ group are deposited in banks as against 35 per cent for the illiterate group, which dominates in the cash on hand share (53 per cent). Graduate+ households keep only 17 per cent cash at home (Figure 4.7). In fact, the liquid cash levels in different household categories are inversely associated with the corresponding levels of education of the chief earner.

Figure 4.7: Preferred Form of Cash Saving by Education: All India

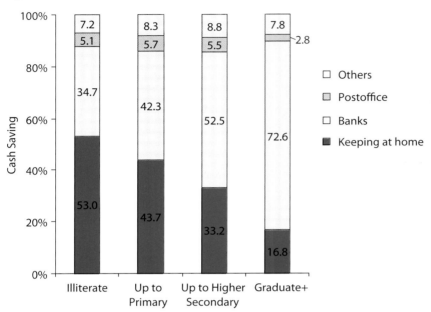

Source: NSHIE 2004–05 data: NCAER–CMCR analysis.

4.2.3 Age of Chief Earner and Surplus Income

As the chief earner (across households) gets older, two trends are observed. First, the motivation to save tends to change; increasingly, the household feels the need to save for old age. Second, in absolute as well as relative terms, the saving level increases.

Households where chief earners are in the 36–45 years age group form the major bulk of households in the country (35 per cent), followed by those in the 26–35 years age group (22 per cent). Households with chief earners in the age group of 66 years and above (66+) constitute just 3 per cent of the population but they make the highest level of savings, that is, Rs 21,196 per annum which is 25 per cent of their annual income (Table 4.4). Savings, both absolute and proportionate, steadily increases up to the 36–45 years age group, then there is a sharp decline in the 46–55 years age group which is followed by a sharp rise in the 56–65 years age segment. The savings of the 66+ years age group is only marginally higher.

Interestingly, in all the categories except the second and last category (66+), the proportionate savings in three modes, viz. cash, financial investments and

Table 4.4: Estimates of Earning, Spending and Savings by Age of Chief Earner: All India

	Less than 25	26–35	36–45	46–55	56–65	More than 65
a. Household income (Rs/annum)	47,588	55,663	61,787	77,237	83,612	85,851
b. Household expenditure (Rs/annum)	39,073	42,198	46,265	56,793	62,416	68,840
c. Surplus income (Rs/annum)						
Financial investment	801	1,625	2,099	1,858	2,099	3,778
Physical investments	1,928	3,741	4,516	3,008	4,516	5,340
Saving in cash	5,785	8,099	13,829	10,656	13,829	12,078
Total	8,515	13,465	20,444	15,522	20,444	21,196
d. Share of surplus income to income (per cent)						
Financial investment	1.7	2.9	3.4	2.4	2.5	4.4
Physical investments	4.1	6.7	7.3	3.9	5.4	6.2
Saving in cash	12.2	14.6	22.4	13.8	16.5	14.1
Total	17.9	24.2	33.1	20.1	24.5	24.7

Source: NSHIE 2004–05 data: NCAER–CMCR analysis.

physical investments are almost identical, nearly 68 per cent cash savings and 22 per cent physical investments. In the 26–35 years age group corresponding shares are 60 per cent and 28 per cent, respectively, and for the 66+ age group, the figures are 57 per cent and 25 per cent, respectively.

All the groups except the 56–65 years age group invest 22 per cent to 23 per cent of their savings in life insurance policies (Figure 4.8). The 56–65 years age group invests only 13 per cent of its savings in life insurance but this is more than compensated by its higher investment (16 per cent) in shares and debentures.

Consumer durable goods are a preferred mode of investment for the youngest earners (less than 25 years) as well as the 26–35 year olds and 36–45 year olds. Investment in this mode ranges between 32 per cent and 39 per cent. The 36–45 year olds invest more in debentures (10 per cent), as do 56–65 year olds. The 66+ age group invests the largest share in consumer goods (52 per cent) at the cost of shares and debentures, and jewellery to some extent. In percentage terms, the youngest chief earners and the 56–65 years age group invest more in jewellery (20 per cent) than other age groups (12 per cent to 15 per cent).

As the chief earners age, the percentage share of savings that is kept at home as cash declines from 45 per cent for the youngest group to 29 per cent for the 56–65 year old age group. Conversely, bank deposit percentages increases from 41 per cent to 60 per cent. At the same time, the 66+ group holds 32 per cent as liquid cash and 57 per cent as bank deposits (Figure 4.9).

Figure 4.8: Distribution of Investment by Age of Chief Earner: All India

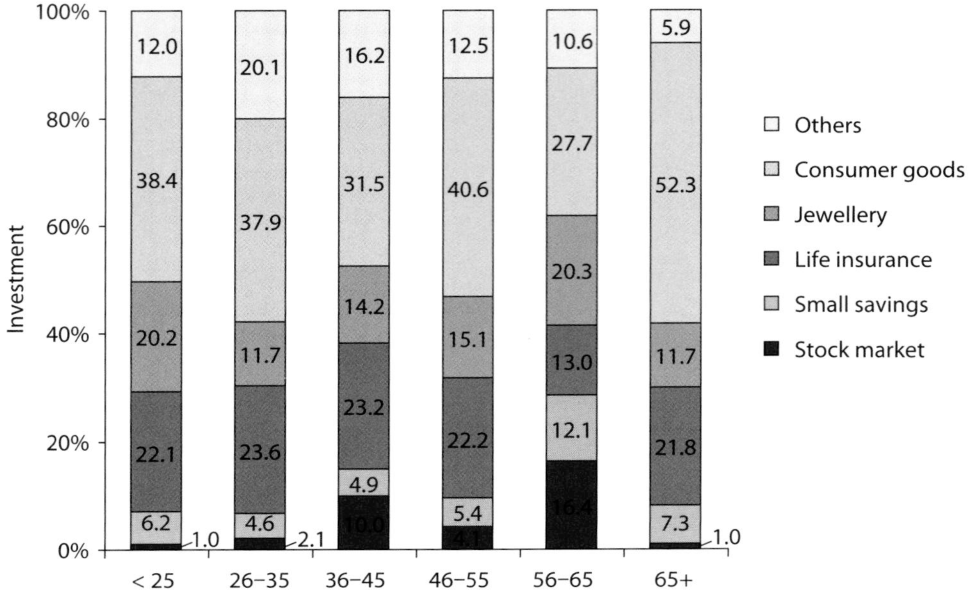

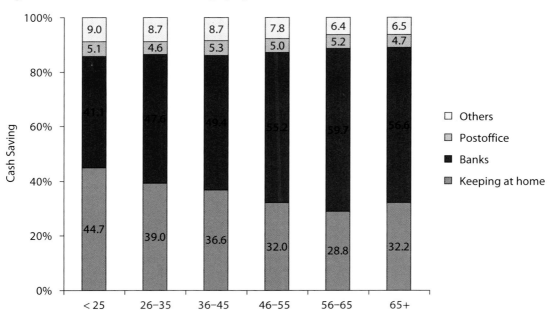

Source: NSHIE 2004–05 data: NCAER–CMCR analysis.

Figure 4.9: Preferred Form of Cash Saving by Age of Chief Earner: All India

Source: NSHIE 2004–05 data: NCAER–CMCR analysis.

4.2.4 State of Residence and Level of Surplus Income

Though around 45 per cent of India's population lives in low income states and another one-third in middle income states, it is the high income states that account for the largest savings in the country. The average income of households in these states is Rs 89,288, of which around 37 per cent is saved (Table 4.5). In absolute terms, the households in high income states save more than four times the amount saved by households in the low income states and nearly twice than that saved by households in the middle income states. In terms of share of surplus income to earnings, the households in low income states save just 15 per cent of their income compared to 25 per cent saving by their counterparts in middle income states. The households in high income states hold 78 per cent, middle income states 61 per cent and low income states 43 per cent of their respective surplus income as liquid cash. Physical investments by these household groups are at the rates of 14 per cent, 24 per cent and 41 per cent, respectively.

Table 4.5: Estimates of Earning, Spending and Savings by State of Residence

	Low income states	Middle income states	High income states
a. Household income (Rs/annum)	52,052	66,737	89,288
b. Household expenditure (Rs/annum)	44,025	49,872	55,887
c. Surplus income (Rs/annum)			
Financial investment	1,330	2,562	2,596
Physical investments	3,254	3,973	4,607
Saving in cash	3,443	10,330	26,197
Total	8,027	16,865	33,401
d. Share of surplus income to income (per cent)			
Financial investment	2.6	3.8	2.9
Physical investments	6.3	6.0	5.2
Saving in cash	6.6	15.5	29.3
Total	15.4	25.3	37.4

Source: NSHIE 2004–05 data: NCAER–CMCR analysis.

While high income states account for the highest proportion invested in shares/debentures (12.5 per cent), it is the middle income states that account for the highest rate of investment in life insurance (Figure 4.10). An average household in middle income states invests nearly 28.7 per cent of its total savings in insurance each year, as against 16 per cent to 19 per cent in low and high income states. The rate of investment in jewellery is also higher in middle income states

(18.5 per cent). While households in low and high income states put in 39 per cent to 40 per cent of their savings into consumer goods, those in middle income states allocate 29 per cent of their savings into consumer durables (Figure 4.10).

Figure 4.10: Distribution of Investment by State of Residence

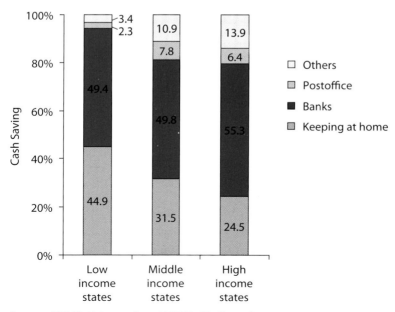

Source: NSHIE 2004–05 data: NCAER–CMCR analysis.

Figure 4.11: Preferred Form of Cash Saving by State of Residence

Source: NSHIE 2004–05 data: NCAER–CMCR analysis.

Households of high income states deposit 55 per cent of their cash savings in bank accounts while in low and middle income states, this figure stands at 50 per cent. Unlike in middle and high income states, a higher proportion of cash savings is kept as liquid cash (45 per cent) by households of low income states (Figure 4.11).

4.3 Personal Savings Help Tide over Economic Hardship

During times of financial crisis, for example, due to the death of the chief earner, illness in the family or job loss, a majority of Indian households draw on their personal savings. Nearly 58 per cent urban households and 54 per cent rural households dip into their personal savings during times of economic hardship. In the event of the death of the chief earner, nearly 55 per cent of Indian households take recourse to own savings for tiding over the crisis (Table 4.6). Almost a fourth of the households opt for a loan from a friend or a relative.

Table 4.6: Measures Taken to Overcome Economic Shock: All India

	Death of chief earner	Major sickness	Crop loss	Business loss
a. Per cent of households who faced economic shocks	3.2	13.8	10.2	2.2
b. First measure taken to overcome economic shock (Per cent of reported households)				
Using own savings	55.3	57.2	48.1	43.5
Loan from friends/relatives	23.7	23.1	15.8	22.6
Selling/mortgaged of land, house, jewellery, and so on	7.1	5.7	7.6	7.9
None	3.5	0.3	6.7	4.5
Loan from employer	1.4	1.7	0.5	0.8
Others	9.0	11.9	21.3	20.8
Total	100.0	100.0	100.0	100.0

Source: NSHIE 2004–05 data: NCAER–CMCR analysis.

A similar trend is observed across the occupational categories of households: 65 per cent of 'regular salary earner', 64 per cent of 'self-employed in non-agriculture', 59 per cent of 'self-employed in agriculture' and 43 per cent of 'labour' households fall back on their personal savings during financial hardship. A good number of agricultural and labour households also sell off their assets to deal with the crisis (8 per cent each).

4.4 Households' Perceptions about Financial Security

4.4.1 Indians are Optimistic about Their Financial Stability

Most Indians are confident of living off their savings after retirement. They are also sure of finding employment in case of job loss. As a result, saving for old age is not a priority. At the all-India level, 12.8 per cent of households feel 'very confident' about the stability of their income, and another 41 per cent are 'confident.' Another 30 per cent each are either 'less confident' or 'not confident at all' while 15.1 per cent do not share their sentiments about their income stability. Traditionally, the extended family and children have pitched in during times of financial difficulty and this mindset is perhaps one of the main reasons for the optimistic outlook. While half of those in rural India are either very confident or confident of the stability of their income, the figure is higher at 63 per cent for urban India.

While there are large differences across various socio-economic groups, the broad trend is the same: a lot more people are confident than those who are not. At the aggregate level, around 44.5 per cent of households headed by those under the age of 25 tend to be confident about the stability of their incomes and this rises to 61.1 per cent in the case of households headed by those in the 56–65 years age group. Around 39.3 per cent of illiterate chief earner households are confident and 78.6 per cent graduate+ households feel the same way.

In the case of the salaried households, three-fourths of them are confident about their financial stability, only 11 per cent, 5 per cent and 9 per cent of such households feel that they are 'less confident,' 'least confident' or 'totally uncertain,' respectively. More labour dependent and agriculture dependent households than those engaged in the non-agricultural activities have 'less/least confidence' or are totally unsure about their financial security. For instance, the percentages of different responses from the labour dependent households are: 26 per cent 'less confident,' 20 per cent 'least confident' and 21 per cent 'totally unsure.' For the households in the 'self-employed in the agriculture' category, the percentages are: 26 per cent 'less confident,' 20 per cent 'least confident' and 22 per cent 'totally unsure' about their financial sources.

4.4.2 Time-frame for Recovering from any Loss of Income

Households sustain themselves on their savings during a financial crisis. The time households perceive it will take them to recover from a loss of income, as opposed to their level of confidence about the stability of their income, is a clear indicator of the kind of financial planning most families undertake. Interestingly, 34 per cent of Indian households believe it will take them less than six months to be able to replace their current incomes in case of a disruption and another 21 per cent feel it will take a year. Therefore, around 55 per cent of Indian households feel it will take six to 12 months to recover from a loss of income, a figure that is relatively equal to the number that feel 'very confident/confident' about their future.

Since incomes from interest on financial savings are not enough to sustain a household for a whole year without any other source of income, this implies that a large number of households that claim to be 'very confident/confident' about the stability of their income plan to draw on their savings, leaving less for their post-retirement life. While the figures vary across different socio-economic groups, the broad trend is the same: the majority believes they can restore their current levels of income within a year of the loss of income.

Almost 39 per cent agricultural households claim they will be able to find alternative income within six months, compared to 34 per cent regular salary earning households, and 37 per cent households each of 'self-employed in non-agriculture' and labour categories. On the other hand, more agriculture dependent and labour dependent households (41 per cent and 40 per cent, respectively) are unable to suggest a time-frame within which they will be able to find alternative income, compared to households of 'self-employed in non-agriculture' and 'regular salary earning' categories (30 per cent and 33 per cent, respectively).

Nearly 38 per cent graduate+ households express confidence that they will be able to find alternative income within six months. This proportion is only slightly higher than for other groups. More illiterate chief earner households are unsure of the time-frame by which they would be able to find alternative income (41 per cent) as compared to graduate+ households (30 per cent). More graduate+ households claim that they would be able to find alternative income (25 per cent) within a year compared to illiterate households (16 per cent).

4.4.3 Drawing on Current Savings in Case of Loss of Income

The fact that households draw on current savings to meet routine expenditure in case of a sudden drop in income levels is borne out by the fact that about 4 per cent of households claim that they can sustain themselves for more than a year if they lose their major source of household income. The proportion differs across various socio-economic groups. Less than 1 per cent of households that depend on labour and agriculture as the main sources of income can sustain themselves for more than a year on their savings, the shares for 'self-employed in non-agriculture' and salary earning categories being 7 per cent and 9 per cent, respectively.

Stretching the savings to last beyond 12 months becomes more of a problem for households that are lower down on the education scale. For instance, as in the case of labour dependent households, 1 per cent households that are headed by illiterate chief earners can sustain themselves for this period, compared to 2 per cent primary educated chief earner households, 4 per cent higher secondary educated chief earner households and 11 per cent graduate+ households.

4.4.4 Misplaced Financial Optimism

India is a country of optimists when it comes to financial security. More than half the Indian households (54 per cent) are confident about their current and future stability. Unfortunately, this financial optimism is not based on facts. An overwhelming 96 per cent of households feel that they cannot survive beyond one year on their current savings in case of loss of a major source of household income and yet 54 per cent households claim that they are financially secure. Urban Indians appear to be even more optimistic than their rural counterparts. This clearly indicates that Indians do not take a long term view of their financial security, and hence, their optimism is misplaced and there is a pressing need for financial literacy for better understanding of their financial risks.

Income Pyramid: Distribution and Income Disparity

five

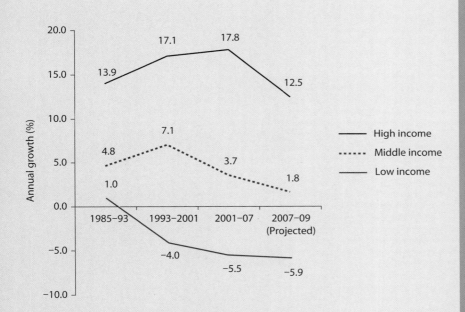

The gap between the top-earning households and the lowest-income earning Indian families is huge. Nearly 70 per cent of the bottom quintile households reside in low income states and 90 per cent of these households are in rural areas. On the other hand, half of all top quintile households also live in rural India. Nearly 60 per cent of the top quintile households are occupied in clerical, sales, service oriented or professional and administrative jobs. In contrast, nearly 70 per cent of the bottom quintile households are engaged in farming activities. Consumer product ownership is skewed heavily towards the top income quintile groups. For instance, while 36 per cent of all households own two wheelers, ownership is significantly higher among households in the top quintile group (71 per cent) compared to the bottom quintile households (8 per cent).

5.1 Understanding Income Distribution Puzzle

The fast changing consumerism in India over the last two decades has made life ever more puzzling for marketers, analysts and policy makers who have been trying to understand the changing dynamics of the Indian marketplace. Gone are the days when Indian consumers could have been neatly slotted into a definite category based on a single indicator, since consumers and consumerism have turned into a more complex proposition looking for more value and satisfaction for their money. For instance, two decades ago, ownership patterns of consumer durables by the highest socio-economic group (SEC-A) consumer and the lowest group (SEC-C) consumer would have been succinctly distinct. Not so anymore. Today, such groups do have access to mobile phones, television sets, computers and other gizmos. Similarly, efficacy of income distribution based on arbitrary absolute household income cut-offs and the use of qualifying labels like 'low–medium–high' is alone no longer effective over a long period of time, when the economy is fast changing. To illustrate, in NCAER's (National Council of Applied Economic Research) income distribution of 1985–86, those that were classified as the 'low income group' have declined significantly as of 2007–08 and expected to cease in the near future.

NCAER regularly uses data from its annual survey to get the shape of the income distribution curve and then superimposes this on gross domestic product

Table 5.1: Estimated Number of Households by Income Class*: All India (Number of Households in Million)

Year	Low income	Middle income	High income	Total
1985–86	83.8	43.3	1.4	128.5
1993–94	90.5	62.9	3.9	157.3
2001–02	65.2	109.2	13.8	188.2
2007–08	46.3	135.9	36.9	219.1
2009–10	41.0	140.7	46.7	228.4

Source: NSHIE 2004–05 data: NCAER–CMCR analysis.
Note: * Income class (Annual household income at 2001–02 prices): Low Income (Less than Rs 45,000); Middle Income (Rs 45,000–Rs 180,000); and High Income (More than Rs 180,000).

(GDP) projections to get estimates of the number of households in different income groups. Based on the various projections of annual GDP growth rates, our calculations show that while economic growth has been pegged at roughly 9.4 per cent during 2005–08, we have assumed a more conservative real net domestic product (NDP) growth which is likely to hit 6.75 per cent during 2008–10 annually.

This exercise has revealed that the number of low income households (those earning under Rs 45,000 per annum at 2001–02 prices) would fall from 84 million in 1985–86 to 65 million in 2001–02; if the GDP next year grows by a little less than 7 per cent, this number will fall to 41 million by the end of the decade. The number of middle income households (Rs 45,000 to Rs 180,000) is estimated

Figure 5.1: Household Income Distribution: All India

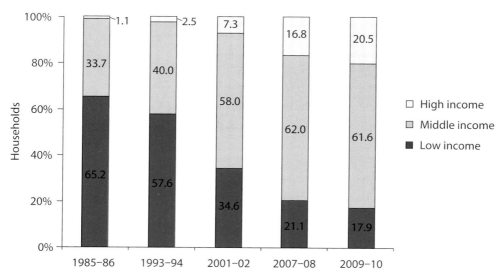

Source: NSHIE 2004–05 data: NCAER–CMCR analysis.

to rise from 43 million in 1985–86 to 109 million in 2001–02 and this will rise to 141 million in 2009–10. The high income households (over Rs 180,000) are projected to rise from just 1.4 million to 13.8 million and will still rise to 47 million in 2009–10 (Table 5.1).

The wheel of fortune continues to spin in India, with each level of household income set to move a notch higher by the end of the decade (Figure 5.1). For the first time, the number of high income households is set to exceed the number of poor households in 2009–10, while more than five million middle income households will hit the high income bracket.

According to our revised forecast, this slow trend in economic growth particularly in 2007–08 and 2009–10 would have the maximum impact on middle income households. However, high income households will continue to grow little slower and lower income households will continue with the declining trend (Figure 5.2).

Another concept related to income distribution which has always been a subject of much debate and controversy is the strength of the *Indian middle class*. Traditionally, both the Indian and foreign media have pegged this figure as ranging from 200 million to 600 million. The difficulty in arriving at an accurate estimate lies in its ambiguous definition and diverse interpretation by users. The World Bank defines middle class as those having purchasing power parity (PPP) per capita

Figure 5.2: Growth in Household Income Distribution: All India

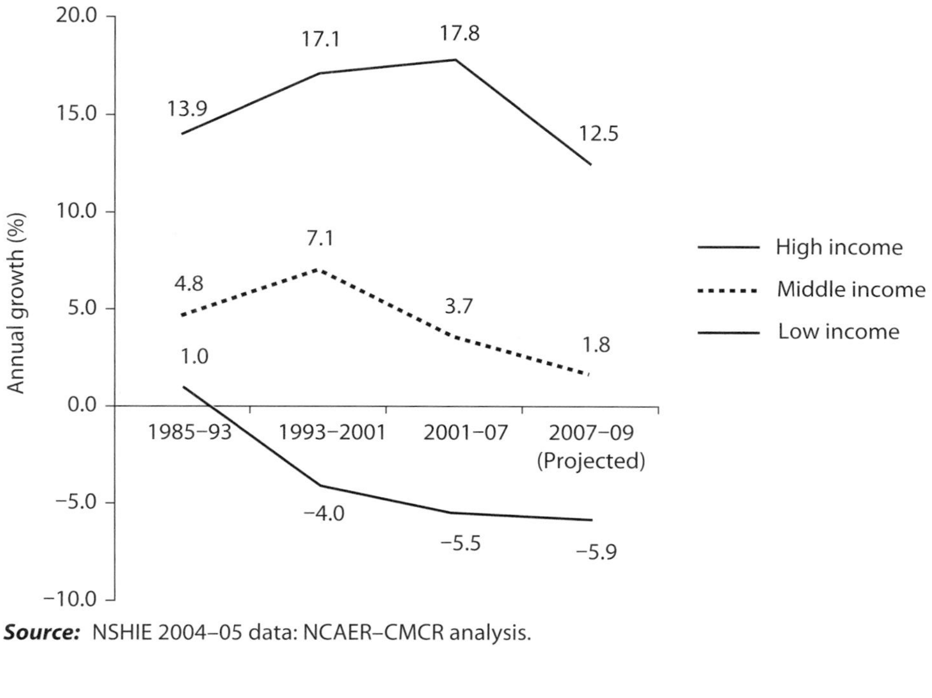

Source: NSHIE 2004–05 data: NCAER–CMCR analysis.

per day between US$10 and US$20, which is much narrower than the NCAER definition attributing the name to those households whose annual incomes lie between Rs 200,000 to one million (US$4,000 to US$21,000 at 2001–02 prices), which is what McKinsey Global Institute used in its *The Bird of Gold* (2007).

As per NCAER definition, between 1995–96 and 2001–02, total middle class homes grew twice in size: from 4.5 million households to 10.7 million and by 2009–10, they are expected to rise to 28.4 million. About two-thirds of the Indian middle class is to be found in urban India and there is not much change in this trend (Table 5.2).

More importantly, while the middle class forms just 11.4 per cent in 2007–08 of the total Indian households, its share of total income is nearly one-fourth and saves more than 55 per cent of its income. The growing clout of the middle class becomes even more apparent when one looks at the ownership patterns of household goods. Nearly 49 per cent of all cars are owned by the middle class, compared to just 7 per cent by the rich. Similarly, 53 per cent of all air-conditioners are owned by middle class homes. Nearly 46 per cent of all credit cards are to be found in middle class households.

What is more, the Indian middle class is far from a homogenous group. While more than half of the urban middle class households are salary/wage earners, the biggest proportion of rural households are self-employed in the agricultural sector.

Table 5.2: Size of Indian Middle Class: NCAER Estimates

Consumer Class (Annual household Income at 2001–02 prices)	Distribution of households (million)		Distribution of households (per cent)		Share of rural (per cent)		Annual growth (per cent)
	2001–02	2009–10	2001–02	2009–10	2001–02	2009–10	
Deprived Below Rs 90,000 (Below US$ 2,000)	135.4 (731)	114.4 (618)	71.9	51.5	81.8	84.2	–2.1
Aspirers Rs 90,000–Rs 200,000 (US$ 2,000–US$ 4,000)	41.3 (221)	75.3 (405)	21.9	33.9	48.5	61.2	7.8
Middle Class Rs 200,000–Rs 10,000,000 (US$ 4,000–US$ 21,000)	10.7 (58)	28.4 (153)	5.7	12.8	35.2	33.4	12.9
Rich Over Rs10,000,000 (Over US$ 21,000)	0.8 (4)	3.8 (20)	0.4	1.7	22.9	22.2	21.4
Total	188.2 (1,014)	221.9 (1,195)	100.0	100.0	71.6	68.8	2.1

Source: NSHIE 2004–05 data: NCAER–CMCR analysis.
Note: Figures in () indicate the size of population.

Patterns of product ownership also show a divergence when it comes to rural and urban middle class households. While only 24 per cent of rural middle class homes own a car, more than 40 per cent do so in urban India. Televisions too are to be found in 90 per cent of all urban middle class homes compared to 62 per cent in rural middle class homes. Though this is an opportunity for marketers, it is clear that addressing the middle class with a one-size-fits-all mindset is unlikely to work.

NCAER's classification of the middle class too has evolved over a period of two decades. Although income is used as the primary criterion to define the middle class, the cultural parameters such as education, patterns of consumption and ownership of selected consumer goods have also been taken into account to understand better the complexities underlying issues related to the middle class. What was started in a bid to capture the income demographics in 1985–86 has evolved into a dynamic model for understanding consumption behaviour. The terms 'middle class,' 'consuming class' and 'middle income households' are often used interchangeably by the users of NCAER data. But a look at Table 5.3 will demonstrate how this demographic has evolved. When annual household income across the three time-periods is taken at 2001–02 prices, it emerges that the middle class of 2001–02 would actually have been categorized as the high income households 20 years ago in real terms. Over the years, the middle class has burgeoned considerably as is evident from Table 5.3. Accordingly, the group that was classified as middle class in 1995–96 and just 25 million strong, has grown to 58 million in 2001–02 and further 153 million by end the current decade.

A few others suggest that the middle class are those who are literally in the middle, that is, those having their incomes approximately between the 33rd

Table 5.3: Evolution of Indian Middle Class: NCAER Estimates

NCAER's definition and income cut-off (Annual household Income at 2001–02 prices)	Estimated households and population (million)			Share to total population/ households (per cent)			Annual growth (per cent)	
	1995–96	2001–02	2009–10	1995–96	2001–02	2009–10	1995–2001	2001–09
Middle income households (Rs 45,000–Rs 180,000) (US$ 900–US$ 3,600)	89 (499)	109 (612)	141 (788)	54.1	58.0	61.6	3.4	3.2
Consuming class (Rs 90,000–Rs 400,000) (US$ 1,800–US$ 8,000)	25 (140)	39 (211)	70 (352)	15.2	20.7	30.8	7.7	7.6
Middle class (Rs 200,000–Rs 10,000,000) (US$ 4,000–US$21,000)	5 (25)	11 (58)	28 (153)	2.7	5.7	12.8	15.5	12.9

Source: NSHIE 2004–05 data: NCAER–CMCR analysis.

and 66th percentiles of income. Expectedly, the numbers swing wildly between 50 million to 600 million. What is more, the nagging worry persists that the middle class being defined by most of these income bands is actually India's upper class.

Typically, income refers to new earnings of individuals and households during a year. It is an indicator of the earning capability of the household, and in combination with consumption data, it should be able to provide useful information for marketers who are seeking to understand key consumer segments, their purchasing power and consumption behaviour. However, the problem with income data is that there is rampant understatement of income which often raises doubts about the interpretation of this data. It also raises concerns about the validity of the data. However, where income data does come in handy is when it is analysed in terms of income distribution by 'quintiles.' That is, to measure income distribution, the households are first ranked from highest to lowest income and then the households are divided into five groups, or quintiles, to determine the share of total income of each quintile, ranging from the bottom (or first quintile) up to the top (or fifth quintile). It provides a clear picture about the different population segments and how they compare with each other.

In a diverse country such as India where there is significant diversity in socio-economic conditions and the gap between the top-earning households and the lowest-income earning families is huge, it becomes necessary to look at the data through the filter of quintiles. Not only that, it becomes even more significant

Table 5.4: Distribution of Income by Per Capita Income Quintiles: All India

Per capita income quintile	Share of each quintile to total income			Ownership of two wheeler (per cent of household own two wheeler)		
	1993–94	2004–05	2009–10	1993–94	2004–05	2009–10
Q5-Top quintile (81 per cent–100 per cent)	36.7	47.9	53.2	17.9	65.5	100.0
Q4-Fourth quintile (61 per cent–80 per cent)	24.7	20.8	18.9	14.2	47.5	80.4
Q3-Third quintile (41 per cent–60 per cent)	18.4	14.4	12.6	9.8	33.4	69.3
Q2-Second quintile (21 per cent–40 per cent)	12.9	10.4	9.2	6.7	20.5	33.6
Q1-Bottom quintile (0 per cent–20 per cent)	7.3	6.5	6.1	4.7	11.0	16.2
Total	100.0	100.0	100.0	10.7	35.6	58.0

Source: NSHIE 2004–05 data: NCAER–CMCR analysis.

when comparing the distance between say the top-earning households in rural and urban India. For instance, in 2004–05, the average annual household income of the top quintile urban households was Rs 168,135 compared to Rs 138,427 in rural India. By contrast, the bottom quintile households in both urban and rural areas had more or less similar average annual household income, that is, Rs 19,799 for urban and Rs 18,967 for rural households.

To compare growth and decline of relative affluence over a longer timeframe, it is imperative that we look at income distribution over quintile groups rather than income groups classified strictly according to absolute income data. Apart from reflecting the huge income inequality gap, analysing income distribution data through this filter gives a perspective of the changing consumer and marketplace dynamics. Consider the issue of regional disparity. Nearly 70 per cent of the bottom quintile households reside in low income states and 90 per cent of these households are in rural areas. On the other hand, half of all top quintile households also live in rural India. Given the coexistence of both types of households in rural areas, marketers would then to need to look at other indicators. For instance, nearly 60 per cent of the top quintile households are occupied in clerical, sales, service oriented or professional and administrative jobs. In contrast, nearly 70 per cent of the bottom quintile households are engaged in farming activities. Such comparisons can provide insights into ownership patterns of products as well.

What is more, for those looking at understanding how GDP growth relates with consumer dynamics, quintile data analysis can provide meaningful insights. To demonstrate this, let us consider how durable ownership of two wheelers has changed over a long term period between 1993–94 and 2004–05. According to NCAER's observed data, two wheeler penetration stood at just 10.7 per cent in 1993–94 whereas in 2004–05, it had grown to 35.6 per cent (Table 5.4). Assuming a GDP growth projection of 6.75 per cent, two wheeler ownership is expected to increase to 58 per cent of the population. That would translate into complete saturation of the top-quintile consumer market by 2009–10 while 70 per cent households in the third quintile group and 16 per cent among the bottom quintile would be owners of two wheelers. Using the per capita income quintile framework thus requires the least assumptions and leaps of faith and is also finds universal acceptance.

5.2 Disparity in the Level of Earning

India has an estimated 205.6 million households of which 61.4 million are urban and 144.2 million are rural. This translates into a total rural population of 732 million and urban population of 295 million. Of the total households (205.6 million) in the country, nearly 45.8 million belong to the top (or fifth) income quintile and 36.6 million belong to the bottom (or first) income quintile. Almost 52 per cent of the top segment households reside in urban India whereas 91 per cent of the bottom segment households reside in rural India.

At the all-India level, the household income rises from Rs 19,041 for the bottom segment to Rs 153,872 for the top segment, showing a phenomenal eightfold increase. For urban areas, the increase is 8.5 times while it is 7.3 times for rural areas. In the second, middle and fourth segments, the household incomes are 1.5, 2.1 and 3.4 times the income of bottom segment, respectively, for rural and urban areas. The top segment also shows a much higher rate of increase over its immediate predecessor (2.0 to 2.5 times) than any other segment. Therefore, the top and bottom segments have their own special significance in the study of income dynamics (Table 5.5).

Table 5.5: Estimates of Households, Population and Income by Income Quintiles

	Q1 Bottom quintile (0 per cent–20 per cent)	Q2 Second quintile (21 per cent–40 per cent)	Q3 Middle quintile (41 per cent–60 per cent)	Q4 Fourth quintile (61 per cent–80 per cent)	Q5 Top quintile (81 per cent–100 per cent)	Total
RURAL						
Population (million)	187.0	170.7	157.1	116.8	100.3	731.9
Households (million)	33.3	32.8	32.0	24.0	22.0	144.2
Household size	5.61	5.2	4.91	4.86	4.56	5.08
Household income (Rs/annum)	18,967	29,212	40,841	64,200	138,427	51,922
URBAN						
Population (million)	18.4	34.8	48.3	88.7	105.1	295.3
Households (million)	3.2	6.6	9.5	18.2	23.8	61.4
Household size	5.70	5.24	5.07	4.87	4.41	4.81
Household income (Rs/annum)	19,799	30,051	42,493	66,599	168,135	95,827
ALL INDIA						
Population (million)	205.4	205.5	205.4	205.5	205.5	1027.3
Households (million)	36.6	39.5	41.5	42.3	45.8	205.6
Household size	5.6	5.2	5.0	4.9	4.5	5.0
Household income (Rs/annum)	19,041	29,353	41,220	65,235	153,872	65,041

Source: NSHIE 2004–05 data: NCAER–CMCR analysis.

In terms of earning levels of these households, nearly 22 million rural households versus 24 million urban households belong to the top (or fifth) income quintile, making these the richest households in the country. There are more rural households that belong to the fourth quintile group (24 million) than in urban India (18 million) translating into populations of 117 million and 89 million, respectively. The density of the affluence is thus higher in urban areas.

The picture that emerges from the bottom three quintiles in rural and urban India is starkly different: rural India has a much higher density of the poorest people in the country. Almost 514 million rural Indians—1.5 times the population of urban India—belong to these three income quintiles. In contrast, only 3.2 million households figure in the bottom quintile, 6.6 million in the second quintile and 9.5 million in the third/middle income quintile in urban India. Together, that makes up for a poor population of 100 million in urban India.

Nearly a quarter of all rural Indians belong to the lowest income quintile compared to just 6 per cent in urban areas. Though in absolute numbers, the number of rural Indians who are in the top quintile group is not very different from those in urban areas—100 million versus 105 million—in terms of their contribution to total income there is a huge gap. Nearly 14 per cent rural Indians belonging to the top quintile group contribute 41 per cent to total rural income against 36 per cent top quintile urban population whose contribution to total urban income is 68 per cent (Table 5.6).

Table 5.6: Distribution of Population and Income by Income Quintiles

Income quintiles	Distribution of population (per cent)			Distribution of income (per cent)			Earning weight		
	Rural	Urban	All India	Rural	Urban	All India	Rural	Urban	All India
Q1-Bottom quintile (0 per cent–20 per cent)	25.5	6.2	20.0	8.4	1.1	5.2	0.33	0.17	0.26
Q2-Second quintile (21 per cent–40 per cent)	23.3	11.8	20.0	12.8	3.4	8.7	0.55	0.29	0.43
Q3-Middle quintile (41 per cent–60 per cent)	21.5	16.4	20.0	17.4	6.9	12.8	0.81	0.42	0.64
Q4-Fourth quintile (61 per cent–80 per cent)	16.0	30.0	20.0	20.6	20.6	20.6	1.29	0.69	1.03
Q5-Top quintile (81 per cent–100 per cent)	13.7	35.6	20.0	40.7	68.0	52.7	2.97	1.91	2.64
Total	100.0	100.0	100.0	100.0	100.0	100.0	1.00	1.00	1.00

Source: NSHIE 2004–05 data: NCAER–CMCR analysis.

The households in the bottom, second and middle segments share hardly 27 per cent of total income estimated generated. However, just 22.2 per cent of households constituting the top segment make all the difference. The earning weight of this segment is 2.97 for rural area and 1.91 for urban area signifying that the group of elites is more affluent in rural areas than in urban areas (Table 5.6).

A hypothetical exercise would help in understanding the huge income gap that exists between households in the bottom most quintile and those in the top quintile (Table 5.7). If a household in the bottom quintile were to move up the income quintile ladder to the topmost group, its income would increase by nearly 708 per cent. Urban households would see a higher jump in their income at the topmost quintile (749 per cent) compared to rural households (630 per cent).

Table 5.7: Impact of Change of Income Quintile on Level of Earnings (Increase in Income taking Bottom Quintile as Base)

Income quintiles	Increase in income (Rs)			Increase in income (per cent)		
	Rural	Urban	All India	Rural	Urban	All India
Q5-Top quintile (81 per cent–100 per cent)	119,460	148,336	134,831	630	749	708
Q4-Fourth quintile (61 per cent–80 per cent)	45,233	46,799	46,194	238	236	243
Q3-Middle quintile (41 per cent–60 per cent)	21,874	22,694	22,179	115	115	116
Q2-Second quintile (21 per cent–40 per cent)	10,245	10,252	10,313	54	52	54
Q1-Bottom quintile (0 per cent–20 per cent) as base income	18,967	19,799	19,041			

Source: NSHIE 2004–05 data: NCAER–CMCR analysis.

5.3 Understanding the Earning Disparity through Demographics

5.3.1 Occupation of Chief Earner and Level of Disparity

Chief earners of a large majority of Indian households are still employed in either agriculture or engaged in manual labour: 30 per cent and 33 per cent, respectively. In rural India, this ratio is even higher: with 40 per cent and 36 per cent employed in farming or manual labour, respectively. While urban households engaged in farming constitute just 3 per cent, a little less than a quarter of all households are engaged in labour. A majority of all households in urban India (38 per cent against the national figure of 18 per cent) are salary earners. Rural India has 10 per cent households who fall in this category. Another 31 per cent of all urban households are engaged in industry or non-farm related self-employment, compared to the national figure of 17 per cent and about 11 per cent for rural India (Table 5.8).

Table 5.8: Distribution of Households by Occupation of Chief Earner and Income Quintiles (Per Cent of Households)

Occupation of chief earner	Q1 Bottom quintile (0 per cent–20 per cent)	Q2 Second quintile (21 per cent–40 per cent)	Q3 Middle quintile (41 per cent–60 per cent)	Q4 Fourth quintile (61 per cent–80 per cent)	Q5 Top quintile (81 per cent–100 per cent)	Total
RURAL						
Regular salary/wages	1.4	3.3	6.1	15.2	34.3	10.2
Self-employment in non-agriculture	4.3	7.4	13.1	18.4	16.9	11.2
Labour	63.1	48.4	31.0	18.0	5.7	36.3
Self-employment in agriculture	30.3	39.8	47.8	44.7	38.8	40.1
Others	0.9	1.1	2.0	3.8	4.4	2.2
Total	100.0	100.0	100.0	100.0	100.0	100.0
URBAN						
Regular salary/wages	10.6	9.7	22.3	37.0	56.2	37.8
Self-employment in non-agriculture	24.0	16.3	33.2	32.8	33.3	30.8
Labour	59.0	67.7	38.4	20.5	2.7	23.5
Self-employment in agriculture	3.3	2.8	1.9	3.8	2.1	2.7
Others	3.1	3.4	4.2	6.0	5.7	5.1
Total	100.0	100.0	100.0	100.0	100.0	100.0
ALL INDIA						
Regular salary/wages	2.2	4.4	9.8	24.6	45.7	18.4
Self-employment in non-agriculture	6.0	8.9	17.7	24.6	25.4	17.1
Labour	62.7	51.6	32.7	19.1	4.1	32.5
Self-employment in agriculture	27.9	33.6	37.3	27.0	19.8	28.9
Others	1.1	1.5	2.5	4.7	5.0	3.1
Total	100.0	100.0	100.0	100.0	100.0	100.0

Source: NSHIE 2004–05 data: NCAER–CMCR analysis.

An overwhelming 93 per cent of all bottom quintile households are engaged in labour and/or agriculture in rural India. In the fourth quintile household group, 18 per cent rural households are engaged in non-farm self-employed activities, another 18 per cent do manual labour and about 45 per cent earn from self-employed agricultural activities. Significantly, more than a third of top quintile households in rural areas earn their income from salaries/wages, which is slightly less than those who do so from self-employed farming activities (39 per cent).

This difference is 15 per cent and 45 per cent, respectively, among fourth income quintile rural households.

More than half of all top income quintile urban households are salaried ones with a third earning their income from non-farm related self-employment. An important aspect of urban income is the growing group of chief earners whose income is from non-farm related self-employment. This group of entrepreneurs/businessmen constitutes nearly a third of each of the middle, fourth and top income quintile urban households. The bottom and second income quintile groups are dominated by labour households in urban India.

In terms of income earned, rural salary for the bottom most quintile is higher (at Rs 23,166) than that for urban areas (Rs 17,192). However, the top quintile salary earners in rural India earn less than their urban counterparts: Rs 145,961 versus Rs 154,373. Household incomes that depend on farm related self-employment in urban and rural areas are not very different for those belonging to the same quintile group. However, the difference in income becomes apparent among the fourth income quintile group: Rs 63,944 for rural and Rs 76,109 for urban. The same is true for the top quintile group where the difference in income is quite significant: Rs 141,204 versus Rs 164,577. Urban households that earn their income from labour earn more than their rural counterparts across all quintile groups (Table 5.9).

Table 5.9: Estimated Household Income by Occupation of Chief Earner and Income Quintiles (Rs Per Annum)

Income quintiles	Regular salary/wages		Self-employment in agriculture		Labour	
	Rural	Urban	Rural	Urban	Rural	Urban
Q1-Bottom quintile (0 per cent–20 per cent)	23,166	17,192	20,012	20,714	18,315	20,712
Q2-Second quintile (21 per cent–40 per cent)	33,991	32,180	31,293	34,270	26,480	28,354
Q3-Middle quintile (41 per cent–60 per cent)	47,319	44,468	42,530	43,122	33,934	37,721
Q4-Fourth quintile (61 per cent–80 per cent)	77,244	70,420	63,944	76,109	51,764	53,031
Q5-Top quintile (81 per cent–100 per cent)	145,961	154,373	141,204	164,577	105,034	106,744
Total	103,687	114,551	54,622	91,218	28,567	39,626

Source: NSHIE 2004–05 data: NCAER–CMCR analysis.

5.3.2 Level of Education of Chief Earner and Level of Disparity

Education levels differ vastly among chief earners in rural and urban areas, and also among the income quintile groups. At an all-India level, 42 per cent of chief earners have studied up to Class 10, 23 per cent are graduates and 18 per cent have studied up to the higher secondary level (Class 12). Urban areas have more graduate chief earners (43 per cent) while the majority of chief earners in rural India have studied up to Class 10 (46 per cent). Looking specifically at income quintile groups, it is obvious that the chief earners of more affluent families belonging to top income quintile in rural as well as urban areas have higher educational qualifications (rural: 39 per cent; urban: 66 per cent). In the bottom quintile rural households, nearly 47 per cent have studied up to Class 10, 28 per cent have done their primary schooling (Class 5) and 9 per cent are illiterates. Urban households in the same group have fewer illiterate chief earners (4 per cent), and many more graduates (19 per cent as against 6 per cent in rural areas) (Table 5.10).

Table 5.10: Distribution of Households by Education Level of Chief Earner and Income Quintiles (Per Cent of Households)

Education level of chief earner	Q1 Bottom quintile (0 per cent–20 per cent)	Q2 Second quintile (21 per cent–40 per cent)	Q3 Middle quintile (41 per cent–60 per cent)	Q4 Fourth quintile (61 per cent–80 per cent)	Q5 Top quintile (81 per cent–100 per cent)	Total
RURAL						
Illiterate	9.2	6.6	4.8	4.1	2.2	5.7
Up to primary (5th)	28.4	19.0	13.5	8.9	5.3	16.2
Up to matric (10th)	46.5	53.5	52.9	43.0	29.1	46.3
Up to higher secondary (12th)	10.2	13.4	17.0	23.8	24.3	16.8
Graduate and above (Graduate+)	5.8	7.5	11.7	20.2	39.1	15.0
Total	100.0	100.0	100.0	100.0	100.0	100.0
URBAN						
Illiterate	3.7	3.2	2.0	1.2	0.3	1.3
Up to primary (5th)	20.5	17.2	8.8	4.6	1.3	6.2
Up to matric (10th)	45.8	51.4	43.8	32.7	14.8	30.2
Up to higher secondary (12th)	11.5	14.5	21.2	23.3	17.9	19.3
Graduate and above (Graduate+)	18.5	13.7	24.2	38.1	65.7	43.0
Total	100.0	100.0	100.0	100.0	100.0	100.0
ALL INDIA						
Illiterate	8.7	6.1	4.1	2.9	1.2	4.4
Up to primary (5th)	27.7	18.7	12.4	7.1	3.2	13.2
Up to matric (10th)	46.4	53.2	50.8	38.5	21.7	41.5
Up to higher secondary (12th)	10.3	13.6	18.0	23.6	21.0	17.6
Graduate and above (Graduate+)	6.9	8.5	14.6	27.9	52.9	23.3
Total	100.0	100.0	100.0	100.0	100.0	100.0

Source: NSHIE 2004–05 data: NCAER–CMCR analysis.

Chief earners in rural areas who have completed their graduation are likely to earn more than their counterparts in urban areas. The only exception is the graduate chief earner of the top quintile rural household whose income is much lower than that of his counterpart in urban areas: Rs 163,206 versus Rs 184,403. The same trend is observed among uneducated chief earners in top quintile rural households and those who have passed their 10th class (Table 5.11).

Table 5.11: Estimated Household Income by Education Level of Chief Earner and Income Quintiles (Rs Per Annum)

Income quintiles	Illiterate		Up to matric (10th)		Graduate and above	
	Rural	Urban	Rural	Urban	Rural	Urban
Q1-Bottom quintile (0 per cent–20 per cent)	14,132	14,870	19,703	21,010	21,310	16,699
Q2-Second quintile (21 per cent–40 per cent)	20,343	20,479	29,979	29,368	34,637	34,477
Q3-Middle quintile (41 per cent–60 per cent)	21,989	31,331	41,142	40,651	49,226	47,733
Q4-Fourth quintile (61 per cent–80 per cent)	30,227	35,019	61,299	60,080	78,641	75,178
Q5-Top quintile (81 per cent–90 per cent)	80,880	95,215	122,272	130,589	163,206	184,403
Total	23,046	32,356	44,133	60,359	97,096	134,800

Source: NSHIE 2004–05 data: NCAER–CMCR analysis.

5.3.1 Sector of Engagement of Households as Major Source of Income and Level of Disparity

As pointed out earlier, there is an increasing shift towards services as the preferred sector of employment. At an all-India level, 48 per cent households are engaged in services (modern as well as traditional) and draw their income from this sector compared to 42 per cent households who are employed in agriculture. In urban India, nearly 77 per cent of all households are involved in the services sector and just 5 per cent in agriculture. In rural India, agriculture still dominates with 58 per cent households drawing their incomes from agriculture compared to 36 per cent of households that depend on services for their annual incomes (Table 5.12).

The share of households that are engaged in traditional services across all income quintiles in rural India ranges from 31 per cent among the first quintile group to 28 per cent among the fourth quintile. The top quintile income groups in rural areas have the least representation in traditional services (22 per cent). Interestingly, modern services have been adopted by the top income quintile group in rural areas with nearly 30 per cent of these households being engaged in modern services. Agriculture continues to be the major source of income for 60 per cent households in the bottom quintile group in rural India as it does for a significant proportion of households across the higher quintile groups as well.

Table 5.12: Distribution of Households by Sector of Engagement and Income Quintiles (Per Cent of Households)

Sector of engagement	Q1 Bottom quintile (0 per cent–20 per cent)	Q2 Second quintile (21 per cent–40 per cent)	Q3 Middle quintile (41 per cent–60 per cent)	Q4 Fourth quintile (61 per cent–80 per cent)	Q5 Top quintile (81 per cent–100 per cent)	Total
RURAL						
Agriculture	59.5	62.9	63.1	55.0	43.2	57.8
Industry	6.9	6.8	6.1	5.2	4.9	6.1
Modern services	2.3	3.4	5.3	11.8	29.9	9.0
Traditional services	31.2	26.9	25.5	28.0	22.0	27.0
Total	100.0	100.0	100.0	100.0	100.0	100.0
URBAN						
Agriculture	8.5	9.1	5.7	6.0	3.3	5.4
Industry	18.5	20.1	18.9	17.6	16.9	17.8
Modern services	11.9	8.4	16.2	24.6	39.2	26.5
Traditional services	61.1	62.4	59.3	51.8	40.7	50.3
Total	100.0	100.0	100.0	100.0	100.0	100.0
ALL INDIA						
Agriculture	55.0	53.9	49.9	33.9	22.4	42.1
Industry	8.0	9.0	9.0	10.5	11.1	9.6
Modern services	3.2	4.3	7.8	17.3	34.8	14.3
Traditional services	33.9	32.9	33.3	38.3	31.7	34.0
Total	100.0	100.0	100.0	100.0	100.0	100.0

Source: NSHIE 2004–05 data: NCAER–CMCR analysis.

The only exception is the top income quintile, where 43 per cent households are engaged in agriculture.

In urban India, services are emerging as the mainstay of household income among the top income quintile group: nearly 80 per cent of all such households are engaged in services (including modern and traditional).

There is no significant variation in household income among rural and urban households in the first and second quintile groups engaged in agriculture, industry and modern services. There is not much variation in the annual average household income for the bottom two quintile groups across urban and rural areas and sector types; it ranges between Rs 16,650 and Rs 30,410 (Table 5.13).

Differences in income are significant for the next group (the third income quintile): while the urban agricultural household in this group earns slightly less than its rural counterpart, those among this group that are engaged in modern services

Table 5.13: Estimated Household Income by Sector of Engagement and Income Quintiles (Rs Per Annum)

Income quintiles	Agriculture		Industry		Modern services	
	Rural	Urban	Rural	Urban	Rural	Urban
Q1-Bottom quintile (0 per cent–20 per cent)	18,870	19,218	18,603	20,412	18,952	16,650
Q2-Second quintile (21 per cent–40 per cent)	29,086	30,410	29,774	30,262	30,162	30,197
Q3-Middle quintile (41 per cent–60 per cent)	40,053	37,903	40,638	41,677	47,284	44,679
Q4-Fourth quintile (61 per cent–80 per cent)	61,564	70,862	63,477	66,290	78,944	70,955
Q5-Top quintile (81 per cent–100 per cent)	138,567	171,406	132,269	164,266	148,977	165,730
Total	46,942	77,338	46,567	91,296	102,345	120,117

Source: NSHIE 2004–05 data: NCAER–CMCR analysis.

in rural and urban India earn much higher incomes (rural: Rs 47,284; urban: Rs 44,679). A point to note is that the rural household engaged in modern services actually earns slightly more than its urban cousin. The same trend is observed for the urban household engaged in modern services in the next income quintile group (fourth): Rs 70,955 compared to its rural counterpart's income of Rs 78,944. The balance tilts in favour of the urban household that is dependent on modern services and belongs to the top income quintile group: here the rural income is Rs 148,977 compared to the urban household income of Rs 165,730. The wide gap in rural and urban incomes is observed across other sectors as well for the top quintile income group.

5.3.4 Occupation Type as Major Source of Household Income and Level of Disparity

Occupation profiles reveal that a majority of the bottom income quintile group households at an all-India level are employed in farm/fishing activities or as production or transport workers. This percentage is as high as 86 per cent. On the other hand, top income quintile households are engaged in diverse occupations, the most significant occupations being farming/fishing, sales jobs, clerical and management professions (Table 5.14).

Consider the occupation profiles for rural and urban areas. Nearly 56 per cent of bottom income quintile households in rural India and 42 per cent among the top income quintile group are employed in farming/fishing/hunting jobs. Nearly 13 per cent of the top income quintile rural households are engaged as professional/technical workers. Sales jobs are more prevalent among the top income quintile groups in urban India (21 per cent) than rural India (12 per cent). More top income quintile households are engaged in administrative/management occupations (14 per cent) in urban areas than in rural ones (5 per cent). Among the bottom income quintile

Table 5.14: Distribution of Households by Occupation of Household and Income Quintiles (Per Cent of Households)

Major profession of households	Q1 Bottom quintile (0 per cent–20 per cent)	Q2 Second quintile (21 per cent–40 per cent)	Q3 Middle quintile (41 per cent–60 per cent)	Q4 Fourth quintile (61 per cent–80 per cent)	Q5 Top quintile (81 per cent–100 per cent)	Total
			RURAL			
Professional, technical and related workers	0.5	0.9	1.5	3.9	12.8	3.3
Administrative, executive and managerial workers	0.1	0.3	0.6	1.1	5.2	1.2
Clerical and related workers	0.3	0.6	1.4	4.8	10.1	2.9
Sales workers	3.3	6.0	10.5	14.6	11.6	8.7
Service workers	2.1	2.8	3.3	4.9	6.7	3.7
Farmers, fishermen, hunters, loggers and related workers	55.8	59.3	60.8	53.4	41.6	55.2
Production and related workers, transport equipment	33.0	25.8	15.4	11.1	7.5	19.9
Workers not classified by occupation	4.9	4.2	6.6	6.1	4.4	5.2
Total	100.0	100.0	100.0	100.0	100.0	100.0
			URBAN			
Professional, technical and related workers	3.5	2.0	3.7	6.0	13.3	7.9
Administrative, executive and managerial workers	2.0	0.7	1.2	3.5	13.6	6.7
Clerical and related workers	2.1	1.8	5.3	12.4	16.0	11.0
Sales workers	16.7	12.8	25.5	24.7	21.2	21.7

Major profession of households	Q1 Bottom quintile (0 per cent–20 per cent)	Q2 Second quintile (21 per cent–40 per cent)	Q3 Middle quintile (41 per cent–60 per cent)	Q4 Fourth quintile (61 per cent–80 per cent)	Q5 Top quintile (81 per cent–100 per cent)	Total
Service workers	6.9	8.5	9.2	11.4	10.7	10.2
Farmers, fishermen, hunters, loggers and related workers	7.6	8.1	4.9	5.1	2.6	4.5
Production and related workers, transport equipment	49.2	52.7	36.1	25.0	16.2	27.6
Workers not classified by occupation	12.0	13.3	14.1	12.0	6.4	10.3
Total	100.0	100.0	100.0	100.0	100.0	100.0
ALL INDIA						
Professional, technical and related workers	0.8	1.1	2.0	4.8	13.1	4.7
Administrative, executive and managerial workers	0.3	0.4	0.8	2.1	9.6	2.8
Clerical and related workers	0.5	0.8	2.3	8.1	13.2	5.3
Sales workers	4.5	7.2	13.9	19.0	16.6	12.6
Service workers	2.5	3.7	4.6	7.7	8.8	5.6
Farmers, fishermen, hunters, loggers and related workers	51.5	50.7	48.0	32.6	21.3	40.0
Production and related workers, transport equipment	34.4	30.3	20.1	17.1	12.0	22.2
Workers not classified by occupation	5.5	5.7	8.3	8.7	5.5	6.8
Total	100.0	100.0	100.0	100.0	100.0	100.0

Source: NSHIE 2004–05 data: NCAER–CMCR analysis.

group in urban areas, half of all households are employed as production/transport workers compared to just 33 per cent among their rural counterparts.

As far as income slabs go, rural household incomes of technical workers in the bottom most quintile group are significantly higher than urban incomes (Rs 21,049 versus Rs 15,815). Farmers and fishermen in the bottom income quintile group earn roughly the same in both rural and urban India (Rs 18,000 to Rs 19,000). Whereas administrative workers in rural India that belong to the top income quintile group have household incomes of just Rs 174,163, their urban counterparts earn as much as Rs 215,067. Professional/technical workers in the top quintile income group in urban areas have average household incomes of Rs 179,117, compared to Rs 159,711 for rural households (Table 5.15).

Table 5.15: Estimated Household Income by Occupation of Household and Income Quintiles (Rs Per Annum)

Income quintiles	Professional, technical and related workers		Administrative, executive and managerial workers		Farmers, fishermen, hunters, loggers and related workers	
	Rural	Urban	Rural	Urban	Rural	Urban
Q1-Bottom quintile (0 per cent–20 per cent)	21,049	15,815	16,767	13,568	18,808	19,219
Q2-Second quintile (21 per cent–40 per cent)	35,034	33,158	34,189	28,058	29,262	28,980
Q3-Middle quintile (41 per cent–60 per cent)	50,265	48,339	48,271	47,421	40,347	37,631
Q4-Fourth quintile (61 per cent–80 per cent)	83,957	73,042	82,695	78,414	62,051	70,033
Q5-Top quintile (81 per cent–100 per cent)	159,711	179,117	174,163	215,067	138,289	170,687
Total	120,080	138,065	135,222	183,803	47,371	74,623

Source: NSHIE 2004–05 data: NCAER–CMCR analysis.

5.3.5 State of Residence and Level of Disparity

It is increasingly becoming clear that high income states are contributing the maximum to national income. At an all-India level, 22 per cent of households are located in high income states, while 34 per cent and 45 per cent households are to be found in the middle and low income states, respectively. Nearly 68 per cent households in the lowest income quintile are those residing in the low income states; 21 per cent of households in the lowest income quintile are from middle income states and just 11 per cent are from high income states. However, in the highest income quintile, around 27 per cent of households are from the poorest states, 38 per cent from the middle income states and 35 per cent from the high income states (Table 5.16).

The most glaring differences in income are visible when we compare the lowest quintile group with the highest income quintile group's earnings. For instance,

Table 5.16: Distribution of Households by State of Residence and Income Quintiles (Per Cent of Households)

	Q1 Bottom quintile (0 per cent–20 per cent)	Q2 Second quintile (21 per cent–40 per cent)	Q3 Middle quintile (41 per cent–60 per cent)	Q4 Fourth quintile (61 per cent–80 per cent)	Q5 Top quintile (81 per cent–100 per cent)	Total
RURAL						
Low income states	70.4	58.3	44.2	40.0	33.6	51.1
Middle income states	20.2	26.8	39.7	39.1	40.6	32.3
High income states	9.5	14.9	16.1	20.8	25.8	16.6
Total	100.0	100.0	100.0	100.0	100.0	100.0
URBAN						
Low income states	48.8	49.8	31.2	28.5	20.8	29.3
Middle income states	29.9	30.4	42.4	40.5	36.3	37.5
High income states	21.3	19.8	26.4	30.9	43.0	33.2
Total	100.0	100.0	100.0	100.0	100.0	100.0
ALL INDIA						
Low income states	68.4	56.9	41.2	35.1	26.9	44.6
Middle income states	21.0	27.4	40.3	39.7	38.4	33.9
High income states	10.5	15.7	18.5	25.2	34.7	21.5
Total	100.0	100.0	100.0	100.0	100.0	100.0

Source: NSHIE 2004–05 data: NCAER–CMCR analysis.

in high income states, the urban households in the top quintile group earn nine times more than their counterparts in the bottom quintile. Similarly, in low income states, top quintile rural households earn about seven times more than the first quintile rural households in such states.

Looked at another way, the high income states have comparatively a higher percentage of poor urban households than poor rural households. To illustrate, 21 per cent of urban households belonging to the first quintile income group are to be found in high income states compared to only 10 per cent of rural households belonging to the same quintile group. Interestingly, low income states also have a higher proportion of rural households belonging to the top income quintile group (34 per cent) compared to urban households (21 per cent). But the low income states have an overwhelming majority of first quintile rural households (70 per cent) whereas middle income states' share of such households is just about 20 per cent.

As has been observed elsewhere, the annual household incomes for the first three quintile groups across low, middle and high income states for rural and urban households do not vary significantly. So the average household income ranges between Rs 17,000 to Rs 21,000 across all states and the rural–urban divide. The second quintile income group too has a more or less similar income band, ranging from Rs 26,000 to Rs 32,000 approximately. In fact, rural and urban households in the low income states have a marginally better income range (Rs 43,000 to Rs 48,000) compared to their counterparts in middle and high income states. For the latter, the income ranges between Rs 42,000 and Rs 43,000 for rural and urban households, respectively. But it is the top quintile income group where the low income states lose out: rural incomes in high income states are nearly Rs 146,000 compared to Rs 139,000 for low income states and urban incomes are about Rs 175,000 for high income states in this group compared to Rs 164,546 for low income states (Table 5.17).

Table 5.17: Estimated Household Income by State of Residence and Income Quintiles (Rs Per Annum)

Income quintiles	Low income states		Middle income states		High income states	
	Rural	Urban	Rural	Urban	Rural	Urban
Q1-Bottom quintile (0 per cent–20 per cent)	19,557	21,765	17,415	16,843	17,890	19,439
Q2-Second quintile (21 per cent–40 per cent)	29,984	31,826	27,613	25,951	29,067	31,884
Q3-Middle quintile (41 per cent–60 per cent)	43,064	47,891	38,104	38,194	41,487	43,020
Q4-Fourth quintile (61 per cent–80 per cent)	67,550	69,514	59,124	59,550	67,302	73,143
Q5-Top quintile (81 per cent–100 per cent)	139,041	164,546	133,028	161,315	146,124	175,622
Total	44,999	80,948	55,604	89,223	66,121	116,421

Source: NSHIE 2004–05 data: NCAER–CMCR analysis.

5.4 Disparity in the Level of Spending

As in the case of earnings, the spending pattern varies significantly across income quintiles. At the aggregate level, households in the top income quintile group spends nearly 56 per cent of the household income on routine as well as non-routine expenses which rises up to 95 per cent for households belonging to the third income quintile group (Table 5.18). As against this, the bottom two quintile groups borrow to meet their routine and non-routine expenses. In absolute terms, the expenditure levels of the top quintile group (Rs 86,040) are almost four times higher than for the bottom quintile group households (Rs 24,923).

The expenditure pattern of Indian households in the lower income groups is skewed towards high expenditure on food items. Food expenses, which comprise 51 per cent of all routine expenditure at the all-India level, rise to 62 per cent in

Table 5.18: Estimates of Income and Expenditure by Income Quintiles: All India

	Q1 Bottom quintile (0 per cent–20 per cent)	Q2 Second quintile (21 per cent–40 per cent)	Q3 Middle quintile (41 per cent–60 per cent)	Q4 Fourth quintile (61 per cent–80 per cent)	Q5 Top quintile (81 per cent–100 per cent)	Total
a. Annual household income (Rs)	19,041	29,353	41,220	65,235	153,872	65,041
b. Annual household expenditure (Rs)						
Food	13,113	15,973	18,621	22,810	30,911	20,733
Non-food	8,074	10,542	14,789	21,896	40,177	19,899
Total (routine)	21,187	26,515	33,410	44,707	71,088	40,632
Non-routine	3,735	4,718	5,860	8,957	14,952	7,926
Total (routine and non-routine)	24,923	31,232	39,270	53,664	86,040	48,558
c. Share of expenditure to income (per cent)						
Food	68.9	54.4	45.2	35.0	20.1	31.9
Non-food	42.4	35.9	35.9	33.6	26.1	30.6
Total (routine)	111.3	90.3	81.1	68.5	46.2	62.5
Non-routine	19.6	16.1	14.2	13.7	9.7	12.2
Total (routine and non-routine)	130.9	106.4	95.3	82.3	55.9	74.7

Source: NSHIE 2004–05 data: NCAER–CMCR analysis.

the case of households in the lowest income quintile, and this falls to 44 per cent in the upper most income quintile. The results also reveal that it is only the households in the top quintile that spend more on non-food items. Households in the remaining quintile groups spend more on food items (Figure 5.3).

Consider this: while the bottom quintile spends Rs 13,113 on food items, its expenditure on non-food items is just Rs 8,074. In contrast, the top 20 per cent group spends Rs 30,911 on food items and a bigger amount on non-food items (Rs 40,177).

Spending patterns on other items such as housing, transport, education, clothing and durables increase substantially for the top 20 per cent households compared to other groups. Expenditure on housing, which is 4.7 per cent at the all-India level, is much lower 3.5 per cent in the case of households in the lowest income quintile and this rises marginally to 5.5 per cent in the topmost quintile.

Figure 5.3: Distribution of Routine Expenditure by Income Quintiles: All India

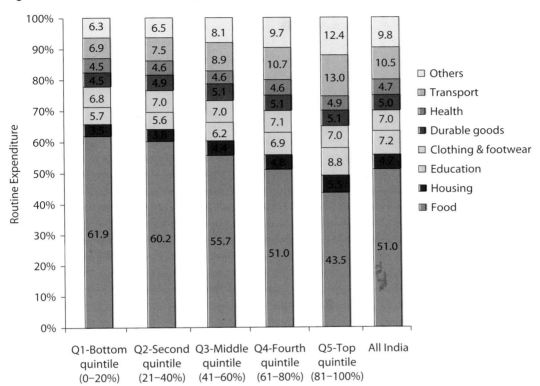

Source: NSHIE 2004–05 data: NCAER–CMCR analysis.

While households in the lowest income quintile spend around 7 per cent of their expenses on transport, this rises to 13 per cent in the topmost income quintile. Education forms 5.7 per cent of the routine expenses of a household in the lowest income quintile as compared to 9 per cent in the case of the topmost income quintile. There is little difference in the case of expenditure on health (between 4.5 per cent and 4.8 per cent), clothing (6.8 per cent to 7.1 per cent) and durables (4.5 per cent to 5 per cent).

Expenses on weddings and other social ceremonies account for around 58.5 per cent of all unusual expenses in households in the lowest income quintile and this falls to 51.8 per cent in the topmost quintile. Medical expenses, similarly, change as a fraction of unusual expenses according to each income quintile (Figure 5.4).

A major proportion of rural households' spending is on food items (Table 5.19). Even among the top quintile households, non-food expenditure is just marginally higher than food expenses (Rs 30,556 versus Rs 26,199). The lowest quintile

Figure 5.4: Distribution of Non-routine Expenditure by Income Quintiles: All India

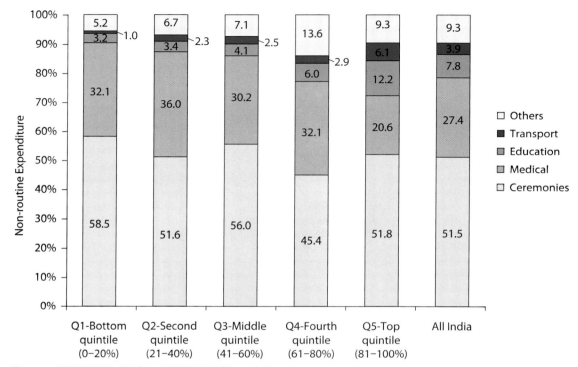

Source: NSHIE 2004–05 data: NCAER–CMCR analysis.

households spend substantially higher amounts on food (Rs 12,715) compared to non-food items (Rs 7,274). After food, transport and education are the two major expenses for top quintile rural households whereas for first quintile rural households 64 per cent of routine expenditure constitutes of food with nearly 7 per cent going towards clothing and footwear. Education expenses constitute just 5.3 per cent of total routine spending for first quintile rural households compared to 8.2 per cent for top quintile rural households (Figure 5.5).

Expenditure on ceremonies is high for both top and bottom quintile rural households: 60 per cent each. Medical expenses are significantly higher for the first quintile rural households, constituting 32 per cent of total unusual expenses while it is 19 per cent for the top quintile households (Figure 5.6).

Food expenses among urban households is lower than that in rural ones but the lower income households in urban areas spend much more on food items than other quintiles. For instance, nearly 51 per cent of all routine expenses of bottom quintile urban households is made up of food items compared to 42 per cent among top quintile households (Figure 5.7). Affluent urban households

Table 5.19: Estimates of Income and Expenditure by Income Quintiles: Rural

	Q1 Bottom quintile (0 per cent–20 per cent)	Q2 Second quintile (21 per cent–40 per cent)	Q3 Middle quintile (41 per cent–60 per cent)	Q4 Fourth quintile (61 per cent–80 per cent)	Q5 Top quintile (81 per cent–100 per cent)	Total
a. Annual household income (Rs)	18,967	29,212	40,841	64,200	1,38,427	51,922
b. Annual household expenditure (Rs)						
Food	12,715	15,781	18,296	22,056	26,199	18,266
Non-food	7,274	9,929	13,569	19,032	30,556	14,788
Total (routine)	19,988	25,710	31,865	41,088	56,755	33,054
Non-routine	3,745	4,670	5,973	9,204	14,950	7,070
Total (routine and non-routine)	23,734	30,380	37,838	50,291	71,705	40,124
c. Share of expenditure to income (per cent)						
Food	66.8	53.8	44.4	33.8	17.0	28.1
Non-food	38.2	33.8	32.9	29.2	19.9	22.7
Total (routine)	105.0	87.6	77.3	63.0	36.9	50.8
Non-routine	19.7	15.9	14.5	14.1	9.7	10.9
Total (routine and non-routine)	124.6	103.5	91.8	77.1	46.6	61.7

Source: NSHIE 2004–05 data: NCAER–CMCR analysis.

also spend more on transport (12.5 per cent) compared to poor households (8.4 per cent).

In absolute terms, top quintile urban households spend Rs 49,063 on non-food items while their expense on food items is Rs 35,263. In contrast, bottom quintile households spend Rs 16,337 on non-food items and Rs 17,222 on food items (Table 5.20).

The top quintile urban households' share of unusual expenditure towards ceremonies is slightly higher (43 per cent) than that of bottom quintile households (45 per cent). Medical expenses as a share of unusual spending is, however, much higher for first quintile households (35.4 per cent) compared to 22.3 per cent for top quintile households. Transport expenses constitute a bigger proportion of top quintile households' spending at 7.6 per cent compared to 3.2 per cent for first quintile households (Figure 5.8).

Figure 5.5: Distribution of Routine Expenditure by Income Quintiles: Rural

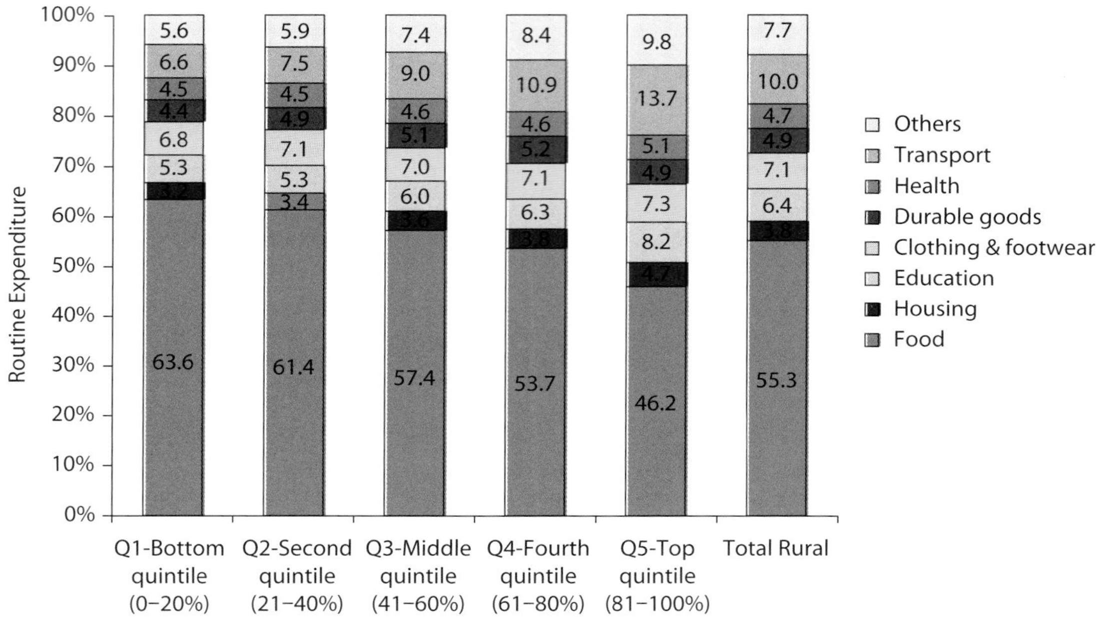

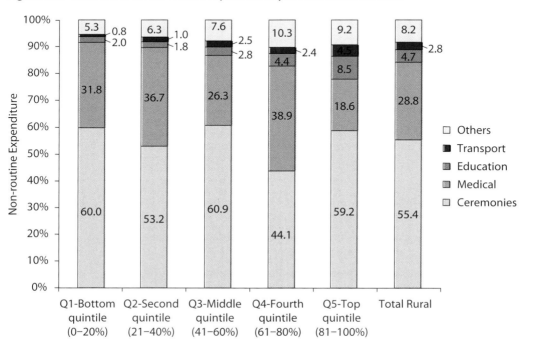

Source: NSHIE 2004–05 data: NCAER–CMCR analysis.

Figure 5.6: Distribution of Non-routine Expenditure by Income Quintiles: Rural

Source: NSHIE 2004–05 data: NCAER–CMCR analysis.

Table 5.20: Estimates of Income and Expenditure by Income Quintiles: Urban

	Q1 Bottom quintile (0 per cent–20 per cent)	Q2 Second quintile (21 per cent–40 per cent)	Q3 Middle quintile (41 per cent–60 per cent)	Q4 Fourth quintile (61 per cent–80 per cent)	Q5 Top quintile (81 per cent–100 per cent)	Total
a. Annual household income (Rs)	19,799	30,051	42,493	66,599	1,68,135	95,827
b. Annual household expenditure (Rs)						
Food	17,222	16,922	19,712	23,805	35,263	26,524
Non-food	16,337	13,570	18,889	25,674	49,063	31,893
Total (routine)	33,559	30,492	38,601	49,478	84,325	58,417
Non-routine	3,635	4,952	5,481	8,633	14,954	9,935
Total (routine and non-routine)	37,194	35,444	44,082	58,111	99,279	68,352
c. Share of expenditure to income (per cent)						
Food	87.0	56.3	46.4	35.7	21.0	27.7
Non-food	82.5	45.2	44.5	38.5	29.2	33.3
Total (routine)	169.5	101.5	90.8	74.3	50.2	61.0
Non-routine	18.4	16.5	12.9	13.0	8.9	10.4
Total (routine and non-routine)	187.9	117.9	103.7	87.3	59.0	71.3

Source: NSHIE 2004–05 data: NCAER–CMCR analysis.

Figure 5.7: Distribution of Routine Expenditure by Income Quintiles: Urban

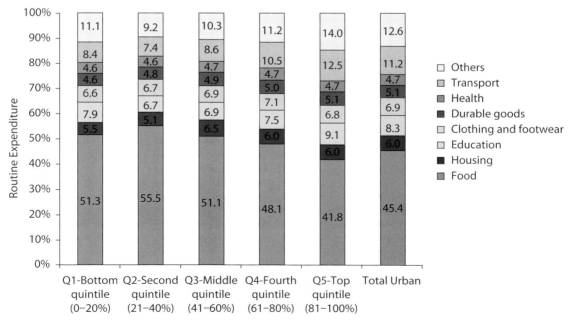

Source: NSHIE 2004–05 data: NCAER–CMCR analysis.

Figure 5.8: Distribution of Non-routine Expenditure by Income Quintiles: Urban

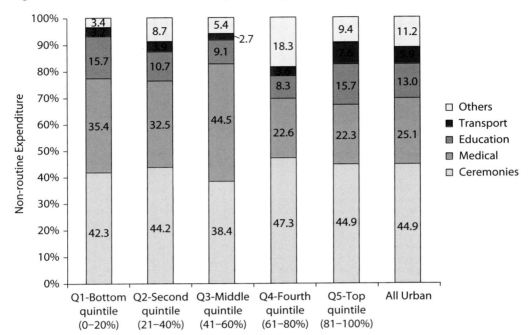

Source: NSHIE 2004–05 data: NCAER–CMCR analysis.

5.5 Saving Behaviour

Saving trends reveal that that nearly 80 per cent of all Indian households save in one form or the other. Nearly 66 per cent own bank accounts and 24 per cent have outstanding loans. A quarter of all households have life insurance policies. Urban and rural trends differ with more urban households (89 per cent) compared to rural ones (80 per cent) saving some money. Many more urban households (81 per cent) than rural ones (59 per cent) have bank accounts. Life insurance ownership too is higher among urban households (38 per cent) as against rural ownership of insurance policies (19 per cent) (Table 5.21).

Differences in saving behaviour among rural and urban households are observed across all quintile groups. For instance, while only 30 per cent of bottom quintile rural households have bank accounts, nearly 45 per cent of their urban counterparts do so. Similarly, life insurance ownership among bottom quintile rural households is 6 per cent while nearly 14 per cent households in the same quintile group in urban areas have insurance policies.

Differences in mode of savings have been observed in rural and urban India. At the all-India level, 36 per cent of all households keep their savings at home.

Table 5.21: Distribution of Households by Income Quintiles (Per Cent of Households)

Saving behaviour	Q1 Bottom quintile (0 per cent–20 per cent)	Q2 Second quintile (21 per cent–40 per cent)	Q3 Middle quintile (41 per cent–60 per cent)	Q4 Fourth quintile (61 per cent–80 per cent)	Q5 Top quintile (81 per cent–100 per cent)	Total
RURAL						
Per cent of households that save	62.1	73.6	82.9	91.7	96.2	79.5
Per cent of households that own accounts	29.9	45.4	63.8	81.9	92.7	59.2
Per cent of households that had loan outstanding	30.3	25.8	24.8	22.2	20.6	25.2
Per cent of households that own life insurance	5.7	8.1	14.9	27.9	48.9	18.6
URBAN						
Per cent of households that save	63.8	70.2	80.9	92.0	98.0	88.8
Per cent of households that own accounts	44.8	48.9	69.0	86.4	96.8	81.5
Per cent of households that had loan outstanding	28.8	23.1	21.6	20.9	18.9	20.9
Per cent of households that own life insurance	13.8	12.0	19.6	33.9	59.3	38.1
ALL INDIA						
Per cent of households that save	62.3	73.0	82.4	91.8	97.1	82.2
Per cent of households that own accounts	31.2	46.0	65.0	83.8	94.8	65.8
Per cent of households that had loan outstanding	30.1	25.3	24.1	21.7	19.7	23.9
Per cent of households that own life insurance	6.4	8.8	16.0	30.5	54.3	24.4

Source: NSHIE 2004–05 data: NCAER–CMCR analysis.

This figure rises to 42 per cent in rural households and drops to 24 per cent among urban households. Similarly, nearly half of all Indian households save in banks (Table 5.22). There are wide variations among urban and rural households, with more urban households (62 per cent) saving in bank deposits compared to rural households (45 per cent).

Table 5.22: Distribution of Households by Mode of Saving and Income Quintiles (Per Cent of Households)

Mode of cash saving	Q1 Bottom quintile (0 per cent–20 per cent)	Q2 Second quintile (21 per cent–40 per cent)	Q3 Middle quintile (41 per cent–60 per cent)	Q4 Fourth quintile (61 per cent–80 per cent)	Q5 Top quintile (81 per cent–100 per cent)	Total
RURAL						
Keep at home	60.7	52.2	40.2	29.6	26.6	41.9
Deposit in bank	28.0	35.5	44.8	56.1	61.6	45.1
Deposit in post office	4.6	5.3	6.9	6.6	3.4	5.4
Others	6.7	7.0	8.2	7.8	8.3	7.6
	100.0	100.0	100.0	100.0	100.0	100.0
URBAN						
Keep at home	41.7	41.8	30.1	24.5	15.6	23.6
Deposit in bank	44.7	45.7	52.2	60.3	72.2	62.4
Deposit in post office	5.5	4.4	5.7	5.3	2.8	4.2
Others	8.2	8.1	11.9	9.8	9.4	9.7
	100.0	100.0	100.0	100.0	100.0	100.0
ALL INDIA						
Keep at home	59.0	50.6	37.9	27.4	20.8	36.0
Deposit in bank	29.5	37.1	46.5	57.9	67.2	50.7
Deposit in post office	4.7	5.2	6.6	6.1	3.1	5.0
Others	6.9	7.1	9.0	8.7	8.9	8.3
	100.0	100.0	100.0	100.0	100.0	100.0

Source: NSHIE 2004–05 data: NCAER–CMCR analysis.

5.6 Ownership Pattern of Consumer Durable Goods

Ownership of consumer goods is often used by analysts to indicate the rate at which certain sections of the population are achieving prosperity. Not surprisingly, product ownership is skewed heavily towards the top income quintile groups. So, while 36 per cent of all households own two wheelers, ownership is higher among the top quintile group (71 per cent) compared to the second or third income quintile groups, which stands at 16 per cent and 28 per cent, respectively. On the other hand, more bottom quintile households possess bicycles (67 per cent) and wrist watches (62 per cent) (Table 5.23).

Table 5.23: Ownership of Selected Consumer Goods by Income Quintiles: All India (Per Cent of Households Owning Product)

Products	Q1 Bottom quintile (0 per cent–20 per cent)	Q2 Second quintile (21 per cent–40 per cent)	Q3 Middle quintile (41 per cent–60 per cent)	Q4 Fourth quintile (61 per cent–80 per cent)	Q5 Top quintile (81 per cent–100 per cent)	All India
Two wheelers	7.6	15.7	27.7	48.1	70.5	35.6
Car	0.6	0.7	1.2	4.2	21.3	6.1
Colour television	6.7	12.4	26.8	52.5	77.3	37.0
Fridge	1.8	2.4	6.4	21.9	53.5	18.5
Television (Black & White)	17.0	32.0	36.8	31.4	17.6	27.0
Bicycle	67.3	72.5	71.2	63.2	49.5	64.3
Wrist watch	62.3	72.6	79.7	87.3	92.1	79.6
Ceiling fan	23.9	42.7	61.6	77.5	87.2	60.3
Pressure cooker	16.9	32.0	44.7	67.5	83.9	50.7
Radio	45.3	48.5	49.7	51.6	51.7	49.5
Credit card	0.6	0.5	0.7	0.8	5.8	1.8
Telephone (L)	2.6	3.8	10.4	25.3	56.9	21.2
Computer	0.2	0.2	0.3	1.0	6.7	1.8
Mobile	1.9	2.7	7.3	18.3	44.7	16.1

Source: NSHIE 2004–05 data: NCAER–CMCR analysis.

Let us consider how product ownership plays out among rural households. Nearly 27 per cent rural households own cars. Of this, 64 per cent are to be found in top income quintile households whereas only 14 per cent second income quintile households have cars. Similarly, colour televisions are to be found in 63 per cent top quintile rural households compared to just 5 per cent bottom quintile rural households. Cell phone ownership has grown exponentially but they are found only among a quarter of top quintile rural households. On the other hand, nearly 2 per cent of bottom quintile urban households own cell phones. Even among fourth quintile rural households, just 10 per cent possess cell phones (Table 5.24).

This is in stark contrast to the urban scenario where nearly 63 per cent of top quintile households and 5 per cent of bottom quintile households have cell phones. Two wheeler ownership is also significantly high among the bottom quintile households in urban India; nearly 19 per cent of these households own a two

Table 5.24: Ownership of Selected Consumer Goods by Income Quintiles: Rural (Per Cent of Households Owning Product)

Products	Q1 Bottom quintile (0 per cent–20 per cent)	Q2 Second quintile (21 per cent–40 per cent)	Q3 Middle quintile (41 per cent–60 per cent)	Q4 Fourth quintile (61 per cent–80 per cent)	Q5 Top quintile (81 per cent–100 per cent)	Rural India
Two wheelers	6.5	14.1	25.3	42.7	64.8	27.3
Car	0.6	0.6	0.4	3.2	12.2	2.8
Colour television	5.1	9.1	21.4	39.9	63.1	24.3
Fridge	1.3	1.4	3.6	10.7	28.7	7.6
Television (Black & White)	15.3	29.4	35.6	36.2	27.2	28.3
Bicycle	68.0	73.8	73.8	66.8	59.5	69.1
Wrist watch	61.2	72.1	78.8	85.6	90.0	76.0
Ceiling fan	19.8	37.0	54.6	66.8	77.1	48.0
Pressure cooker	14.0	27.8	37.7	54.6	72.3	38.1
Radio	45.5	50.4	52.6	56.6	60.6	52.3
Credit card	0.7	0.5	0.5	0.4	1.9	0.7
Telephone (L)	2.2	1.9	8.3	19.5	46.4	13.1
Computer	0.2	0.1	0.1	0.4	2.7	0.6
Mobile	1.6	1.7	5.4	10.2	25.1	7.5

Source: NSHIE 2004–05 data: NCAER–CMCR analysis.

Table 5.25: Ownership of Selected Consumer Goods by Income Quintiles: Urban (Per Cent of Households Owning Product)

Products	Q1 Bottom quintile (0 per cent–20 per cent)	Q2 Second quintile (21 per cent –40 per cent)	Q3 Middle quintile (41 per cent –60 per cent)	Q4 Fourth quintile (61 per cent –80 per cent)	Q5 Top quintile (81 per cent –100 per cent)	Urban India
Two wheelers	18.7	23.8	35.9	55.3	75.8	54.9
Car	1.1	1.7	3.8	5.6	29.6	14.0
Colour television	23.2	28.6	45.1	69.1	90.4	66.9
Fridge	7.2	7.5	15.8	36.7	76.4	44.2
Television (Black & White)	34.5	44.8	40.9	25.1	8.8	23.8
Bicycle	59.8	66.0	62.7	58.3	40.2	52.9
Wrist watch	72.2	74.7	83.0	89.6	94.0	87.9
Ceiling Fan	66.2	71.2	85.0	91.7	96.6	89.0
Pressure cooker	46.0	52.7	68.1	84.5	94.6	80.4
Radio	43.4	39.2	40.0	45.0	43.5	42.9
Credit card	0.1	0.3	1.0	1.3	9.3	4.2
Telephone (L)	6.5	13.5	17.2	32.9	66.5	40.0
Computer	0.3	0.5	1.1	1.8	10.4	4.8
Mobile	5.2	7.6	13.6	29.1	62.9	36.2

Source: NSHIE 2004–05 data: NCAER–CMCR analysis.

wheeler and this percentage rises significantly to 76 per cent among top quintile households. Colour television is perhaps the other ubiquitous consumer item: while nearly 90 per cent of all top quintile households have colour televisions, it dips to 69 per cent for fourth quintile households. Nearly a quarter of bottom quintile urban households possess colour televisions (Table 5.25).

Reference

McKinsey Global Institute. 2007. *The Bird of Gold: The Rise of India's Middle Class.* Available from http://www.mckinsey.com/mgi/publications/india_consumer_market/index.asp. Accessed on 22 February 2010.

Rural Well-being

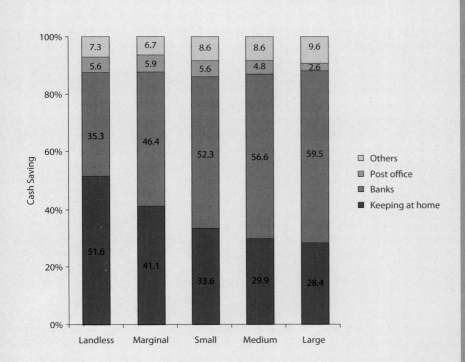

six

Legend:
- ☐ Others
- ☐ Post office
- ☐ Banks
- ■ Keeping at home

	Landless	Marginal	Small	Medium	Large
Others	7.3	6.7	8.6	8.6	9.6
Post office	5.6	5.9	5.6	4.8	2.6
Banks	35.3	46.4	52.3	56.6	59.5
Keeping at home	51.6	41.1	33.6	29.9	28.4

Cash Saving

Rural India accounts for 70 per cent of India's population, 56 per cent of the national income, 64 per cent of total expenditure and one-third of total saving. The traditional vision of rural economies as purely agricultural is clearly obsolete. Share of agriculture in rural economy has dropped from 74 per cent in 1970 and 41 per cent in 1993 to 40 per cent in 2007–08. What is more, a significant proportion of salaried (38.7 per cent) and non-agricultural self-employed households (46.1 per cent) are located in rural areas. While an overwhelming share of illiterate households are based in rural areas (88.5 per cent), there are also 36.1 per cent households whose chief earners are graduates. The average household income of the large farm-owning households is about four times that of the landless households. Landless households end up spending more on medical expenses (28.7 per cent of all non-routine expenditure) and less on education (4.5 per cent) compared to their richer counterparts who spend 15 per cent and 8 per cent, respectively.

It is often said that India lives in its villages. This is as true today as it was in 1947 when India became an independent country. However, there have been significant changes in the past 60 years in the countryside that make today's rural India a far more vibrant and dynamic economy than ever. With nearly 70 per cent of the country's population residing in the over 620,000 villages scattered over the length and breadth of the country, rural India continues to wield huge influence over the country's policy makers.

Rural India accounts for 70 per cent of India's population, 56 per cent of national income, 64 per cent of total expenditure and one-third of total saving. In real terms (at 1999 prices), the size of rural economy will be about Rs 16,000 billion in the year 2012–13 which was Rs 12,000 billion in 2007–08. The traditional vision of rural economies as purely agricultural is clearly obsolete. The share of non-farm income will be about two-third by 2012–13 of rural economy. The term 'non-farm' encompasses all the non-crop agricultural activities. It includes manufacturing activities, electricity, gases, construction, mining and quarrying, trade, transportation and services in rural areas. It supplements employment to small and marginal farm households, especially during the slack season, and reduces income inequalities and rural–urban migration which has fallen from 6.5 per cent in 1981 to 2.8 per cent in 2001.

The same set of households mostly give different stories when dissected using various indicators such as income, expenditure, education and occupation levels, ownership of goods and services, and so on. There has not been sufficient analytical effort made by data providers to classify Indian households through integrating various indicators in a meaningful way. Income data when viewed through the filter of socio-economic characteristics such as occupational profile of the chief earner, education level, age group, employment sector can provide invaluable insights into consumption and income trends. For instance, for a clearer understanding, let us consider some of the key occupations in which chief earners of rural households are engaged. And how this impacts their earning levels, and the propensity to spend and save.

There are 144 million rural households (translating into a population of 732 million) in India. Of these, 58 million are headed by chief earners who are engaged in self-employed activities in agriculture and their annual household income is about Rs 54,000. The next largest group of households is those headed by chief earners who are manual labourers. There are 52.4 million labour households earning an average annual income of Rs 28,000 approximately. Nearly 16 million households are engaged in self-employment in non-farm occupations while 15 million are regular salary/wage earning households. These two groups have annual incomes of Rs 67,000 and Rs 103,000, respectively.

How do the rural households, particularly the salary/wage and self-employed non-farm earning ones, compare with their urban counterparts? There are 19 million urban households that are engaged in self-employed non-agricultural activities and their annual income is about Rs 118,000, which is 1.5 times that of their rural counterparts. Urban India also has more regular wage/salary earning households–about 23 million–and these have an annual income of Rs 114,000. These two groups of rural households would form prime targets for marketers of consumer goods and services. Admittedly, these households would be scattered over a larger geographical area than urban households. But the point to consider here is that these rural households have a higher earning weight, that is, they have a higher share of income than other household types in rural India.

Now let us consider consumption patterns. Just as urban incomes are higher than rural ones, so are expenditure levels. A rural salary earning household spends about Rs 63,000 annually compared to Rs 78,000 spent by its urban counterpart. While the rural salary earning household spends 61 per cent of its income on routine and non-routine expenses, this works out to 68 per cent for the urban salary earning household. It also implies that these rural households have more surplus income for saving. For labour households in rural and urban India, the difference is less stark whereas it is most prominent among rural agricultural households that spend nearly 80 per cent of their income on routine and non-routine expenses compared to its urban counterpart which spends just 66 per cent on similar expenses.

Consider the absolute amounts spent by different types of rural households: food expenditure for salary earning households is almost Rs 25,000 per year compared to Rs 15,000 for labour households and 19,000 for self-employed non-farm households. Non-food expenditure too differs significantly for these three household types with salary earners spending as much as Rs 26,000 while labour households and self-employed non-agriculture households spending Rs 9,000 and Rs 16,000, respectively.

On dissecting product ownership by households of various occupation types across urban and rural India, we can gain valuable insights into consumption patterns. For instance, a little less than half of all urban salaried households compared to a little less than a quarter of all rural households own cellular phones. Similarly, refrigerators are owned by nearly 58 per cent of all urban salaried households compared to just 24 per cent of all rural salaried households. Colour televisions are to be found in 83 per cent such households in urban India whereas 57 per cent rural salaried households own colour televisions. Three times more salaried households in urban areas own cars than their rural counterparts.

The picture that is presented here is just a tiny glimpse into rural consumer behaviour. Looking at rural household data through a number of filters can provide rich insights into the changing dynamics of the Indian rural market. Such analysis can be the basis of smarter rural marketing strategies that can result in better outcomes and sales revenues. It is for marketers to discover the potential of the untapped consumer base that the rural market presents and harness it with a winning combination of strategies.

Increasingly, marketers are looking to rural consumers in a bid to grow sales of their products. Rural India is a major part of India's domestic consumption story not just because it has 70 per cent of India's population, but because it already has 56 per cent of India's income, 64 per cent of expenditure and 33 per cent of India's savings. What is more, a significant proportion of salaried (38.7 per cent) and non-agricultural self-employed households (46.1 per cent) are located in rural areas. While an overwhelming share of illiterate households are based in rural areas (88.5 per cent), there are also 36.1 per cent households whose chief earners are graduate+ (Table 6.1).

Product ownership among rural households too is undergoing significant change. For instance, nearly 73.6 per cent of all black-and-white televisions sold in India are owned by rural households. Higher priced products such as refrigerators are also finding more buyers in rural areas with nearly 28.7 per cent of refrigerators being sold to rural households. Similarly, nearly 46 per cent of colour televisions, 53.9 per cent of two wheelers and 43.5 per cent of telephone instruments have been purchased by rural households.

Table 6.1: Understanding Dynamics of Rural Consumer

	Demographics	Share of rural to total (per cent)	Consumer goods	Share of rural to total stock (per cent)
Economic profile	Household	70.1	Computer	21.6
	Population	71.3	Fridge	28.7
	Income	56.0	Credit card	29.4
	Expenditure	57.0	Car	31.7
	Surplus income	33.0	Mobile	32.6
Occupation profile	Salaried	38.7	Telephone (L)	43.5
	Self-employed in non-agriculture	46.1	Television (Colour)	46.0
	Labour	78.4	Pressure cooker	52.6
	Agriculturists	97.2	Two wheeler	53.9
Education profile	Illiterate	88.5	Ceiling fan	55.9
	Up to primary (5th)	82.2	Wrist watch	67.0
	Up to matric (10th)	70.1	Television (Black and White)	73.6
	Up to higher Secondary (12th)	55.7	Radio	74.1
	Graduate and above	36.1	Bicycle	75.4

Source: NSHIE 2004–05 data: NCAER–CMCR analysis.

6.1 Size of Land Holding and Level of Earnings

The linkage between economic status of a household and land possessed[1] is perhaps stronger for those living in rural areas than it is in urban India. Land ownership has been inextricably linked with social status and hierarchy in our villages. In fact, owning land translates into empowerment for a rural household, which has little to do with the value of the land per se, but implies membership of a certain social strata. A little over 38 per cent of households (55.3 million) in rural India do not possess any land (Table 6.2) while 31 per cent (44 million) have less than 1 hectare. The share of large farmers–those with more than 10 hectare–is only 2.2 per cent. Households that do not own any land form the largest group with smallest family size of 4.71 members. The family size increases with size of land holding to 6.12 for large farmers.

Size of land possessed has as much impact on earning levels as occupation. A vast bulk of landless households (70 per cent), are headed by labourers (Figure 6.1).

---

[1] Land possessed = Land owned + Land rented-in – Land rented-out.

Table 6.2: Estimates of Households, Population and Income by Land Class*: Rural

Land class	Households (million)	Population (million)	Household size	Average household income (Rs per annum)	Per capita income (Rs per annum)
Landless	55.3	260.4	4.71	38,237	8,126
Marginal	44.0	223.9	5.09	46,312	9,097
Small	19.4	101.7	5.24	58,484	11,162
Semi-medium	14.2	78.9	5.55	73,702	13,275
Medium	8.1	47.8	5.92	99,858	16,880
Large	3.1	19.2	6.12	109,082	17,831
Total Rural	144.2	731.9	5.08	51,922	10,227

Source: NSHIE 2004–05 data: NCAER–CMCR analysis.
Note: * Land class: Landless: 0 hectare; Marginal farmers: 0.1 hectare–1 hectare; Small farmers: 1 hectare–2 hectare; Semi-medium farmers: 2 hectare–4 hectare; Medium farmers: 4 hectare–10 hectare; Large farmers: Over 10 hectare.

Among households with large land holdings, a majority earn their income from agricultural activities (72.5 per cent) compared to just 3.5 per cent landless households who earn their income from farming. Nearly a quarter of marginal land holding households also depend on labour as a major source of income. In fact, nearly 81 per cent each of the medium and semi-medium farm holding households are dependent on agriculture for their income.

Figure 6.1: Distribution of Rural Households by Major Source of Income and Land Class

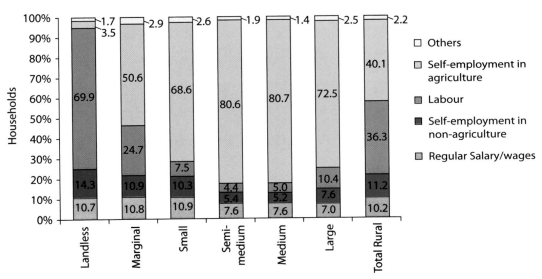

Source: NSHIE 2004–05 data: NCAER–CMCR analysis.

The average income of the landless household is Rs 38,237, while semi-medium farm holdings (between 2 hectare and 4 hectare) earn roughly two times, and medium holdings earn roughly 2.6 times of the income of landless households. The large farmer households have an average annual household income of Rs 109,082, which is roughly three times the earnings of the landless households.

6.2 Size of Land holding and Level of Spending

Households possessing large land holdings have the highest annual income as well as the highest annual consumption expenditure (Table 6.3). The average household income of large land owners is Rs 109,082 and they spend more on non-food items (Rs 28,748) than on food items (Rs 23,752). The next group of high earners and spenders is medium land holding households. Earning about Rs 99,858 per year, these households spend Rs 65,833 of which Rs 27,080 are spent on non-food items and Rs 24,881 on food items. Landless households are the lowest in the earning–spending hierarchy. This category of rural households earns about Rs 38,237 annually and spends Rs 31,515. They spend more on food items (Rs 15,418) rather than on non-food items (Rs 11,472).

Percentage income spent on food items decreases as we move from landless class (40.3 per cent) to the large farmer class (21.6 per cent) The landless households as well as marginal and small farmers spend a higher share of their routine expenditure on food, while the medium and larger farmers spend at less rates. The semi-medium land holding household spends equally on food and non-food items. The non-routine expenditure of a large farmer is 3.5 times that of the landless household, and three times that of a medium land holding household (Table 6.3).

Table 6.3: Estimates of Expenditure by Land Class

Land class	Average annual household income (Rs)	Average annual household expenditure (Rs) Routine		Non-routine	Total	Share of expenditure to income (per cent)
		Food	Non-food			
Landless	38,237	15,418	11,472	4,624	31,515	82.4
Small	46,312	17,973	12,845	6,806	37,624	81.2
Marginal	58,484	20,207	16,144	7,154	43,505	74.4
Semi-medium	73,702	22,632	21,779	11,343	55,754	75.6
Medium	99,858	24,881	27,080	13,873	65,833	65.9
Large	109,082	23,752	28,748	16,478	68,977	63.2
Total rural	51,922	18,266	14,788	7,070	40,124	77.3

Source: NSHIE 2004–05 data: NCAER–CMCR analysis.

Annual food expenses constitute 57.3 per cent of routine expenditure of landless households and this falls to 45.2 per cent for large land holding households. Expenditure levels in respect of health and consumer durables show little variation over the land holding size categories. The expenditure on transport for medium and large land holders (14 per cent) is much higher than that for the landless, marginal and small land holder categories (8 per cent to 10 per cent). Education also accounts for slightly higher outlays for the two top land holder categories (7 per cent to 8 per cent) compared to the bottom categories (6 per cent) (Figure 6.2).

Expenditure on weddings and other social ceremonies account for around 57.3 per cent of all unusual expenses for landless households and this rises to 73.0 per cent in large land holding households (Figure 6.3). There is, however, not much variation among the landless to medium land holder categories. The differences further widen with respect to medical expenses. For instance, medical expenses account for 29.5 per cent of unusual expenditure for landless households and this reduces to 12.5 per cent for large land holder households. Variations between the top and bottom categories are also evident. The landless and marginal land holder households spend 4 per cent of their income on education, while the small to medium categories spend 5 per cent and the large land holder spends 7 per cent.

Figure 6.2: Distribution of Routine Expenditure

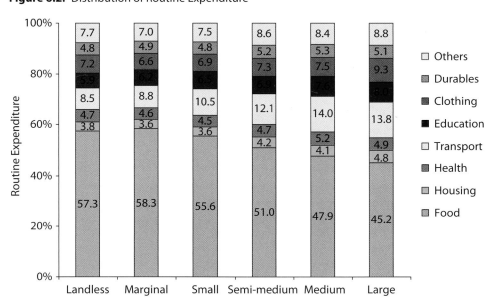

Source: NSHIE 2004–05 data: NCAER–CMCR analysis.

Figure 6.3: Distribution of Unusual Expenditure

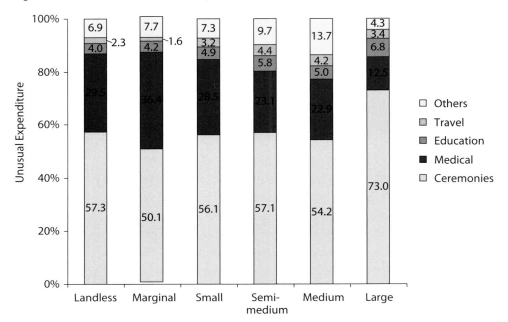

Source: NSHIE 2004–05 data: NCAER–CMCR analysis.

6.3 Size of Land Holding and Saving Patterns

The landless form a major bulk of rural households in the country and save the least at Rs 6,722. The large land holders, on the other hand, have the largest surplus income at Rs 40,105 (37 per cent of income), which is more than six times that of landless households. The medium land holding households save nearly 28.6 per cent of their income, which works out to Rs 23,788 per annum (Table 6.4). The share of cash savings does not show much variation among the different land holding categories.

The landless households spend much less on physical investments compared to marginal and small land holders as well as medium and large land holders. The bigger the land holding size, the investment in durables increases proportionately. A higher proportion of the surplus income is put into life insurance by the landless as compared to the large land holding households (Figure 6.4).

Landless households keep the major portion of their cash savings as cash on hand (52 per cent) and 36 per cent in bank deposits. In contrast the large land holding category deposits 60 per cent in bank and only 28.0 per cent is kept at

Table 6.4: Estimates of Surplus Income by Land Class: Rural

	Landless	Marginal	Small	Medium	Large
a. Household income (Rs/annum)	38,237	46,312	58,484	83,203	109,082
b. Household expenditure (Rs/annum)	31,515	37,624	43,505	59,415	68,977
c. Surplus income (Rs/annum)					
Financial investment	1,234	764	1,678	2,068	3,456
Physical investments	1,191	2,194	3,802	6,779	11,481
Saving in cash	4,297	5,730	9,500	14,941	25,167
Total	6,722	8,688	14,979	23,788	40,105
d. Share of surplus income to income (per cent)					
Financial investment	3.2	1.6	2.9	2.5	3.2
Physical investments	3.1	4.7	6.5	8.1	10.5
Saving in cash	11.2	12.4	16.2	18.0	23.1
Total	17.6	18.8	25.6	28.6	36.8

Source: NSHIE 2004–05 data: NCAER–CMCR analysis.

Figure 6.4: Preferred Forms of Financial Investment by Land Class: Rural

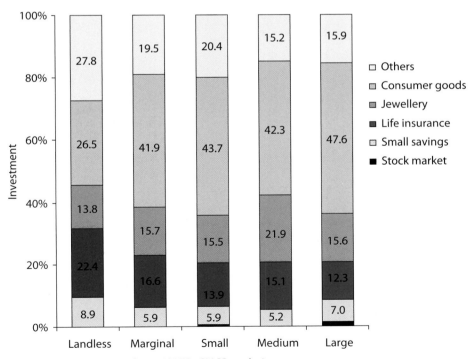

Source: NSHIE 2004–05 data: NCAER–CMCR analysis.

home as cash (Figure 6.5). The cash saving pattern of the medium sized land holder is quite similar to that of large land holding household.

Though it seems most improbable, it is the landless that have the least outstanding loans and the landed categories that have the most. First, it is possible that the landless have fewer reasons to borrow as compared to the landed, and second, the collateral they offer is so low that few are willing to lend to them. Around 23 per cent of the landless in the country have outstanding loans, and the figure goes up to 25.1 per cent in the case of marginal and to 35.5 per cent in the case of large land holders.

The awareness of insurance stands at a high 78 per cent on an all-India level with more urban households (90 per cent) aware about insurance than rural households (73 per cent). Households that have larger land holdings are more aware of insurance than those with relatively smaller land holdings or the landless: 66 per cent of households among the landless and 75 per cent among marginal farmers

Figure 6.5: Preferred Form of Cash Saving by Land Class: Rural

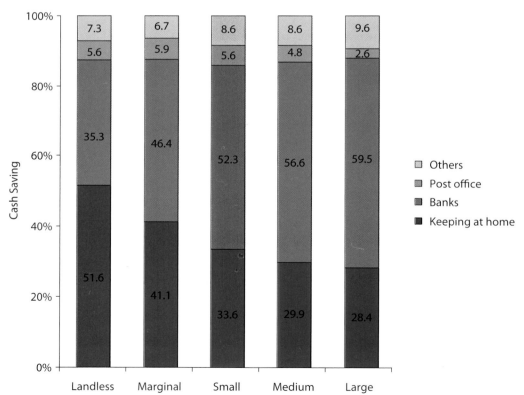

Source: NSHIE 2004–05 data: NCAER–CMCR analysis.

are aware of insurance. This percentage rises to 86 per cent and 87 per cent, respectively, among medium and large farmers.

At the aggregate level, a quarter of all households (24 per cent) own life insurance. More urban households (38 per cent) than rural (19 per cent) own life insurance products. Nearly 47 per cent of large land holders own life insurance products. This only reinforces the fact that life insurance ownership is closely associated with affluence. Nearly 39 per cent of medium sized land holders are also life insurance owners. Policy ownership among households that own small land holdings stands at 27 per cent. Nearly 86 per cent of landless households and 81 per cent of households of the marginal land holders do not possess any insurance product.

The two biggest land holding groups—medium and large—pay the highest premiums in absolute terms at Rs 5,894 and Rs 11,283, respectively, and the face values of life insurance policies owned by them are also the highest: at Rs 109,318 and Rs 210,984, respectively.

6.4 Impact of Size of Land Holding on Earning, Spending and Saving

While the landless households constituting 35.6 per cent of rural households contribute 28.3 per cent share to rural income, 30.2 per cent share to expenditure and 21.9 share to savings, large land holders—comprising just 2.6 per cent of rural households—contribute 4.6 per cent share to income, 3.7 share to expenditure and 7.4 share to savings. Accordingly, the earning weights, spending weights and saving weights of the large land holding category are much higher compared to the landless segment (Table 6.5).

Table 6.5: Impact of Size of Land Holding on Earning, Spending and Saving across Land Classes

	Percentage of				Earning weight	Spending weight	Saving weight
	Population	Income	Expenditure	Saving			
Landless	35.6	28.3	30.2	21.9	0.79	0.85	0.61
Marginal	30.6	27.2	28.6	22.5	0.89	0.94	0.73
Small	13.9	15.2	14.6	17.1	1.09	1.05	1.23
Semi-medium	10.8	14.0	13.7	15.0	1.30	1.27	1.39
Medium	6.5	10.8	9.2	16.2	1.65	1.41	2.47
Large	2.6	4.6	3.7	7.4	1.74	1.43	2.82
Total	100.0	100.0	100.0	100.0	1.00	1.00	1.00

Source: NSHIE 2004–05 data: NCAER–CMCR analysis.

6.5 Pattern of Ownership of Selected Consumer Durable Goods

Product ownership trends reveal that the lower end consumer durables have high penetration. Nearly 69 per cent of all rural households own bicycles. Wrist watches (76 per cent) and radio (52 per cent) are the other durables that are to be found in rural homes (Table 6.6). Colour televisions and two wheelers are increasingly finding more buyers among rural homes. Significantly, 34 per cent marginal land holding households, 53 per cent semi-medium land holders and 63 per cent medium land holders have two wheelers. The percentage of large land holding households that own two wheelers is 55 per cent, but 10 per cent of these households (compared to 9 per cent for medium land holders) have cars.

Table 6.6: Ownership of Selected Consumer Goods by Land Class (Per Cent Households Owning Product)

	Landless	Small	Marginal	Semi-medium	Medium	Large	Rural
Two wheelers	16.9	20.5	34.5	53.4	62.5	55.0	27.3
Car	1.5	1.9	3.3	4.6	9.2	10.0	2.8
Colour television	18.9	20.8	28.2	35.7	42.4	45.8	24.3
Fridge	6.1	5.4	8.0	11.2	17.1	19.6	7.6
Television (B&W)	23.1	27.6	33.4	37.6	37.1	35.2	28.3
Bicycle	65.0	72.6	73.2	70.4	68.6	63.5	69.1
Wrist watch	71.3	73.5	82.6	84.3	87.1	88.1	76.0
Ceiling fan	42.0	42.7	52.8	64.7	69.6	67.9	48.0
Pressure cooker	30.6	35.3	43.2	54.4	56.4	55.8	38.1
Radio	47.9	52.9	57.3	57.7	56.5	57.9	52.3
Credit card	0.2	0.2	0.8	2.7	3.3	2.9	0.7
Telephone (L)	9.6	9.5	14.3	21.2	30.9	36.4	13.1
Computer	0.6	0.4	0.4	0.7	1.4	1.4	0.6
Mobile	5.1	5.2	8.6	14.1	18.0	17.3	7.5

Source: NSHIE 2004–05 data: NCAER–CMCR analysis.

Perceptions about Financial Security

As has been noted earlier, Indians tend to save for emergencies and not for their old age, as they are quite sure about their ability to live off their savings after retirement, and also confident of getting alternative employment within months of any eventual job loss. Expectedly, households with large land holdings are 'confident' or 'most confident' about their financial security. Nearly half of the largest land holding households feel 'confident' and more than a quarter (27 per cent) feel they are 'most confident.' Among households that own medium and small land holdings, the confidence level is quite high as well: 49 per cent are 'confident' of being able to meet their financial needs. Surprisingly, even among landless households, nearly 33 per cent are upbeat about their financial security. However, a higher percentage of households among this group (60 per cent) reveal that they are either 'less confident,' 'least confident' or 'totally uncertain' about their financial stability (23 per cent 'less confident' and 18 per cent 'least confident').

Again, landless households are the most upbeat about finding alternative source income within six months (36 per cent) compared to 37.2 per cent for large land holders. But a larger proportion of such households are uncertain about their ability to find alternative source of income (39 per cent). There is, however, not much difference among the other groups.

The possibility that households will draw on current savings to meet routine expenditure in case of a sudden drop in income levels is borne out by the fact that about 5 per cent of households claim that if they lose their major source of household income, they can sustain themselves beyond a year. While the proportion differs across landowning groups, nearly a third of landless households claim that they can sustain themselves for up to six months, while only 4 per cent feel they would be able to sustain themselves beyond 12 months. The highest proportion (14 per cent) of households being able to stretch their savings to last them beyond 12 months is found in the largest land holding category.

Urban Well-being

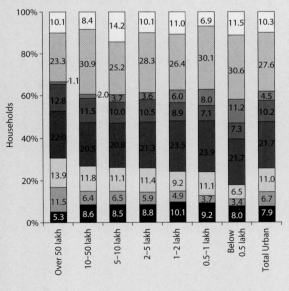

Households (y-axis)

Category	Over 50 lakh	10–50 lakh	5–10 lakh	2–5 lakh	1–2 lakh	0.5–1 lakh	Below 0.5 lakh	Total Urban
Workers not classified by occupation	10.1	8.4	14.2	10.1	11.0	6.9	11.5	10.3
Production and related workers	23.3	30.9	25.2	28.3	26.4	30.1	30.6	27.6
Farmers, fishermen, hunters, loggers and related workers	1.1	2.0	3.7	3.6	6.0	8.0		4.5
Service workers	12.8	11.5	10.0	10.5	8.9	7.1	11.2	10.2
Sales workers	22.0	20.5	20.8	21.3	23.5	23.9	7.3	21.7
Clerical and related workers	13.9	11.8	11.1	11.4	9.2	11.1	21.7	11.0
Administrative, executive and managerial workers	11.5	6.4	6.5	5.9	4.9	3.7	6.5	6.7
Professional, technical and related workers	5.3	8.6	8.5	8.8	10.1	9.2	3.4	7.9
							8.0	

On a conservative estimate, 45 per cent of Indians would be living in towns and cities by 2050. This means that 379 million people may be added to urban spaces over the next 40 years, which is more than the present population of the United States. Urban residents are the most educated, they have the highest incomes, and consequently, account for the highest share of savings in the country. Around 51 per cent of the households in the top 20 cities have at least one graduate in a household, and it is just 15 per cent in the villages. As a result, nearly half of those employed in the top 20 cities tend to have salaried jobs in comparison to just 10 per cent in villages. India simply cannot afford urban development to languish. India's top 20 cities account for just 10 per cent of the country's population, but this population earns 31 per cent of the country's income, spends 21 per cent, and so, accounts for 60 per cent of the surplus income. India needs to place urban development—particularly infrastructure—squarely alongside rural priorities, recognising in part that both are interdependent.

The twentieth century witnessed a rapid shift of population from rural to urban areas[1] in most countries of the world. A mere 13 per cent of the global population lived in urban areas in 1900, which increased to 29 per cent in 1950 and to about 50 per cent by the close of the twentieth century (United Nations 2006). However, the pattern of urbanisation is quite uneven between the developed and developing countries. Majority of the population of developed countries lives in urban areas whereas in the developing countries, the majority lives in rural areas. While this figure is currently much lower for India, things are changing. For instance, the urban population in India at the beginning of the twentieth century was only 25.8 million, constituting 10.8 per cent of total population in 1901, which increased to 286.1 million, making 27.8 per cent of total population in 2001. The net addition in urban population was five million during 1921–31, which rose to 18 million during 1941–51 and sharply increased to 50 million during 1971–81, and grew further to 69 million between 1991 and 2001. On a conservative estimate, 45 per cent of Indians would be living in her towns and cities

---

[1] There is no thumb rule to divide rural and urban, and the practice is followed diversely across the countries of the world. In the present context, we followed the Census 2001 definition. According to Census 2001, urban areas include: *(i)* All places with a municipality, corporation, cantonment board or notified town area committee, and so on; and *(ii)* All other places which satisfy the following criteria: *(a)* Minimum population of 5000, *(b)* At least 75 per cent of male working population engaged in non-agricultural pursuits and *(c)* A population density of at least 400 persons per square kilometre.

by 2050. This means that 379 million people may be added to urban spaces over the next 40 years–more than the present population of the United States.

India has had a contentious relationship with its cities. The romanticised notion that 'India lives in its villages' has obscured the trend and need for urbanisation. The 1951 census report even made the mystifying remark that India's towns and cities were 'accidents of history and geography.' It is only now in the era of globalisation that urban centres have been recognised as important drivers of the economic growth and innovations and the overall trend is much more complex than we acknowledge. The diversity of income, spending, savings and demographic patterns across different town sizes reveals that generalisation about urban development in India is no longer sufficient. The increasing concentration of population in cities, particularly in large cities, has been the striking feature of India's urbanisation during the last century. For instance, in 1901, nearly one-fourth of urban population lived in cities with a population of 100,000 or more, which went up to 45 per cent in 1951 and increased up to 69 per cent in 2001.

7.1 Why India's Cities Matter?

Urban residents are the most educated, they have the highest incomes, and consequently, account for the highest share of savings in the country. India's top 20 cities[2] account for just 10 per cent of the country's population, but this population earns 31 per cent of the country's income, spends 21 per cent, and so, accounts for 60 per cent of the surplus income (Table 7.1). The next lot of cities account for

Table 7.1: Economic Matrix of India (Share of Total Per Cent)

	Urban			Rural	All India
	Top 20 cities	Other cities	Total		
Households	10.7	20.1	30.7	69.3	100.0
Population	9.9	19.7	29.5	70.5	100.0
Income	30.8	13.1	44.0	56.0	100.0
Expenditure	21.1	15.0	36.1	63.9	100.0
Surplus income	59.8	7.7	67.5	32.5	100.0

Source: NSHIE 2004–05 data: NCAER–CMCR analysis.

---

[2] Top 20 cities: Mega cities (8): Delhi, Mumbai, Chennai, Kolkata, Banglore, Hyderabad, Ahmedabad and Pune; Boomtowns (7): Surat, Kanpur, Jaipur, Lucknow, Nagpur, Bhopal and Coimbatore; and Niche cities (5): Faridabad, Amritsar, Ludhiana, Chandigarh and Jalandhar. For more details, see Shukla and Purushothaman (2008).

20 per cent of the population, 13 per cent of income and almost 8 per cent of surplus
income or savings. Rural areas account for 70 per cent of population, 64 per cent
of expenditure and just a third of the country's surplus income. It is obvious then
that India's savings can grow only as the country's urbanisation progresses. Given
this, the promise of creating more urban centres would be a more effective way
to progress the rural India.

The reason for such an argument is quite clear once we look at the data closely.
Around 51 per cent of households in the top 20 cities have at least one graduate
(that means, at least a tenth of the population in these cities consists of graduates).
The figure is 38 per cent for other cities, and it is just 15 per cent in the villages
(Figure 7.1). As a result, nearly 49 per cent of those employed in the top 20 cities
tend to have salaried jobs, and another 32 per cent are self-employed. In comparison, other cities and rural areas that have a smaller proportion of graduates,
tend to have a much smaller proportion of either the salaried or self-employed:
32 per cent of those in other cities are salaried and the figure is just 10 per cent in
villages. In the case of self-employed in non-agriculture, the figure is 30 per cent
for smaller towns and a mere 11 per cent in rural India (Figure 7.2).

Figure 7.1: Distribution of Households by Highest Literacy in the Household

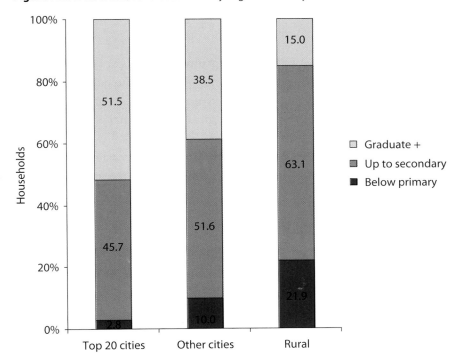

Source: NSHIE 2004–05 data: NCAER–CMCR analysis.

Figure 7.2: Distribution of Households by Major Source of Household Income

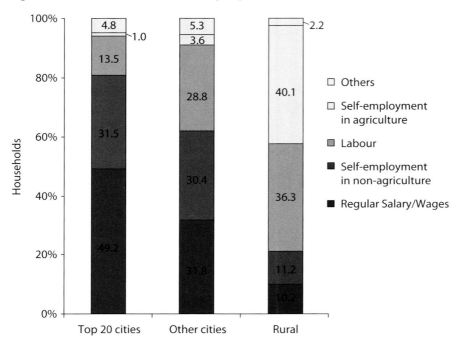

Source: NSHIE 2004–05 data: NCAER–CMCR analysis.

When looked from another angle, the inequality levels appear very high in the top 20 cities: 53 per cent of households in the topmost income quintile are to be found in the top 20 cities. The figure is 30 per cent in the other cities and just 12 per cent in rural India. The Gini coefficient, a measure of inequality, is 0.41 for the top 20 cities and 0.43 for other cities and rural areas (Figure 7.3).

This occupation structure coupled with the variability in earnings across the top 20 cities and rural areas is what causes big differences in income and savings levels. So, for instance, an average graduate earned approximately Rs 180,000 per year in the top 20 cities as compared to just Rs 91,000 in rural areas (Table 7.2). The difference, in fact, is higher for illiterates as well: the average earning of an illiterate was Rs 70,000 per annum in the top 20 cities versus just Rs 22,500 in rural areas.

For those with regular jobs, the ratio of salaries in rural areas to that in top 20 cities was 0.62 (Rs 96,394 versus Rs 154,455). It was 0.38 in the case of the self-employed and 0.47 in the case of labourers. As a result, the average earning of those in the bottom most quintile in the top 20 cities was Rs 43,878 as compared to Rs 19,536 in rural areas; for the topmost quintile, the earnings were Rs 301,734 and Rs 135,936, respectively.

Figure 7.3: Distribution of Households by Per Capita Income Quintile

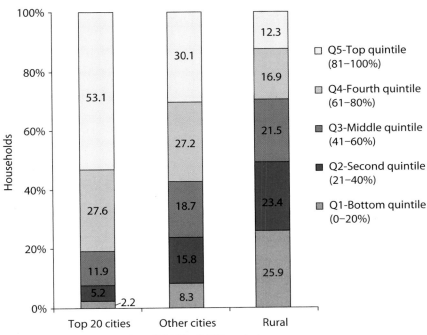

Source: NSHIE 2004–05 data: NCAER–CMCR analysis.

An interesting finding is that the top 20 cities are not, in any way, more diverse than rural areas, with the ratio of the household earnings in the top quintile to that in the lowest quintile being around 6.9 in both the cases.

From the point of view of India's marketing firms, the top 20 cities and their growth are clearly of paramount importance. In the case of colour televisions,

Table 7.2: Disparity in Level of Earnings and Saving

Household characteristics	Annual mean household income (Rs)		Ratio (Rural/cities)	Share of saving to total income (per cent)	
	Top 20 cities	Rural		Top 20 cities	Rural
Illiterate	70,199	22,432	0.32	53	23
Graduate+	1,79,242	90,746	0.51	52	42
Regular salary/wages	1,54,455	96,394	0.62	53	47
Self-employment in non-agriculture	1,68,779	64,448	0.38	52	37
Labour	59,509	28,219	0.47	37	19
Q1-Bottom quintile (0 per cent–20 per cent)	43,878	19,536	0.45	–20	–4
Q5-Top quintile (81 per cent–100 per cent)	3,01,734	1,35,936	0.45	70	57

Source: NSHIE 2004–05 data: NCAER–CMCR analysis.

Figure 7.4: Ownership of Selected Consumer Durable Goods (Per Cent of Households Owning Products)

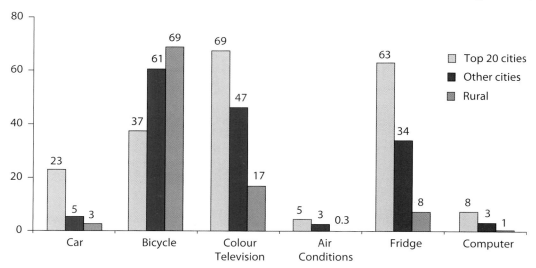

Source: NSHIE 2004–05 data: NCAER–CMCR analysis.

for instance, 68 per cent of households in the top 20 cities own these products (Figure 7.4). The figure is a low 47 per cent in the other cities and a mere 17 per cent in rural areas. For cars, the figures are 23 per cent, 5 per cent and 3 per cent, respectively; for refrigerators, the figures are 63 per cent, 34 per cent and 8 per cent, respectively.

Around 94 per cent households in the top 20 cities reported that they save some part of their earnings. The figure is 85 per cent in other cities and 79 per cent for rural India. Fewer rural households hold accounts in any financial institutions, with percentages pegged at 59 per cent for rural India and 92 per cent for the top 20 cities. A fourth of all rural households have outstanding loans, and the corresponding figure for the top 20 cities is 17 per cent. More households in the top 20 cities (43 per cent) than rural areas (19 per cent) own life insurance products (Figure 7.5). An estimate of household expenditure on health and education can be obtained from Figure 7.6.

With 67 per cent of households in the top 20 cities and 46 per cent in rural areas putting their cash saving in bank deposits, the impact on cash savings is obvious. Almost 43 per cent rural Indians prefer to keep their cash saving at home which is much lower (20 per cent) in the case of the top 20 cities. Households opting for post office deposits account for just 4 per cent to 5 per cent, irrespective of the location of such households (Figure 7.7).

In the earlier chapters, we saw that higher educational qualification and better profession in promising sectors lead to higher levels of income and savings

Figure 7.5: Ownership of Selected Financial Services (Per Cent of Households Owning Services)

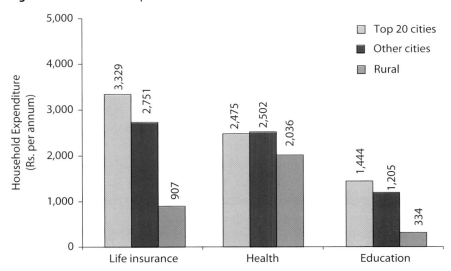

Source: NSHIE 2004–05 data: NCAER–CMCR analysis.

of urban households. Since larger cities and towns have better job opportunities, avenues for personal development and advancement and scope for entering the growing sectors of employment, the households situated in such cities are more likely to earn and save at much higher levels than relatively smaller ones. Let us

Figure 7.6: Household Expenditure on Health and Education

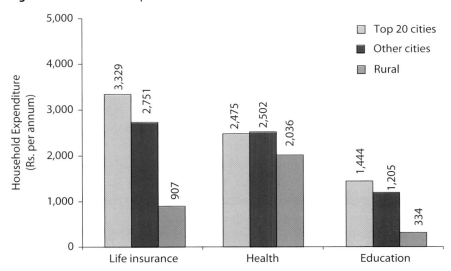

Source: NSHIE 2004–05 data: NCAER–CMCR analysis.

Figure 7.7: Preferred Forms of Saving

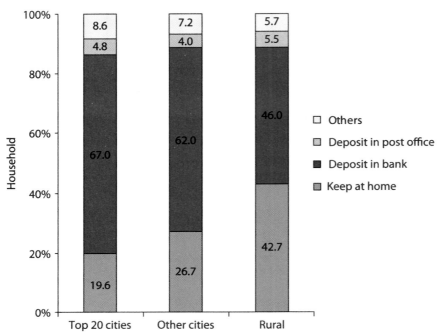

Source: NSHIE 2004–05 data: NCAER–CMCR analysis.

check out this hypothesis by analysing the patterns of earning, spending and savings of urban households across different town sizes.

7.2 Size-class of Towns and Level of Earning

Out of a total of 61.4 million urban households, a little less than a quarter of these households are to be found in cities with populations of over 50 lakh (Table 7.3). Their average household income is higher than the average urban household at Rs 127,516 per annum versus Rs 95,827. Nearly 11.2 million (or 18 per cent of all urban households) are located in towns with populations between 10 lakh and 50 lakh. The average annual household income of this category of towns is slightly higher than the average urban household income (at Rs 99,360). The largest towns (by population size) thus account for nearly 40 per cent of the total urban households, that is, nearly 121 million people.

It may be noted that the average earnings of households in the top two categories of cities is higher by 79 per cent and 32 per cent, respectively, over the smaller town income (population less than 0.5 lakh). Per capita income also displays the

Table 7.3: Estimates of Households, Population and Income by Town Class

Town class (population size in lakh)	Households (million)	Population (million)	Household size	Average household income (Rs per annum)	Per capita income (Rs per annum)
Over 50	14.5	64.8	4.48	127,516	28,483
10–50	11.2	55.9	5.01	99,360	19,832
5–10	6.6	31.8	4.83	89,503	18,519
2–5	8.2	38.9	4.74	85,678	18,067
1–2	6.1	28.9	4.71	82,560	17,511
0.5–1	4.8	23.8	4.93	78,401	15,892
Below 0.5	10.1	51.3	5.09	75,225	14,789
Total Urban	61.4	295.3	4.81	95,827	19,935

Source: NSHIE 2004–05 data: NCAER–CMCR analysis.

same trend. The per capita incomes of the three highest size categories are 93 per cent, 34 per cent and 25 per cent higher than that of the small town per capita income.

7.3 Size-class of Towns and Spending Pattern

In terms of expenditure, households in the largest towns are the big spenders: their annual expenditure is Rs 81,665 compared to the average urban household expenditure level of Rs 68,352. However, in terms of share of expenditure to income, it is lower than the average urban household level: 64 per cent versus 71 per cent, respectively.

Table 7.4 gives the details of routine and non-routine expenditure incurred by households, according to the size-classes of the cities/towns in which they are situated. Interestingly, the households in the largest towns have a lower share of non-food expenditure (relative to their income) than those of households in the smaller towns. For instance, the urban households in town sizes of 10 lakh to 50 lakh spend nearly 36 per cent of their income on non-food expenditure. Even the households in the smallest towns (with population of less than 0.5 lakh) spend 32 per cent of their income on non-food items and 30 per cent on food items. By contrast, households in the largest towns spend a quarter of their income on food items.

The total expenditures incurred by households in largest two categories of cities are 41 per cent and 29 per cent more than that incurred by a household of a

Table 7.4: Estimates of Expenditure by Town Class

Town class (population size in lakh)	Average household expenditure (Rs per annum)				Share of expenditure to income (per cent)			
	Routine		Non-routine	Total	Routine		Non-routine	Total
	Food	Non-food			Food	Non-food		
Over 50	32,659	38,971	10,035	81,665	25.6	30.6	7.9	64.0
10–50	26,898	35,433	8,867	71,199	27.1	35.7	8.9	71.7
5–10	26,058	30,672	11,083	67,814	29.1	34.3	12.4	75.8
2–5	23,697	30,141	9,712	63,549	27.7	35.2	11.3	74.2
1–2	23,986	28,164	9,704	61,855	29.1	34.1	11.8	74.9
0.5–1	23,575	27,505	9,925	61,005	30.1	35.1	12.7	77.8
Below 0.5	22,863	24,408	10,550	57,821	30.4	32.4	14.0	76.9
Total Urban	26,524	31,893	9,935	68,352	27.7	33.3	10.4	71.3

Source: NSHIE 2004–05 data: NCAER–CMCR analysis.

smallest town category. Although the expenditures on food and non-food items are more in higher size-classes in the absolute terms, the expenditure shares of these components to household income are relatively smaller in larger towns than smaller ones. However, the non-routine expenditures in the two topmost town classes are significantly lower, both in absolute terms and as percentages of the total expenditure which probably indicates the level of better infrastructure and services in larger cities.

The households in the smaller towns spend a marginally higher percentage of their income on food items as compared to those in the bigger towns. Across all items of routine expenditure–housing, education, clothing and footwear, durables, health care, transport–there is not much difference in the share of the households' spend levels across different town classes. However, when it comes to non-routine expenditure, households in the smallest towns (0.5 lakh population) spend almost half of their non-routine expenditure on ceremonies compared to 42 per cent in the largest towns. In contrast, households in big towns spend nearly 17 per cent of their non-routine expenditure on education compared to just 12 per cent for the town classes with population less than 0.5 lakh. Transport is not significantly higher for the households in the largest towns.

The annual food expenses constitute 48.4 per cent of household's routine expenditure in small towns (population below 0.5 lakh), 45.6 per cent in cities with population over 50 lakh and 43.2 per cent in cities where the population is between 10 lakh and 50 lakh (Figure 7.8). Expenditure levels in respect of clothing and consumer durables show little variation among the different size-class categories. However, there is a higher rate of spending on housing component in

Figure 7.8: Distribution of Routine Expenditure

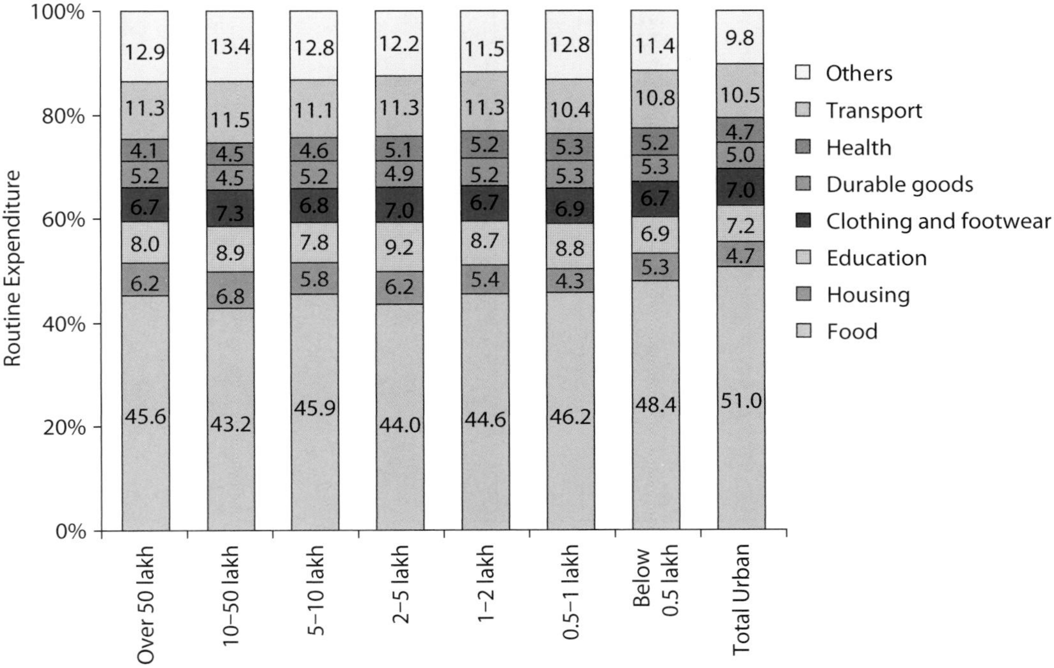

Source: NSHIE 2004–05 data: NCAER–CMCR analysis.

cities as compared to towns in the country. Interestingly, the households in the three topmost city types spend at comparatively lower rates on health care than in cities with population below five lakh. This, points to the availability of better medical facilities, at reasonable rates, in high class cities. Also, by spending almost at the same level, the households in the two topmost classes of cities provide better education to the youngsters than those situated in lower class cities and towns. These two points clearly mean well-being of the people living in high class cities.

Expenditure on weddings and other social ceremonies account for around 50.4 per cent of household's unusual expenses in small towns, whereas in top two categories of cities (over 50 lakh, and 10 lakh to 50 lakh population) this entails 41.8 per cent and 49.4 per cent, respectively (Figure 7.9). Medical expenses form 25.3 per cent of unusual expenditure in small towns and 22.9 per cent in the top cities. Transport expenditure accounts for 10.5 per cent of the households' unusual expenses in top cities which is much higher than the percentages spent in other classes of cities and towns.

On education also, households in the cities with over 50 lakh population spent a much higher share (17.2 per cent) because of their affordability coupled with

Figure 7.9: Distribution of Non-routine Expenditure

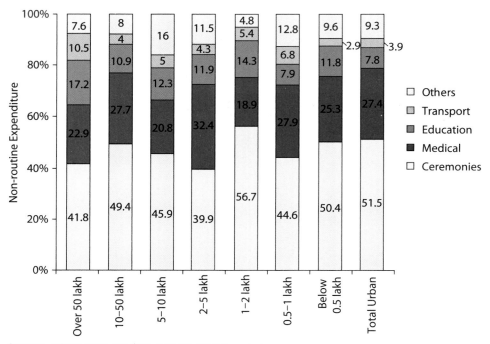

Source: NSHIE 2004–05 data: NCAER–CMCR analysis.

higher cost of education in such cities, as compared to a household in a small town which spends 11.8 per cent of the unusual expenses at its disposal.

7.4 Size-class of Towns and Saving pattern

The largest towns have the highest savings at Rs 45,852 per annum. This is a little less than twice that that saved by households in the second rung of towns (10 lakh to 50 lakh population) but approximately three times the savings of households in the smallest towns (0.5 lakh population). This shows that the savings rate in the largest cities is about 36 per cent and it gets reduced to 21 per cent for the smallest cities (Table 7.5).

The pattern of utilisation of surplus income in different town size-classes shows that financial investments range from Rs 2,955 for the lowest size class to Rs 7,243 for the highest class. Similarly, physical investments range from Rs 3,762 for the lowest size-class to Rs 7,906 for the highest class. The share of physical invest-ments is comparatively higher in two lakh+ cities. Level of financial investments is comparatively higher in larger cities than in smaller cities. Similarly, in the case

Table 7.5: Estimates of Surplus Income by Town Class

Town class (population size in lakh)	Surplus income (Rs/annum)				Share of surplus income to income (per cent)			
	Financial investment	Physical investment	Saving in cash	Total	Financial investment	Physical investment	Saving in cash	Total
Over 50	7,243	7,906	30,657	45,852	5.7	6.2	24.0	36.0
10–50	2,755	6,751	18,635	28,161	2.8	6.8	18.8	28.3
5–10	1,179	6,627	13,887	21,689	1.3	7.4	15.5	24.2
2–5	2,147	5,659	14,321	22,129	2.5	6.6	16.7	25.8
1–2	4,733	4,247	11,790	20,706	5.7	5.1	14.3	25.1
0.5–1	3,586	4,059	9,810	17,397	4.6	5.2	12.5	22.2
Below 0.5	2,955	3,762	9,092	15,764	3.9	5.0	12.1	21.0
Total Urban	3,857	5,912	17,706	27,475	4.0	6.2	18.5	28.7

Source: NSHIE 2004–05 data: NCAER–CMCR analysis.

of cash savings, note that the larger cities perform better than smaller towns, and among the cities, the two highest size-classes have much higher rates of saving than the remaining cities.

Households in the smallest towns share the same trait with the biggest saving urban households: about two-third of their savings is in cash. However, just 2 per cent of households in the smallest towns invest in the stock markets compared to 11 per cent households in the largest towns. Nearly 32 per cent households in the smallest towns prefer to invest in life insurance policies compared to 24 per cent households in the largest towns. More households (41 per cent) in the mid-sized towns (2 lakh to 5 lakh population) prefer life insurance policies.

Coming to financial investments, it can be observed that investments in life insurance policies are much higher in towns with population below two lakh than in large cities. In 10 lakh+ cities, there is much less investment in jewellery compared to rest of the cities and towns (Figure 7.10). In the case of consumer durables, it is in general higher across town categories with the exception of the largest cities where the lower rate of spending on durables (30 per cent) is compensated by spending a higher share of the total investment on stocks and debentures (11.4 per cent), with smallest towns (0.5 lakh to one lakh) having the lowest share (hardly 2 per cent) in stocks.

Across all town classes, a majority of households prefer to keep their cash in banks. The percentage is slightly higher (63 per cent) for the largest towns as against 57 per cent for the smallest towns. More households in the smallest towns (29 per cent) compared to the largest towns (18 per cent) prefer to keep the cash at home (Figure 7.11).

Figure 7.10: Preferred Forms of Financial Investment by Town Class

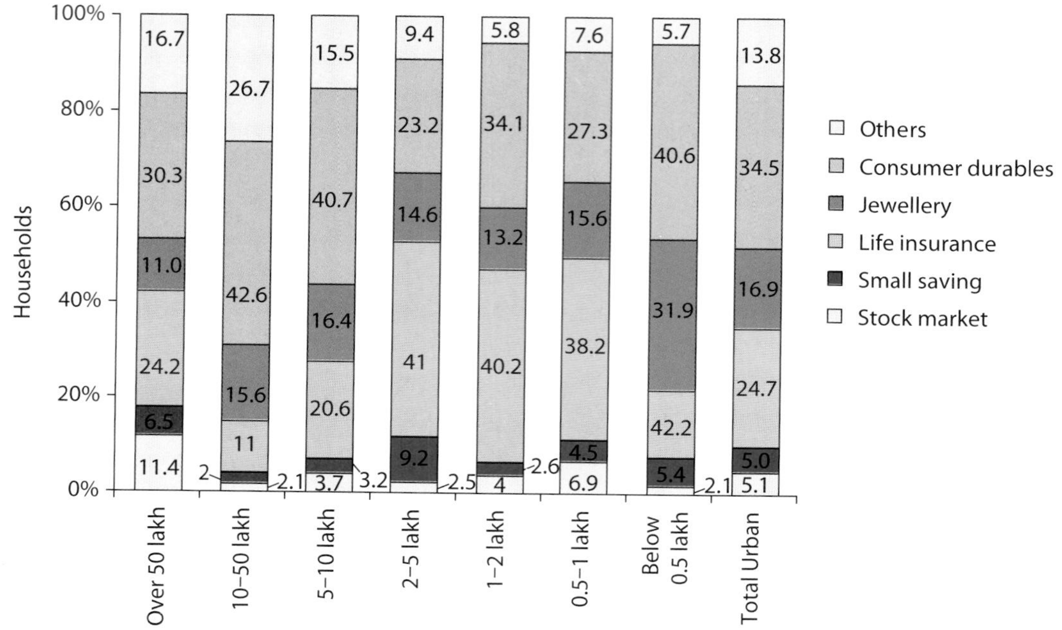

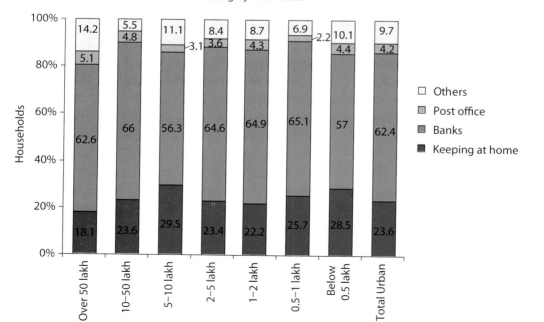

Source: NSHIE 2004–05 data: NCAER–CMCR analysis.

Figure 7.11: Preferred Form of Cash Saving by Town Class

Source: NSHIE 2004–05 data: NCAER–CMCR analysis.

7.5 Impact of Size-class of Towns on Earning, Spending and Saving

The largest towns are the biggest contributors to urban income, expenditure and saving. Nearly 22 per cent population living in these towns contributes 31 per cent of the total urban income, 28 per cent of urban expenditure and 39 per cent of urban surplus income. By contrast, 19 per cent population residing in the second rung of towns (10 lakh to 50 lakh population) contributes 19 per cent each towards urban income, expenditure and surplus income. The smallest towns (with populations of less than 0.5 lakh) have a share of 17.4 per cent of urban population but their share of urban income, expenditure and saving is just 12.9 per cent, 13.9 per cent and 10.4 per cent, respectively (Table 7.6).

It can be seen that the earning weights and saving weights in respect of largest cities are far ahead of the remaining size-classes. The households of cities with 10 lakh to 50 lakh population have their population share nearly equal to their shares in income and surplus income, thus recording unit earning weight and saving weight. The households of the largest cities and the class just below it are at much higher levels of affluence and well-being than those in smaller cities in the country.

The largest towns continue to attract people from all over the country, and migration is not just from rural areas but also from smaller towns to the bigger ones. The metropolitan cities hold out the promise of more income and this is clearly borne out by our analysis.

Let us consider the impact on an urban household's income level, if it were to move from the smallest town (population of less than 0.5 lakh) to a bigger town. The average household income would increase by almost Rs 3,177 if the move

Table 7.6: Impact of Size of Town on Earning, Spending and Saving

Town class (population size in lakh)	Percentage distribution of				Earning weight	Spending weight	Saving weight
	Population	Income	Expenditure	Saving			
Over 50	21.9	31.3	28.1	39.3	1.43	1.28	1.79
10–50	18.9	18.8	18.9	18.6	0.99	1.00	0.98
5–10	10.8	10.0	10.6	8.4	0.93	0.99	0.79
2–5	13.2	11.9	12.4	10.7	0.91	0.94	0.82
1–2	9.8	8.6	9.0	7.5	0.88	0.92	0.77
0.5–1	8.0	6.4	7.0	5.0	0.80	0.87	0.62
Below 0.5	17.4	12.9	13.9	10.4	0.74	0.80	0.60
Total Urban	100.0	100.0	100.0	100.0	1.00	1.00	1.00

Source: NSHIE 2004–05 data: NCAER–CMCR analysis.

Table 7.7: Impact of Size-class of Town on Level of Earnings (Percentage Increase over Base Income)

Town class (population size in lakh)	Increase over base income (Rs)	Percentage increase
Over 50	52,292	69
10–50	24,135	32
5–10	14,278	19
2–5	10,454	14
1–2	7,335	10
0.5–1	3,177	4
Below 0.5 lakh (Base income)	75,225	

Source: NSHIE 2004–05 data: NCAER–CMCR analysis.

was to the next town class in the hierarchy (Table 7.7). However, if the household moved to the second largest town size (10 lakh to 50 lakh population), the increase in average household income would amount to Rs 24,135. And if the shift were to take place to the largest town size (with population of over 50 lakh), the increase would be a whopping Rs 52,292 (or a 69 per cent increase).

7.6 Pattern of Ownership of Selected Consumer Durable Goods

The propensity for buying consumer goods is similar among households across all town classes. In terms of routine expenditure, nearly all urban households spend about 5 per cent of their routine expenditure on purchasing consumer durables. Product ownership trends reveal that the penetration of high-end products like two wheeler, car, colour television and refrigerator is much higher in five lakh+ cities than in smaller sized cities and towns. For instance, cars are owned more by households in the largest towns, though ownership of two wheelers is quite significant among urban households across all town classes. Poor transport services in smaller towns may actually be fuelling demand for two wheelers in smaller towns. Nearly 44 per cent households in towns with less than 0.5 lakh population own two wheelers, which is 15 percentage points less than the largest towns (59 per cent). Smaller towns have a way to go before they catch up with the 50 lakh+ population cities in terms of ownership of cars, which is 7 per cent and 24 per cent, respectively (Table 7.8).

Credit card ownership continues to be low across all town classes, with just 7 per cent households in the biggest cities owning credit cards. The same trend is observed for computers as well. With half of all big city households owning landline phones, the percentage is steadily increasing among smaller towns as well. Colour television ownership has gone up to almost 50 per cent of urban

Table 7.8: Ownership of Selected Consumer Goods by Town Class (Per Cent of Households Owning Product)

Products	Town class (population size in lakh)							Total urban
	Over 50	10–50	5–10	2–5	1–2	0.5–1.0	Below 0.5	
Two wheelers	59.0	64.0	56.8	55.0	48.2	50.6	43.8	54.9
Car	23.6	16.7	12.5	11.0	7.7	8.0	7.1	14.0
Colour television	81.9	72.6	67.8	62.8	59.2	56.6	51.2	66.9
Fridge	64.1	51.2	42.8	39.6	33.6	29.4	25.9	44.2
Television (B&W)	14.2	22.1	24.4	27.7	28.8	29.5	30.3	23.8
Bicycle	30.6	55.4	54.8	60.3	54.9	64.1	68.1	52.9
Wrist watch	92.5	89.8	86.8	87.3	84.5	84.7	83.9	87.9
Ceiling fan	88.8	88.4	80.5	78.7	76.0	71.1	68.1	80.4
Pressure cooker	19.8	17.7	16.7	16.6	16.1	14.4	13.4	16.7
Radio	47.6	32.6	39.6	38.3	41.9	45.8	52.8	42.9
Credit card	7.2	7.4	2.0	1.7	2.8	3.7	1.0	4.2
Telephone (L)	50.2	40.6	41.6	38.0	35.3	35.7	30.3	40.0
Computer	7.6	5.8	5.5	4.4	2.9	2.8	1.9	4.8
Mobile	53.8	41.7	32.1	29.8	30.4	27.7	20.5	36.2

Source: NSHIE 2004–05 data: NCAER–CMCR analysis.

households in the smallest towns, whereas in the largest cities, nearly 82 per cent of households own colour televisions.

7.7 Economic Well-being by Town Size-classes

In this section we shall examine the earning, expenditure and saving levels of different household groups, based on various household characteristics such as the chief earner's source of income, education level and state of residence; and the nature of work pursued and the sector of engagement of households for their earnings. Major groups under each characteristic are chosen for assessing their performance in terms of income, expenditure and saving in different classes of towns.

7.7.1 Occupation of Chief Earner

In the context of urban areas, the 'regular salary,' 'self-employed in non-agriculture' and 'labour' occupation groups have been considered for discussion as they are not only the most numerous groups but are also the major earners

Figure 7.12: Distribution of Households by Occupation of Chief Earner and Town Class

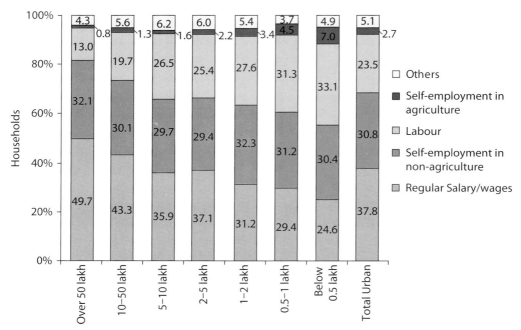

Source: NSHIE 2004–05 data: NCAER–CMCR analysis.

and savers of urban India (Figure 7.12). The top four largest town classes have a higher percentage of households engaged in regular salaried jobs, whereas in the smaller towns, a higher percentage of households earn their money from non-farm income related activities or labour. Significantly, in the largest cities, half of all households earn their income from regular salaried jobs compared to a quarter of households in the smallest towns.

It can be seen that all the groups have the highest earning, expenditure and surplus income if they are working in largest cities (Table 7.9). The salary dependent households earn Rs 103,930 in small towns but in the largest cities, they earn 23 per cent more (Rs 127,743). Such households spend Rs 83,764 in the largest cities, which is 26 per cent more than the expenditure incurred by their counterparts in small towns (Rs 66,583). Similarly the surplus income in the largest cities is Rs 43,979 which is 18 per cent more than in small towns (Rs 37, 347). As against this, the households engaged in non-agriculture activities earn Rs 165,562, spend Rs 96,566 and generate a surplus income of Rs 68,996, which is 181 per cent more than the surplus income obtainable in small towns.

In the largest cities, the labour dependent households also generate 2.5 times as much surplus income as generated in small towns. In general, the earning and surplus income levels of salary dependent and self-employed (non-agriculture)

Table 7.9: Estimates of Income, Expenditure and Surplus Income by Occupation of Chief Earner and Town Class

Occupation of chief earner	Town class (population size in lakh)							Total urban
	Over 50	10–50	5–10	2–5	1–2	0.5–1.0	Below 0.5	
Income (Rs per household per annum)								
Regular salary/wages	127,743	111,267	116,835	105,873	106,540	103,000	103,930	114,551
Self-employment in non-agriculture	165,562	120,344	99,580	104,742	98,927	95,046	91,644	118,419
Labour	46,522	43,752	40,541	36,496	34,923	38,764	37,274	39,626
Expenditure (Rs per household per annum)								
Regular salary/wages	83,764	78,539	82,340	74,917	74,403	71,055	66,583	77,995
Self-employment in non-agriculture	96,566	76,853	73,067	71,874	68,600	80,067	67,153	78,489
Labour	37,569	42,498	38,987	36,732	34,002	33,392	34,709	36,854
Surplus Income (Rs per household per annum)								
Regular salary/wages	43,979	32,728	34,495	30,956	32,137	31,945	37,347	36,555
Self-employment in non-agriculture	68,996	43,491	26,513	32,868	30,327	14,978	24,490	39,930
Labour	8,953	1,255	1,554	–236	921	5,372	2,564	2,772
Share of expenditure to income (per cent)								
Regular salary/wages	65.6	70.6	70.5	70.8	69.8	69	64.1	68.1
Self-employment in non-agriculture	58.3	63.9	73.4	68.6	69.3	84.2	73.3	66.3
Labour	80.8	97.1	96.2	100.6	97.4	86.1	93.1	93.0
Share of surplus income to income (per cent)								
Regular Salary/wages	34.4	29.4	29.5	29.2	30.2	31.0	35.9	31.9
Self-employment in non-agriculture	41.7	36.1	26.6	31.4	30.7	15.8	26.7	33.7
Labour	19.2	2.9	3.8	–0.6	2.6	13.9	6.9	7.0

Source: NSHIE 2004–05 data: NCAER–CMCR analysis.

households are much higher in five lakh+ cities than in the lower class cities and towns. But the position of the self-employed (non-agriculture) households is far better than salary dependent households in terms of the percentage benefits over their small town counterparts. The share of income spent by the self-employed category is considerably lower in 10 lakh+ cities than in lower class cities and towns. This enables this category to accrue a much higher share of their income (36 per cent to 42 per cent) as surplus income in such large cities. In contrast, the surplus income share of salary dependent households has reduced from 36.6 per cent in small towns to 34.4 per cent in the largest cities because of spending a larger share of their income (66 per cent to 71 per cent) than the self-employed category (58 per cent to 64 per cent). The labour households in India's cities and towns, except the largest cities, spend out most part of their income and have hardly any money left to save. In the largest cities, they are, however, able to save 19.2 per cent of their income. This analysis shows that the self-employed and labour categories settled in largest cities are financially much better off than their counterparts in 10 lakh+ towns.

Interestingly, the expenditure level of households that earn their income from self-employed non-farm activities is somewhat more than that of salaried house-holds in smaller towns, even though their surplus income is lower. In terms of share of expenditure to income, the self-employed households have a higher spend ratio in smaller towns, while in the biggest towns, it is the salaried house-holds that are spending a higher percentage of their income. The self-employed households are bigger savers in the top two categories of town classes, whereas in smaller towns, the salaried households save a higher proportion of their income. Coming to variability across source of income categories, we find that the that salary dependent household's income is more or less the same multiple of a labour household's income in a small town as well as a large city, but in the case of the self-employed category, it is 3.56 times in the largest cities as against 2.46 multiples in small towns, suggesting the impact of size-class of towns.

7.7.2 Education Level of Chief Earner

In the largest towns, nearly 37 per cent households are headed by chief earn-ers who are graduates or have attained higher education followed by households headed by matriculates (36 per cent). In the smallest towns, nearly 38 per cent households are headed by chief earners who have studied till Class 10. Across all town classes, roughly a third of all households are headed by chief earners who have studied up to class 10. Significantly, most urban towns have a very small population of illiterate households: just 3 per cent in the biggest towns to 12 per cent in smallest town class (Figure 7.13).

Here we considered to focus on the performance of graduate+ households, and those with matriculates as chief earners vis-á-vis the 'up to primary' households. A graduate household in the biggest cities earns the highest income (at Rs 177,022). Its counterpart in the smallest town earns roughly Rs 50,000 less. This disparity exists across all education levels by town classes. Chief earners who are educated only till the primary level and reside in the largest towns earn about twice the income of their counterparts in the smallest towns (Rs 85,837 versus Rs 50,919, respectively). Accordingly, this impacts their expenditure and saving patterns as

Figure 7.13: Distribution of Households by Education Level of Chief Earner and Town Class

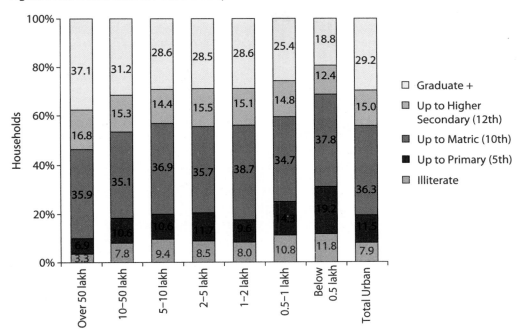

Source: NSHIE 2004–05 data: NCAER–CMCR analysis.

well (Table 7.10). For instance, the share of expenditure to income of the primary educated chief earner household is 68 per cent in the largest cities as against 88 per cent in the smallest towns. Similarly, the former has a surplus income of Rs 27,697, which is more than five times that of the latter (Rs 6,162).

A comparison of the graduate households in the largest and smallest towns reveals that though the households in the largest towns have a surplus income of Rs 72, 694 compared to just Rs 45,240 in the smallest towns, as a share to income, this works out to 41 per cent and 35.1 per cent, respectively. So even though they are earning less than their counterparts in the largest towns, the graduate households of the smallest towns are saving marginally less. It seems that the better educated households even in the smallest towns are thriftier than those who are not so well educated.

It can be appreciated that graduate+ households have the highest income (Rs 177,022), both across the educational groups and the town size-classes, the income being 37 per cent more than the a small town household's income. However, the two low education categories, 'up to primary' and 'matric' have registered a higher increase–68 per cent and 43 per cent–over their counterparts in small towns. In the largest cities, the incomes of graduate+ households and the 'matric' category are 79 per cent and 13 per cent, respectively, more than that of the 'up to primary'

Table 7.10: Estimates of Income, Expenditure and Surplus Income by Education Level of Chief Earner and Town Class

Education level of chief earner	Town class (population size in lakh)							Total urban
	Over 50	10–50	5–10	2–5	1–2	0.5–1.0	Below 0.5	
Income (Rs per household per annum)								
Up to primary (5th)	85,837	65,072	57,611	44,487	47,136	54,393	50,919	58,015
Up to matric (10th)	95,624	85,599	69,536	68,339	63,721	65,939	66,957	76,948
Graduate+	177,022	139,474	137,029	133,134	128,298	117,033	128,733	145,859
Expenditure (Rs per household per annum)								
Up to primary (5th)	58,141	52,189	50,590	42,744	42,251	51,762	44,757	48,665
Up to matric (10th)	65,507	62,124	57,524	55,518	51,087	57,341	53,544	58,552
Graduate+	104,328	94,722	92,223	89,656	91,251	79,585	83,493	94,112
Surplus Income (Rs per household per annum)								
Up to primary (5th)	27,697	12,883	7,021	1,744	4,885	2,630	6,162	9,350
Up to matric (10th)	30,117	23,474	12,012	12,821	12,634	8,597	13,413	18,396
Graduate+	72,694	44,753	44,806	43,477	37,047	37,448	45,240	51,747
Share of expenditure to income (per cent)								
Up to primary (5th)	67.7	80.2	87.8	96.1	89.6	95.2	87.9	83.9
Up to matric (10th)	68.5	72.6	82.7	81.2	80.2	87	80.0	76.1
Graduate+	58.9	67.9	67.3	67.3	71.1	68	64.9	64.5
Share of surplus income to income (per cent)								
Up to primary (5th)	32.3	19.8	12.2	3.9	10.4	4.8	12.1	16.1
Up to matric (10th)	31.5	27.4	17.3	18.8	19.8	13	20.0	23.9
Graduate+	41.1	32.1	32.7	32.7	28.9	32	35.1	35.5

Source: NSHIE 2004–05 data: NCAER–CMCR analysis.

category as against 86 per cent and 20 per cent in small towns. This clearly shows that in the largest cities, the income disparity has decreased to a large extent because of better career advancement opportunities available over there.

The lowest educated group in the largest cities, which earns 68 per cent more but spends only 30 per cent more than its spending in a small town, is the one which is getting the maximum benefit of urbanisation: its surplus income is 4.5 times that of its counterpart in a small town as against 2.24 and 1.61 times surplus income generated by matric and graduate+ households, respectively. The surplus incomes of graduate+ and matric households are 2.62 and 1.09 times that of the lowest education category in the largest cities as against 7.34 and 2.18 times in small towns. This once again shows that the disparity in disposable income is at a much lower level in the largest cities as compared to lower class cities/towns. In general, the share of surplus income in total income is much higher in the largest cities than lower class towns and the reverse is the case with expenditure share.

Much smaller distances among surplus income shares in respect of the largest cities relative to small towns further corroborate the hypothesis of economic disparity reduction in the largest cities. A graduate+ household makes a surplus income of 41 per cent as against the two low education categories (each at 32 per cent).

7.7.3 Sector of Engagement as Source of Income for Households

Traditional services are a major source of income for a dominant section of urban households across all town classes. Nearly half of all urban households in the over 50 lakh population cities are engaged in traditional services. However, the biggest cities have many more households (30 per cent) compared to the smallest towns (20 per cent) that earn their income from modern services. Clearly, then, the largest cities offer better employment opportunities. Industry as a sector of engagement is accessed by nearly 23 per cent of households in the second rung cities (10 lakh to 50 lakh) while 17 per cent households in the smallest towns draw their income from industry (Figure 7.14).

The range of income offered by traditional services in larger towns is definitely higher than those in the smallest towns. For instance, the average annual income of a household that is engaged in traditional services in the largest towns

Figure 7.14: Distribution of Households by Sector as Source of Income for Households and Size of Town Class

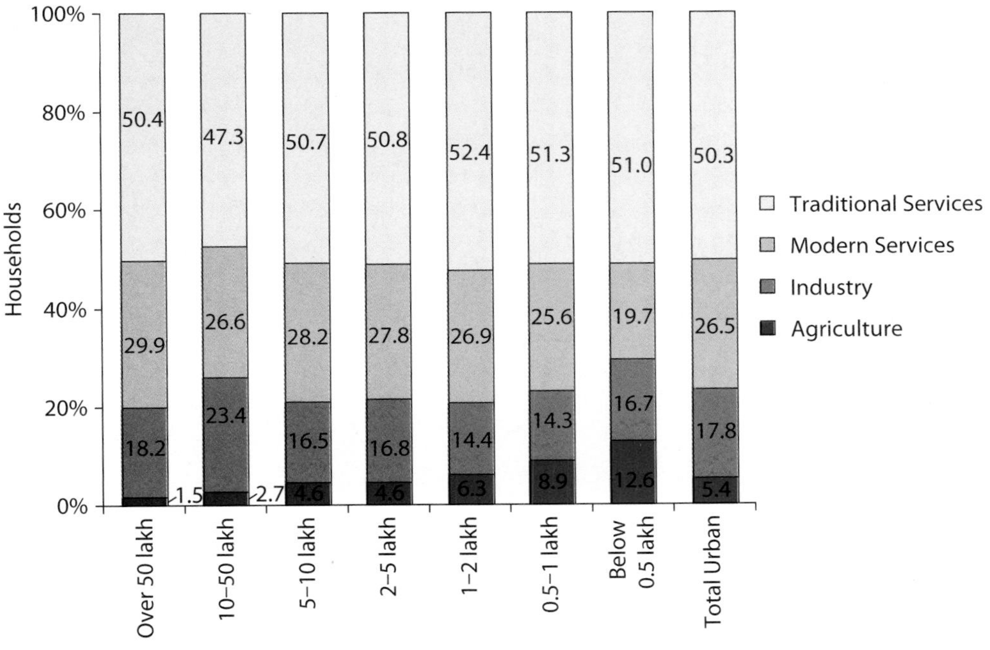

Source: NSHIE 2004–05 data: NCAER–CMCR analysis.

is about Rs 120,846, whereas in the smallest town, its counterpart earns little more than half that amount (Rs 66,120). A similar disparity is evident in income earned from modern services in the big cities (Rs 145,856) versus that in the smallest cities (Rs 103,450).

Households that earn their income from modern services are bigger spenders across all town classes. In contrast, households that earn from industry across all town classes are the smallest savers. Interestingly, in the biggest cities, the share of expenditure to income and share of saving to income are roughly the same, irrespective of the sector from which they earn their income. However, in the smallest towns, the biggest savers are those who are engaged in modern services followed by those who are employed in traditional services.

The three most populous sectors as source of income for urban households, namely, traditional services, modern services and industry have been considered for discussion (Table 7.11). It can be appreciated that the households of modern

Table 7.11: Estimates of Income, Expenditure and Surplus Income by Sector as Source of Income for Households and Town Class

Sector of engagement	Town class (population size in lakh)							Total urban
	Over 50	10–50	5–10	2–5	1–2	0.5–1.0	Below 0.5	
Income (Rs per household per annum)								
Industry	119,029	100,703	77,296	86,525	65,801	59,820	72,631	91,296
Modern services	145,856	113,935	117,832	104,303	116,468	108,970	103,450	120,117
Traditional services	120,846	89,169	79,797	76,669	70,477	69,391	66,120	86,578
Expenditure (Rs Per household per annum)								
Industry	77,137	68,049	64,612	63,452	55,340	47,166	57,654	65,375
Modern services	90,869	82,138	82,663	77,920	77,550	77,686	70,532	81,715
Traditional services	78,062	65,968	61,413	56,513	54,899	58,010	50,175	62,636
Surplus Income (Rs per household per annum)								
Industry	41,892	32,653	12,684	23,073	10,461	12,654	14,977	25,921
Modern services	54,987	31,797	35,168	26,383	38,917	31,285	32,917	38,402
Traditional services	42,784	23,201	18,384	20,156	15,577	11,381	15,945	23,942
Share of expenditure to income (per cent)								
Industry	64.8	67.6	83.6	73.3	84.1	78.8	79.4	71.6
Modern services	62.3	72.1	70.2	74.7	66.6	71.3	68.2	68.0
Traditional services	64.6	74.0	77.0	73.7	77.9	83.6	75.9	72.3
Share of surplus income to income (per cent)								
Industry	35.2	32.4	16.4	26.7	15.9	21.2	20.6	28.4
Modern services	37.7	27.9	29.8	25.3	33.4	28.7	31.8	32.0
Traditional services	35.4	26.0	23.0	26.3	22.1	16.4	24.1	27.7

Source: NSHIE 2004–05 data: NCAER–CMCR analysis.

services sector have the highest income (Rs 145,856); both across the sectors and the town size-classes, the income is 41 per cent more than a small town household's income (Table 7.11). However, the traditional services and industry sectors have registered a higher rate increase–83 per cent and 63 per cent–over their counterparts in small towns. In the largest cities, it is the industry and traditional services groups that earn 63 per cent and 83 per cent, respectively more, but spend only 34 per cent and 55 per cent, respectively more, than their spending in a small town. They get the maximum benefit of urbanisation: their surplus income is 2.7 to 2.8 times that of their counterpart in a small town as against 1.67 times surplus income generated by modern services category of households.

The surplus incomes of modern services and traditional services groups are 1.31 and 1.02 times that of the industry group in the largest cities as against 2.20 and 1.06 times in small towns. This once again shows that the disparity in disposable income has come down in the largest cities. In general, the share of surplus income in total income is much higher in largest cities than lower class towns and the reverse is the case with expenditure share. Note the narrowing down of distances among surplus income shares in respect of the largest cities relative to small towns as proof of the hypothesis of economic disparity reduction in largest cities.

7.7.4 Occupational Types of Households

A little more than a quarter of all urban households across all town classes are employed in some kind of production related job. While the national average is about 28 per cent, there are some marginal variations across town classes. The largest towns have roughly about 23 per cent of households employed in production jobs, while 30 per cent households in towns with populations of between 0.5 to one lakh have production/transport equipment related jobs. The next large chunk of households (about 22 per cent) is employed in sales jobs. More administrative, executive and managerial workers (11.5 per cent) are to be found in the largest towns (population size of over 50 lakh), while the smallest towns have only 3.4 per cent households that have administrators, managers or executives as their chief earners (Figure 7.15).

The highest earning category of households is the one that has chief earners who are administrative or managerial staff. Their average household income at the national level is Rs 183,803. If such a household lives in a town size with population of more than 50 lakh, it is likely that its average income would be even higher than the national average at Rs 200,070. Such workers who reside in the smallest towns earn slightly less than the national average at Rs 193,292. The next high earning category is the professional/technical worker household living in a metropolitan city with an annual average income about Rs 175,169. Its counterpart in the smallest town would

Figure 7.15: Distribution of Households by Type of Occupation Pursued by Households and Town Class

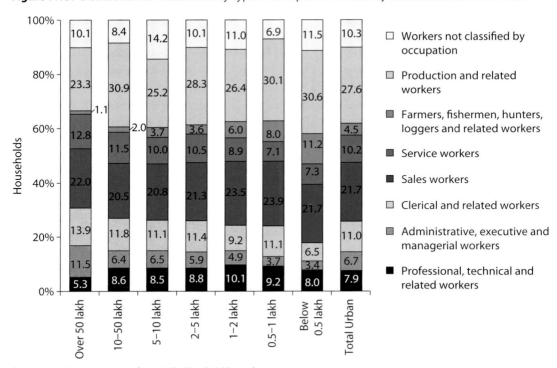

Source: NSHIE 2004–05 data: NCAER–CMCR analysis.

earn about Rs 113,535. Sales worker households are next in the line up: those in the biggest towns have average incomes of Rs 148,455 compared to their counterparts in the smallest towns with average incomes of Rs 83,005.

Not surprisingly, expenditure patterns too reflect the disparity that is observed in income trends. So, professional worker households in the largest towns spend a little more than their counterparts in the smallest towns. However, in terms of savings, the professional worker households in the smallest towns save 33.1 per cent of their income compared to 32.8 per cent that their slightly better off counterparts in the largest towns save. Similarly, while the administrative and executive households of the largest towns spend Rs 115,970 compared to Rs 105,505 spent by their counterparts in the smallest towns, the share of expenditure to income is 58 per cent in the case of the former and 54.6 per cent in the case of the latter. Similarly, saving trends reveal that the share of surplus income at 42 per cent is much lower for richer households in the largest towns than their counterparts in the smallest towns whose share of surplus income to earnings is 45.4 per cent.

We have seen earlier that the administrative and managerial workers, and the professional and technical workers are the two most performing categories in terms of household earnings. The income, expenditure and saving levels of these groups are compared here with those of sales workers which serves as the control group. As expected, the households of administrative and managerial workers have the highest income (Rs 200,070), both across occupational groups and town size-classes, which is just 3 per cent above the a small town household's income (Table 7.12). However, the professional and technical workers, and sales workers

Table 7.12: Estimates of Income, Expenditure and Surplus Income by Nature of Occupation Pursued by Households and Town Class

Occupation of household	Town class (population size in lakh)							Total urban
	Over 50	10–50	5–10	2–5	1–2	0.5–1.0	Below 0.5	
Income (Rs per household per annum)								
Professional, technical and related workers	175,169	135,541	146,288	132,944	131,013	132,134	113,535	138,065
Administrative, executive and managerial workers	200,070	196,605	164,456	160,196	149,625	130,049	193,292	183,803
Sales workers	148,455	109,191	92,575	93,360	92,051	88,284	83,005	106,842
Expenditure (Rs per household per annum)								
Professional, technical and related workers	117,736	93,629	106,189	85,434	91,889	86,496	75,954	93,840
Administrative, executive and managerial workers	115,970	111,595	101,314	106,318	101,877	84,053	105,505	109,264
Sales workers	84,063	73,412	70,635	65,766	64,032	72,098	61,736	71,632
Surplus Income (Rs per household per annum)								
Professional, technical and related workers	57,433	41,912	40,099	47,510	39,124	45,638	37,582	44,225
Administrative, executive and managerial workers	84,099	85,010	63,142	53,878	47,748	45,996	87,787	74,539
Sales workers	64,391	35,778	21,940	27,594	28,019	16,186	21,269	35,211
Share of expenditure to income (per cent)								
Professional, technical and related workers	67.2	69.1	72.6	64.3	70.1	65.5	66.9	68.0
Administrative, executive and managerial workers	58.0	56.8	61.6	66.4	68.1	64.6	54.6	59.4
Sales workers	56.6	67.2	76.3	70.4	69.6	81.7	74.4	67.0
Share of surplus income to income (per cent)								
Professional, technical and related workers	32.8	30.9	27.4	35.7	29.9	34.5	33.1	32.0
Administrative, executive and managerial workers	42.0	43.2	38.4	33.6	31.9	35.4	45.4	40.6
Sales workers	43.4	32.8	23.7	29.6	30.4	18.3	25.6	33.0

Source: NSHIE 2004–05 data: NCAER–CMCR analysis.

categories have registered higher growth rates–54 per cent and 79 per cent, re-spectively–over their small town counterparts. In the largest cities, the incomes of administrative and managerial workers, and professional and technical workers households are only 35 per cent and 18 per cent, respectively, higher than that of sales workers category, as against 133 per cent and 37 per cent, respectively, in the small towns. This clearly reveals income disparity reduction resulting from urbanisation. In the largest cities, the sales workers category–which earns 79 per cent more but spends only 36 per cent more than its counterpart in a small town–is the one which gets the benefit of urbanisation with its surplus income showing a twofold increase over that of its counterpart in a small town. The administrative and managerial workers, and professional and technical workers getting 4.13 and 1.77 times surplus incomes relative to the sales workers category in small towns have come much closer in the largest cities where the corresponding rates are 1.31 and 0.89, respectively. This also shows that the disparity in disposable income has come down in the largest cities. Note further that the surplus income shares in re-spect of the largest cities have also narrowed down their pair-wise distances in the largest cities, further supporting the hypothesis of economic disparity reduction.

7.7.5 Prosperity of States and Their Towns

As they say, success breeds success. This is particularly true of the richer states that have spawned more larger towns that offer their citizens better income earn-ing opportunities. While the low income states do not have even a single town with a population of over 50 lakh, the middle income states have 51 per cent of their households living in the largest towns and the high income states have about 49 per cent of their residents living in such large cities. Low income states, on the other hand, have more towns in the smallest town category (below 0.5 lakh population) and nearly 42 per cent of the population of these states lives in these towns (Figure 7.16).

The average annual income of a household living in the largest towns of a high income state is significantly more (Rs 143,527) than that of a household living in the smallest town of a high income state (Rs 97,710), signifying that larger towns have more income generating opportunities, and the smaller towns of even high income states have much fewer options to offer to their citizens in terms of income generation (Table 7.13). The households residing in the smallest towns of low in-come states fare much worse than their counterparts in the high income states and the difference in income is almost Rs 35,000. Similar trends are observed in expenditure patterns as well, with the households in the smallest towns of high income states spending somewhat more than their counterparts in the low income

Figure 7.16: Distribution of Households by State of Residence and Town Class

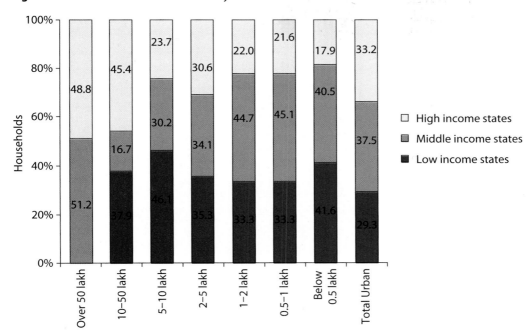

Source: NSHIE 2004–05 data: NCAER–CMCR analysis.

states. Surplus income or savings pattern reveals that households in the smallest towns of high income states saves three times more than households in the same category in low income states.

At the other end of the scale too, a similar trend is observed: households in towns of population size 10 lakh to 50 lakh in high income states save almost twice the amount that their counterparts do in low income states. In terms of expenditure, the households in towns belonging to low income states spend slightly more than their counterparts living in high income states. What seems to be happening is that the share of expenditure to income is much higher across all town classes for low income states as compared to those living in similar town sizes in high income states. Conversely, the share of savings to income is higher for households across all town sizes in high income states when compared to households in similar town classes in low income states.

The households of high income states have the highest income (Rs 143,527), both across state of residence groups and town size-classes, the income being 47 per cent more than a small town household's income. It is interesting to note that the households in middle income states have also registered the same rate of growth in the largest cities and the disparity in income between rich and less rich states persists even in the largest cities. In earlier sections, we have seen that

Table 7.13: Estimates of Income, Expenditure and Surplus Income by State of Residence and Town Class

State category	Town class (population size in lakh)							Total urban
	Over 50	10–50	5–10	2–5	1–2	0.5–1.0	Below 0.5	
Income (Rs per household per annum)								
Low income states	–	92,877	91,261	85,823	80,909	63,959	64,597	80,948
Middle income states	112,244	74,381	77,533	83,297	82,860	74,310	76,206	89,223
High income states	143,527	113,938	101,317	88,172	84,442	109,144	97,710	116,421
Expenditure (Rs per household per annum)								
Low income states	–	75,905	69,362	62,923	62,196	59,727	52,692	64,311
Middle income states	79,085	58,413	64,439	63,957	64,035	53,403	61,180	66,932
High income states	84,371	71,956	69,097	63,818	56,912	78,824	62,134	73,523
Surplus Income (Rs per household per annum)								
Low income states	–	16,972	21,899	22,900	18,713	4,232	12,818	16,636
Middle income states	33,160	15,968	13,094	19,340	18,826	20,908	17,880	22,291
High income states	59,156	41,982	32,220	24,354	27,529	30,320	33,614	42,898
Share of expenditure to income (per cent)								
Low income states	–	81.7	76	73.3	76.9	93.4	81.6	79.4
Middle income states	70.5	78.5	83.1	76.8	77.3	71.9	80.3	75.0
High income states	58.8	63.2	68.2	72.4	67.4	72.2	63.6	63.2
Share of surplus income to income (per cent)								
Low income states	–	18.3	24.0	26.7	23.1	6.6	10.1	20.6
Middle income states	29.5	21.5	16.9	23.2	22.7	28.1	18.4	25.0
High income states	41.2	36.8	31.8	27.6	32.6	27.8	19.7	36.8

Source: NSHIE 2004–05 data: NCAER–CMCR analysis.

the disparities in income and savings due to education, and sector of employment narrow down in largest cities. This is not happening in respect of state differences because the largest cities in richer states will have more opportunities than in comparatively less advanced states. The consequence is obvious: the households in high income states have been able to save a much higher share of their income (41.2 per cent) than in middle income states (29.5 per cent)–the disparity has only widened rather than narrowing down. In middle income states, the surplus income of a largest city household is 1.85 times that of a small town household, while in high income states, the increase is 1.76 times. This shows that a largest city household in middle income states has not received much additional advantage over its counterpart in high income states. In middle income states, a largest city household spends a higher percentage of its household income (70.5 per cent) than in high income states (58.8 per cent), both the fractions being the least in their respective groups. By virtue of spending at lower rates, largest city households in high income states account for higher rates of surplus income compared to middle income states, which only adds to the disparity in surplus income between states.

References

Shukla, Rajesh and Roopa Purushothaman. 2008. *The Next Urban Frontier: Twenty Cities to Watch.* New Delhi: National Council of Applied Economics Research; Mumbai: Future Research Capital.

United Nations. 2006. *World Urbanisation Prospects: The 2005 Revision.* New York: Population Division, United Nations.

Annexure: Concepts, Definitions and Survey Methodology

A.1 Concepts and Definitions

A household is the basic unit of analysis in this book. Most of the quantitative classificatory factors such as income, expenditure, investment, surplus income, amount of life insurance payments, and so on, refer to the household as a whole. However, certain other characteristics used for analysis such as occupation, age, education and source of income pertain only to the chief earner of the household. The main concepts and measures used in this study have been defined below.

A.1.1 Household

A group of persons normally living together and taking food from a common kitchen constitutes a household. The members of a household may or may not be related by blood or marriage. Servants, permanent labourers and unrelated members are treated as members of the household in case they take their meals regularly from the same kitchen. If a person was out for more than six months during the reference period (2004–05), he/she was not treated as a member of the household. Those entering the household on account of marriage or other alliances and new born babies are counted as members of the household, even if they had lived with the household for less than six months.

A.1.2 Household Size

The number of resident members of a household is its size. It includes temporary stay-away members, but excludes temporary visitors and guests.

A.1.3 Head of the Household

The head is the main decision-maker in the family and the person best informed about the family's finances. Usually, he/she is the chief earner or the oldest member in the household. The household members were expected to inform the interviewer who they regard as their head/chief earner.

A.1.4 Rural and Urban Areas

The rural and urban areas of the country are taken from Census 2001, for which the required information is available with the Survey Design and Research Division of the National Sample Survey Organisation (NSSO). The lists of Census villages as published in the Primary Census Abstracts (PCA) constitute the rural areas. The lists of cities, towns, cantonments, non-municipal urban areas and notified areas constitute urban areas. The definition of urban areas adopted for this study is the same as that used in the 2001 Census. Accordingly, urban areas include:

- All places with a municipality/corporation, cantonment board or a notified town area committee;
- All other places satisfying the following criteria:
  - Minimum population of 5,000,
  - At least 75 per cent of the male workforce is engaged in non-agricultural pursuits, and
  - A population density of over 400 per sq km (1,000 per sq mile).

A.1.5. Household Income

In broad terms, income refers to regular receipts such as wages and salaries, income from self-employment, interest and dividends from invested funds, and pensions or other benefits from social insurance and other current transfers receivable. Income represents a partial view of economic well-being and comprises the regular or recurring receipts of household economic accounts. It provides a measure of resources available to the household for consumption and savings.

- **Regular salaries and wages:** Regular salaries and wages are the earnings that a person working in other's farm or non-farm enterprises (both household and non-household) gets in return on a regular basis (and not on the basis of daily or periodic renewal of work contract).

- **Self-employed in non-agriculture:** Persons/households who are engaged in their own non-farm enterprises are defined as self-employed in non-agriculture (craft/business/professionals, and so on).
- **Agricultural labour:** An individual following one or more of the following agricultural operations in the capacity of labourer or hire or in exchange, whether paid wholly in cash or kind or partly in cash and partly in kind.
- **Casual wage labour:** A person casually engaged in non-farm enterprises (both household and non-household) and getting in return wages according to the terms of daily or periodic work contract is treated as casual wage labour.
- **Self-employed in agriculture:** Persons/households who are engaged in their own farm are defined as self-employed in agriculture.
- **Income from other sources:** This comprises incomes such as rent from land, rent from providing accommodation and capital for production, net interest received (income from bonds, deposits and savings), dividend (income received from stock holdings and mutual fund shares), employer-based private pension (payments received from companies/government after retirement), government social insurance and social assistance benefits, and so on.

A.1.6 Major Source of Household Income (Major Occupation)

In the event that members of a household engage in only one type of income source, the nature of the income source in order to earn livelihood is the primary occupation for the household. In the event that the household is pursuing two or more economic activities, the principal occupation is considered to be the economic activity that contributes maximum to household income.

A.1.7 Routine Consumption Expenditure

Household consumption that includes the value of all goods and services provided in kind by the employer or as a result of home production (including the value of imputed rent for owner-occupied dwellings), which were already included in total income. Consumption expenditure is classified into eight groups:

- **Food:** While recording consumption, care should be taken to include consumption on ceremonies, parties, and so on. If the household makes any transfer payment in terms of commodities (like cereals, beverages, fruits, vegetables pulses, and so on), the quantity of such commodities should not be shown under domestic consumption of the payer household. For this survey, the portion out of that receipt consumed by the recipient household during the reference period was shown against the consumption of the recipient household.

- **Housing:** For the reference period, information was collected on expenditures such as rent, taxes, maintenance, other household services, water bills, and so on. The actual expenditure incurred towards the purchase of these items—used for non-productive purposes—was considered as the consumption expenditure of the household. Expenditure in both cash and in kind was taken into account. Consumption was recorded in terms of an average per month.
- **Health expenses** (fee on medical facilities/medical labs/medicines): These items include expenditure on medicines and medical goods, payments made to doctors, nurses, and so on, on account of professional fees and those made to hospital, nursing home, and so on, for medical treatment.
- **Transport** (road/air/fuel/repair/insurance/licence): Expenditure incurred on account of journeys undertaken and/or transportation of goods made by airways, railways, bus, tram, steamer, motor car (or taxi), motorcycle, auto-rickshaw, bicycle, rickshaw (hand-drawn and cycle) horse-cab, bullock cart, hand-cart, porter or any other means of conveyance. In case of owned conveyance, the cost of fuel (petrol, mobile oil, diesel, and so on) for power-driven transport and animal feed for animal-drawn carriage were also taken into account.
- **Education:** This was meant for recording expenses incurred in connection with education like purchase of books, stationeries, school fees, boarding, school transportation, and so on. It also included fees paid to educational institutions (for example, schools, colleges, universities, and so on) on account of tuition (inclusive of minor items like game fees, library fees, fan fees, and so on) and payment to private tutors.
- **Clothing and footwear:** Information on the value of consumption of all items of clothing and footwear were collected in (whole number of) Rupees.
- **Consumer durable goods:** Expenditure incurred on purchase of consumer durables and cost of raw materials and services for construction and repairs of durable goods for domestic use were collected against this item. Expenditure included both cash and kind. Expenditure incurred on purchase of durable goods for giving gifts was also included.

A.1.8 Unusual Household Expenditure

It includes occasional but large annual expenditures on social ceremonies (marriage, birth and other social events), health/medical, higher education, leisure and holiday travel, jewellery, and so on.

A.1.9 Surplus Income

Surplus income refers to the current income less current routine consumption expenditure and unusual expenditure.

A.1.10 Investment

The annual investment made by all the members of household in stock markets (shares/debentures/bonds), small savings, insurance, and so on.

A.1.11 Reference Period

The information was collected primarily for the year April 2004–March 2005. For questions where the reference period was mentioned as 'last month', it was defined as 30 days preceding the date of enquiry.

A.1.12 Period of Survey

Primary data was collected during 1 October 2005 and 28 February 2006.

A. 2 Coverage

Primary survey of households was undertaken in 24 major states/union territories (UTs) of India covering both rural and urban areas of Andhra Pradesh, Assam, Bihar, Chandigarh, Chhattisgarh, Delhi, Goa, Gujarat, Haryana, Himachal Pradesh, Jharkhand, Karnataka, Kerala, Madhya Pradesh, Maharashtra, Meghalaya, Orissa, Pondicherry, Punjab, Rajasthan, Tamil Nadu, Uttaranchal, Uttar Pradesh and West Bengal. Territories that were excluded were Jammu & Kashmir, Sikkim, Arunachal Pradesh, Nagaland, Manipur, Mizoram, Tripura, Andaman & Nicobar Islands, Daman & Diu, Dadra & Nagar Haveli and Lakshadweep. Remaining states were left out due to operational difficulty. These states account for only 3 per cent to 4 per cent of the country's total population.

A.3 Sample Design

A three-stage stratified sample design has been adopted for the survey to generate representative samples. Sample districts, villages and households formed the first, second and third stage sample units, respectively, for selection of the rural sample, while cities/towns, urban wards and households were the three stages of selection for the urban sample. Sampling was done independently within each state/UT and estimates were generated at the state/UT level. Estimate for all India was arrived at through an aggregation of estimates for all states/UTs. The sample sizes at first, second and third stages in rural and urban areas were determined on the basis of available resources and the derived level of precision for key estimates from the survey, taking into account the experience of NCAER in conducting the earlier surveys.[1]

Within a state, there are variations with respect to social and economic characteristics; the bigger a state, the larger the variation. In the National Sample Survey (NSS) within a state, regions are formed considering the homogeneity of crop pattern, vegetation, climate, physical features, rainfall pattern, and so on. An NSS region is a group of districts within a state similar to each other in respect of agro-climatic features. In the present survey within a state, NSS regions formed the strata for both rural and urban sampling.

A.3.1 Selection of the Rural Sample

In the rural sample design, a sample size of 250 districts was allocated to the 64 NSS regions within the 24 covered states/UTs in proportion to the total number of districts in an NSS region. From each of the NSS regions, the allocated number of districts was selected, as the first-stage sample units, with probability proportional to size and replacement, where rural population of each district as per Census 2001 was used as size measure.

---

[1] All India Rural Household Survey on Saving, Income and Investment (1962); Survey on Urban Income and Saving (1962); Market Information Survey of Households (1985–2001); Micro-Impact of Macro and Adjustment Policies (1994–95); Rural Economic and Demographic Survey (1970, 1980 and 1999). All surveys conducted by NCAER.

Villages formed the second stage of selection procedure. District-wise lists of villages are available from Census 2001 records along with population. A total sample of 1,976 villages (second-stage sampling units) was allocated to the selected 250 districts, approximately in proportion to rural population of each selected district. The allocated number of sample villages in a selected district was chosen with equal probability sampling approach.

In each of the selected villages, approximately 100 households were selected following equal probability sampling approach for listing purpose and preliminary survey. During this preliminary survey, information on land possessed and principal source of income of the listed household was collected for use in stratifying the listed households into eight strata as follows:

- **Stratum 1:** Principal source of income was self-employment in agriculture and land possessed was 0 acres to 2 acres;
- **Stratum 2:** Principal source of income was self-employment in agriculture and land possessed was 2 acres to 10 acres;
- **Stratum 3:** Principal source of income was self-employment in agriculture and land possessed was above 10 acres;
- **Stratum 4:** Principal source of income was labour (agricultural/other casual);
- **Stratum 5:** Principal source of income was self-employment in non-agriculture and land possessed was 0 acres to 2 acres;
- **Stratum 6:** Principal source of income was self-employment in non-agriculture and land possessed was above 2 acres;
- **Stratum 7:** Principal source of income was regular salary/wages and other sources and land possessed was 0 acres to 2 acres; and
- **Stratum 8:** Principal source of income was regular salary/wages and other sources and land possessed was above 2 acres.

From each of the above eight strata, two households were selected by following equal probability sampling approach. In case, any of the strata was found to be missing (no household), then households from previous stratum, where additional households were available, were selected so as to get 16 sample households in a selected village.

Following the above sampling design in rural areas, the realised sample of 31,446 households out of preliminary listed sample of 211,979 households was spread over 1,976 villages in 250 districts and 64 NSS regions covering the 24 states/UTs (Table A1).

Table A1: Profile of the Rural Sample

State	Number of NSS Regions	Stage I Total districts	Stage I Sample districts	Stage II Total villages	Stage II Sample villages	Stage III Listed households	Stage III Sample households
Himachal Pradesh	1	12	6	17,495	32	2,736	512
Punjab	2	17	8	12,278	48	4,983	768
Chandigarh	1	1	1	23	5	500	78
Uttaranchal	1	13	6	15,761	30	3,044	480
Haryana	2	19	9	6,764	47	4,862	752
Delhi	1	9	1	158	6	668	88
Rajasthan	4	32	16	39,753	118	12,036	1,888
Uttar Pradesh	4	70	29	97,942	274	30,356	4,384
Bihar	2	37	18	39,018	196	21,721	3,136
Meghalaya	1	7	5	–	10	991	160
Assam	3	23	11	25,124	67	6,419	1,072
West Bengal	4	17	9	37,955	123	12,438	1,968
Jharkhand	1	18	9	29,354	59	5,930	944
Orissa	3	30	14	47,529	86	9,958	1,376
Chhattisgarh	1	15	7	19,744	49	4,924	784
Madhya Pradesh	6	45	22	52,117	132	14,092	2,112
Gujarat	5	25	12	18,066	90	10,659	1,440
Maharashtra	6	33	16	41,095	157	18,057	2,512
Andhra Pradesh	4	22	12	26,614	160	16,619	2,560
Karnataka	4	27	14	27,481	103	11,969	1,648
Goa	1	2	2	347	10	1,166	160
Kerala	2	14	7	1,364	63	6,368	848
Tamil Nadu	4	30	14	15,400	101	10,443	1,616
Pondicherry	1	4	2	92	10	1,040	160
ALL INDIA	64	522	250	571,474	1,976	211,979	31,446

A.3.2 Selection of the Urban Sample

According to Census 2001, there are about 4,850 cities/towns in the states/UTs (excluding Jammu & Kashmir). The population of cities/towns in India varies from less than 5,000 to over 10 million. In the urban sample design, within the 24 covered states/UTs, the 64 NSS regions were again treated as strata. In each

Table A2: Sampling Fraction for City/Town Groups

Town class	Town population ('000)	Total towns	Sample towns	Sampling fraction
I	> 10000	3	3	1.00
II	5000–10000	3	3	1.00
III	1000–5000	29	29	1.00
IV	500–1000	37	37	1.00
V	200–500	98	98	1.00
VI	100–200	219	56	0.26
VII	50–100	396	44	0.11
VIII	20–50	1,135	28	0.02
IX	< 20	2,270	44	0.02
Total		4,190	342	0.08

NSS region, towns were categorised into five groups based on their population, namely, big towns and small towns. There are 170 cities with a population exceeding 200,000. All the cities were selected with a probability of one. The remaining cities/towns were grouped into four strata on the basis of their population size and from each stratum a sample of towns was selected independently.

A progressively increasing sampling fraction with increasing town population class was used for determining the number of towns to be selected from each stratum. From each NSS region, the allocated number of small towns was selected by following an equal probability sampling procedure. The sampling fraction was used at the state level (Table A2).

A total sample size of 2,255 urban wards was allocated among the selected small/big towns in proportion to the number of wards in the respective towns. The allocated number of wards was selected from each sample town following equal probability sampling approach. Thus, towns and wards formed the first- and second-stage sample units in the urban sample design.

Like in the rural sample design, within a selected ward, a sample of about 100 households was selected for listing and preliminary survey, following equal probability sampling approach. In the preliminary survey, at the time of listing of the sample households, information on household size, household consumption expenditure for last month or the monthly per capita expenditure (MPCE) and the principal source of household income were collected for use in stratifying the listed households into seven strata as follows:

- **Stratum 1:** Principal source of income was regular salary/wage earnings and sources like remittances, pension, and so on, and MPCE of Rs 800 or less;

- **Stratum 2:** Principal source of income same as in Stratum 1, but MPCE between Rs 801 and Rs 2500;
- **Stratum 3:** Principal source of income same as Stratum 1, but MPCE above Rs 2500;
- **Stratum 4:** Principal source of income was self-employment and MPCE less than Rs 800;

Table A3: Profile of Urban Sample

State	Number of NSS Regions	First stage of selection		Second stage of selection		Third stage of selection	
		Total towns	Sample towns	Total blocks	Sample blocks	Listed households	Sample households
Himachal Pradesh	1	56	2	22	5	502	70
Punjab	2	157	12	472	74	7,596	1,036
Chandigarh	1	1	1	21	10	1,000	140
Uttaranchal	1	76	3	129	18	1,881	252
Haryana	2	97	13	596	74	7,543	1,036
Delhi	1	4	1	289	60	7,197	840
Rajasthan	4	216	19	851	114	11,568	1,596
Uttar Pradesh	4	670	51	2,036	316	31,975	4,424
Bihar	2	120	14	444	75	7,973	1,050
Meghalaya	1	10	1	6	6	600	84
Assam	3	110	5	100	20	1,940	280
West Bengal	4	239	18	–	142	14,620	1,988
Jharkhand	1	95	10	860	68	6,896	952
Orissa	3	132	8	322	45	4,501	630
Chhattisgarh	1	84	8	473	44	4,412	616
Madhya Pradesh	6	368	19	799	114	11,516	1,596
Gujarat	5	190	19	572	146	14,615	2,044
Maharashtra	6	347	35	2,220	273	31,553	3,822
Andhra Pradesh	4	173	27	1,172	195	20,426	2,730
Karnataka	4	237	22	905	153	18,819	2,142
Goa	1	38	2	12	4	440	56
Kerala	2	98	13	1,019	79	8,030	1,106
Tamil Nadu	4	68	37	2,272	207	21,937	2,898
Pondicherry	1	4	2	23	13	1,273	182
ALL INDIA	64	4,190	342	15,615	2,255	238,813	31,570

- **Stratum 5:** Principal source of income was self-employment and MPCE between Rs 801 and Rs 2500;
- **Stratum 6:** Principal source of income was self-employment and MPCE above Rs 2500; and
- **Stratum 7:** Principal source of income was casual labour (agricultural or non-agricultural).

From each of the above strata, two households were selected at random with equal probability of selection. If there was no household in any of the strata, the shortfall was compensated from the previous stratum, where additional households were available, so as to get 14 sample households from each selected ward in urban sector for a detailed survey.

Following the above sampling design in urban areas, the realised sample of 31,570 households, out of the preliminary listed sample of 238,813 households, was spread over 2,255 urban wards in 342 towns and 64 NSS regions covering the 24 states/UTs (Table A3).

Index

About the Author and the Institute

Rajesh Shukla is Director of NCAER–Center for Macro Consumer Research (NCAER–CMCR). He is a Statistician, who has specialised in sample survey and data analysis. He has been involved for over 15 years in primary and secondary data based socio-economic studies (baseline, impact evaluation and longitudinal) and has executed over 25 national level studies covering a range of topics such as household income, expenditure and saving; tourism, science and technology, public understanding of science, youth as human resource and energy.

He has worked as technical advisor to several reputed national and international institutions such as United Nations Committee on Tourism Statistics, WTO, Spain; McKinsey Global Institute, Washington; Government of Sultanate of Oman; Asian Development Bank, Manila; Yale Centre for Consumer Insight, and so on. He has been engaged in compiling, integrating and analysing GESIS longitudinal datasets of European Countries. He is part of the collaborative research on 'Construction of Global Indicators of Science and Technology' at the London School of Economics since 2002.

He has authored seven books, more than 25 research reports, a number of research papers and popular articles. Some of his distinctive publications include *First India Science Report* (NCAER, 2004–05), *Domestic Tourism Survey* (Ministry of Tourism and Culture, Government of India, 2002–03), *Tourism Satellite of India* (Ministry of Tourism, 2006), *The Great Indian Middle Class* (NCAER, 2005), *The Great Indian Market* (NCAER, 2004) and *The Next Urban Frontier: Twenty Cities to Watch* (NCAER, 2008).

Visit the author at www.ncaer-cmcr.org

The **National Council of Applied Economic Research (NCAER)** is an independent interdisciplinary policy research institute founded in 1956 committed to assist government, civil society and the private sector to make informed policy choices. NCAER was created to provide objective data and analysis to support India's economic development through public policy and private initiative.

Household demand is one of the key pillars of the Indian economy. Business strategists and policy makers require continuous knowledge, insight and foresight in this area. NCAER has been active in providing authoritative analyses on this topic for more than two decades now. In a move to deepen its commitment to this, in 2010, NCAER has created a dedicated research centre called NCAER–Centre for Macro Consumer Research (NCAER–CMCR), with the objective of building and disseminating seminal knowledge about India's consumer economy.

The goal of the Centre is to be an important and vibrant resource for scholars, academicians, market analysts and corporations from round the world. The Centre will leverage and build on the excellent and widely acclaimed work already being done in this arena by NCAER. Some of the landmark publications in the recent past includes *The Great Indian Middle Class* (2004), *The Great Indian Market* (2005), *How India Earns, Spends and Saves* (2007) and *Next Urban Frontier: Twenty Cities to Watch* (2008).

To know more about the NCAER–CMCR, please log in www.ncaer-cmcr.org